Praise for
40 Thieves on Saipan

"I am thankful that someone took the time to tell our story. Otherwise the world would never know the 40 Thieves; how we lived, what we went through, and how some of us died. I remember every one of my buddies and pray for them every day."
—Roscoe Mullins, one of the 40 Thieves

"*40 Thieves on Saipan* is not Hollywood's version of World War II combat. It's a gritty, heart-stopping description of what it was really like for individual Marines fighting in unspeakably brutal conditions against a ruthless enemy in the Pacific. It is also a needed reminder that most of America's heroes were not born that way. They are ordinary Americans who, when faced with a dangerous enemy, responded with extraordinary bravery and courage."
—Jim Michaels, author of *A Chance in Hell: The Men Who Triumphed over Iraq's Deadliest City and Turned the Tide of War* and former Marine infantry officer

"As the WWII generation fast disappears, this book is a timely reminder of what those men endured. *40 Thieves on Saipan* strips away the rosy-hued Hollywood vision of what combat in that war was like. It reports by the firsthand accounts of the soldiers themselves; there was very little glory and lots of horror in the savage fighting in the Pacific Theater. The deep but largely unspoken camaraderie of the men who made up this elite unit of warriors was quietly moving. The inability of the men who survived the war to readjust to civilian life after all they had seen and done is a toxic byproduct of the war that has gone unrecognized for too long. This book is a fascinating and important addition to the WWII canon and has a special resonance for me since my uncle, my namesake, fought and died there as an original member of the unit."
—Donald Evans, nephew of Donald Evans, one of the 40 Thieves

"Our father never talked about the war, but to know now what he went through made us realize why he sometimes acted the way he did. When we boys would do something wrong and got into trouble, Dad got upset very quickly and let us know about it in no uncertain terms. But then he'd immediately go to his workshop: he had to walk away to control his anger by working at something he enjoyed. All of us boys are proud to be his sons, and my grandson, who is only nine, can't wait to read about his Great Grandpa's War."

—Larry, Don, and Lonnie, Jr. Jackson, sons of Lonnie Jackson, one of the 40 Thieves

"I appreciate Joseph for telling our story and bringing to light the stories and sacrifices of the men who fought by my side. Heroes like Dyer and Evans who paid the ultimate price for freedom. *40 Thieves on Saipan* breathes life into the past, and illuminates the humor, sacrifice, and valor of us young Marines who were the Sixth Regiment's Scout-Sniper Platoon."

—Marvin Strombo, one of the 40 Thieves

"*40 Thieves* captures that difference between regular combatants and the warriors who make up special operations forces. Not especially suited for inspections and parades, but perfectly geared for courageous improvisation and constant out-of-the-box thinking, these proto-operators are shown to be the team players they needed to be. Rambo need not apply. These men, as *40 Thieves on Saipan* shows us, were thinking-warriors and fiercely committed to each other and the mission. This remains the standard for our elite forces to this day."

—Kevin St. Jarre, combat intel team leader with the U.S. Army and author of the Night Stalkers series

"*40 Thieves on Saipan* means a lot to me, allowing people to see what these men went through for our country and how it affected their lives. Nightmares plagued my dad for the rest of his life, and losing his buddies to war affected him greatly. He often said to me, 'Junior, every day of my life is a bonus.' He was one proud Marine. God bless him."

—Al Yunker, Jr., son of Al Yunker, one of the 40 Thieves

"A son's curiosity of his father's service during World War II leads to the uncovering of an all-but-forgotten piece of U.S. Marine Corps history. How Frank Tachovsky, Colonel USMC Retired, as a lieutenant recruited a group of young Marines and molded them into an elite fighting unit, the Sixth Marine Regiment's Scout-Sniper Platoon. They served with distinction and uncommon valor during the Battle of Saipan in the Pacific Campaign and were known as the 40 Thieves, a well-earned nickname for their effectiveness as an elite combat unit as well as for their light-fingered antics."

—Clyde Kusatsu, actor and national vice president of Los Angeles SAG-AFTRA

"My father, Warren "Hobart" Tipton, was a proud member of the 40 Thieves. He told me many tales of thievery, training at Parker Ranch, the Garapan bike patrol, but very little of the combat. He was a very young Marine, turning eighteen on the day the platoon landed on Saipan. He inspired me to do some of the goofy stuff I did when I was a Marine in Vietnam, mostly to the detriment of Air Force and Army inventories. *40 Thieves on Saipan* fills in many blanks Dad left open most likely because of the pain of recalling the death of friends and living through terrifying events as essentially just a kid."

—Chris Tipton, son of Warren "Hobart" Tipton, one of the 40 Thieves

"When Joseph first visited Bob, researching for the book, memories were unleashed, memories he had not shared with anyone, not even his family. We all knew about his nightmares, always chasing the enemy who killed his buddy, Red. This book breathes live into forty special young Leathernecks and their intrepid lieutenant. Well done, Joseph and Cynthia."

—Alma Smotts, wife of Bob Smotts, one of the 40 Thieves

"To the families of every one of the 40, our fathers were truly the Greatest Generation, and the elite of the Few and the Proud."

—Andrew Orozco, son of Jesus Orozco, one of the 40 Thieves

"As a kid growing up in the 60s, I only knew my Uncle Don from old family photos packed in trunks I discovered in the attic. I thought of him as one of the tough, stalwart characters depicted in the 'Fightin' Marines' and 'Sgt Rock' comic books I enjoyed so much. Some might say he was a 'hero.' What I found was a heroic man filled with loyalty and fierce dedication to his Marine brothers in arms, and they for him. This is their story. A story that should be heard lest their sacrifices be diminished and forgotten in other dust-filled attics. The authors of *40 Thieves on Saipan* have given these truly remarkable men a voice again. Semper Fi."

—Steve Evans, nephew of Donald Evans, one of the 40 Thieves

40 Thieves on Saipan

40 THIEVES ON SAIPAN

The Elite Marine Scout-Snipers in One of WWII's Bloodiest Battles

JOSEPH TACHOVSKY
with CYNTHIA KRAACK

REGNERY
HISTORY

Regnery History™ is a trademark of Salem Communications Holding Corporation
Regnery® is a registered trademark of Salem Communications Holding Corporation

ISBN 978-1-68451-048-1
eISBN 978-1-68451-067-2

Library of Congress Control Number: 2019955288

Published in the United States by
Regnery History
An Imprint of Regnery Publishing
A Division of Salem Media Group
300 New Jersey Ave NW
Washington, DC 20001
www.RegneryHistory.com

Manufactured in the United States of America

10 9 8 7 6 5 4 3 2 1

Books are available in quantity for promotional or premium use. For information on discounts and terms, please visit our website: www.RegneryHistory.com.

DEDICATION

Las Islas de los Ladrones

In 1521 while en route to India, Ferdinand Magellan's expedition arrived at a remote group of islands in the Pacific now known as the Marianas. Finding the native Chamorros to be adept at the art of thievery, his Spanish mariners named the archipelago Las Islas de los Ladrones, "The Islands of Thieves."

Centuries later, during World War II, a different group of thieves invaded the Marianas.

On June 15, 1944, the Sixth Marine Regiment's elite Scout-Sniper Platoon spearheaded the invasion of Saipan, the Empire of Japan's bulwark in the Pacific. Nicknamed "The 40 Thieves" by their peers, this fledgling Special Operations platoon, a precursor to Green Berets and Navy SEALs, wreaked havoc in, around, and mostly behind the front lines. Working deep within enemy territory, where firing a weapon would be their last option, the 40 Thieves had been specially trained in "Silent Killing" techniques. This is the true story of their war, which was terribly up close and personal.

Saipan was the first link in the chain of Japanese home islands that would lead to Tokyo, and the Imperial Army would defend this mountainous terrain to the last man. The Battle for Saipan would be the bloodiest of the Pacific war to date.

We are grateful for the memories and documents that were shared with us by the still-surviving members of the 40 Thieves. This story is dedicated to the men who lived, fought, and died beside them.

*"The Marines I have seen around the world
have the cleanest bodies, the filthiest minds,
the highest morale, and the lowest morals of any
group of animals I have ever seen.*

Thank God for the United States Marine Corps."

—Eleanor Roosevelt

CONTENTS

A NOTE FROM THE AUTHORS

40 Thieves on Saipan is a historical account based on the oral histories, photographs, personal letters, and other documentation willingly shared by surviving members of the platoon and placed in the context of research to authenticate dates, technical information, and other facts. For purposes of readability, some letters included in the book have been condensed to eliminate extraneous material. The original letter from Bill Emerick, which Bill Knuppel read to his platoon mates (see Chapter Twenty-eight) has not survived, so we have included a recreation of it based on Knuppel's memory of its contents. Two characters in *40 Thieves on Saipan* are fictionalized. "Dottie" is a composite figure representing many young women who wrote to men serving overseas in World War II. "Paul Lewis" is a pseudonym for a member of the platoon whom fellow Thieves were reluctant to identify for reasons that will become clear over the course of this story.

Four Woodpeckers

*"Most of this you try to put out of your mind, because it's
nothing you want to think about. You try to forget, but
you relive it every day for the rest of your life."*

—Bob Smotts

June 21, 1944
Saipan

Everybody knew it was a bad idea. And everybody knew what to expect, being sent out miles ahead of the front lines into heavy jungle. Eighteen-year-old Scout-Sniper Bobbie Gene Smotts had heard his buddies joke about it. The guys who had survived Guadalcanal and Tarawa would wisecrack, "The third time's the charm."

Saipan being just his second combat, Smotts felt invincible. He'd go anywhere he was sent and do anything he was told.

And each time his name got called for a mission, he was aware of what could happen. Somebody could get killed. That was part of the bargain.

But not him. Never him. The rough-and-tumble young Okie could take care of himself. Growing up on the Osage Reservation, he had been taught to track, hunt, and shoot from the time he could hold a rifle. With the .22 his parents bought from a Spiegel catalogue, he could shoot the eye out of a rabbit at seventy yards.

As the sun set on June 21, 1944, Smotts sat sleepless in his foxhole, a bad feeling in his gut. Scuttlebutt had it that his lieutenant's request for a phosphorus shelling of the next day's target area had been denied by their colonel. And that afternoon he had overheard his Ares-like corporal say to another squad leader, "We've been lucky so far...all of us. But we aren't Supermen. Tomorrow we may not be so lucky."

Morning dawned on June 22, 1944, the seventh day after landing on Saipan, and a red morning sky backlit the foreboding pitch-black peaks of Tipo Pale and the rocky hills that formed the island's jagged backbone. Tipo Pale's hulking mass of barbed coral, jagged brush, and thick foliage provided countless hiding spots for the Japanese and their woodpeckers—the Marines' nickname for the Imperial Army's Nambu Type 92 heavy machine gun, with its staccato peck-peck-pecking sound. Smotts's foxhole buddy Jesus Orozco maintained that the fierce weapon spat bullets in such a fast and tight pattern that it could cut a man in half in a matter of seconds. He'd seen it happen.

At 0600, the push for the mountain began.

Throughout the morning Marine line troops methodically progressed toward Tipo Pale, bypassing pockets of stiff resistance. Cleaning out those trouble spots, a task considered to be one of the most dangerous jobs in the Corps, fell to the Sixth Regiment's Scout-Sniper Platoon, the elite of the elite, handpicked from hundreds of volunteers. The leader of the forty-man unit had specifically chosen men with brig time. "If a man had spent any office hours for brawling" the platoon's lieutenant explained, "or had a black mark on his record for being in fights, that showed he'd been in trouble and could handle himself. The guy that wins the fight is thrown in the brig. The other guy goes to the infirmary. The guy in the brig is the kind of guy I want."

To his superiors, Smotts had adamantly professed innocence for his role in clearing out a bar full of doggies and swabbies during an earlier stationing in New Zealand. But when asked about his brig time during his Scout-Sniper interview, he found it tough to not smile while replying, "No comment."

On Saipan Smotts frequently got tagged to be on point during missions because of his uncanny sense of smell, honed back home on the Osage Reservation. The Japanese fighters had a distinct odor he could track.

Searching the packs of dead enemy soldiers, it was normal to find bottles of cologne. At first Smotts thought that was curious, but later he figured it was their way of taking a bath in the absence of water. The cologne and their predominantly rice diet gave the enemy an unusual odor—not foul, just distinctive. So in the deep, dense jungle when the hot, thick air was still, Smotts knew if the Japanese were there.

But today, with a steady breeze blowing, this sensory skill would be of no help.

At 1232 Smotts led the Scout-Snipers up a dirt road that snaked its way along the base of Tipo Pale. His platoon was on its way to a finger of a ravine where K Company had been decimated by several well-placed machine guns—seventy-two men, almost a third of its troops, dead or wounded.

Twenty yards ahead of the main body, Smotts silently and cautiously hobbled along; several days of wet socks had brought on a bad case of jungle rot. Limping slightly, he listened for the sound of a bolt being drawn back, looked for a glint of metal in the tangled roots of a banyan tree, and inhaled deeply, just in case.

Reaching a small box canyon, he paused before entering. The path had leveled off into an open area. To his right the road fell off abruptly into a gully full of fifteen-foot-tall trees choked with kudzu vines. On the left, a sheer wall mottled with thick foliage hemmed the other side. Every few feet were fissures that had been cut into the gnarled walls to create the only cover from a blistering tropical sun. Looking into the empty, tranquil canyon, Smotts observed no signs of a skirmish and thought this couldn't have been where K caught it.

Normally the constant noise of gunfire and explosions could be heard from somewhere on the island at all hours of the day or night. Now only a noiseless wind rustled the leaves.

Smotts found the stillness odd.

His tired eyes followed the path he would soon take. Letting the sling on his Springfield out all the way, he switched the safety off. With the rifle

Private First Class Bobbie Gene Smotts.
Courtesy of Bob Smotts

on his hip ready to fire and his ears wide open, Smotts slowly moved forward into the canyon, methodically scanning the mottled face of the sheer wall.

He reached the other side and waited for the rest of his platoon to come into view. Silently he raised his left hand as a signal for them to proceed.

While some of his buddies tentatively entered the canyon at ten-yard intervals, Smotts slid into the shade of one of the fissures to escape the close heat. He lit a cigarette.

The cool smoke felt refreshing as he drew it deep into his lungs. Slipping out of the fissure to check on his buddies' progress, he exhaled just as the foliage of the trees suddenly stopped rustling. His eyes darted toward the new quiet.

Quickly he drew another deep breath—and smelled that distinctive odor.

Before he could yell out a warning, sheets of bluish-white flame erupted from the walls of the box canyon.

Four woodpeckers opened fire.

It was too late.

CHAPTER ONE

A Mustang

"Out of all the lieutenants in the Sixth, Ski was chosen to form and train this platoon. He'd paid his dues on Tarawa and the Solomons and was highly decorated. It was my understanding that he was a Mustang. That's the most respected you can get as an officer, to come up through the ranks like he done."

—Bob Smotts

January 11, 1944
Sixth Marine Regiment, Parker Ranch, Territory of Hawaii

He wouldn't be asked. He would be told. But had he been asked, First Lieutenant Frank Tachovsky would have accepted. Declining a job offer was never an option in the Corps.

Since entering combat, the former Pennsylvania steelworker had gained a reputation as a rugged Marine. Frank was a "Mustang," having risen rapidly through the ranks from buck private to first lieutenant. Both the men he served with and the men who made the decisions recognized his quick mind and ability to remember the smallest details with accuracy. In training or battle, he displayed a certain kind of toughness, a determination to make orders happen. Like a true mustang he had a wild streak. He was more resourceful and possessed better survival instincts than his fresh-out-of-school counterparts. The boys he led appreciated that. They showed it by never referring to him by his rank, but respectfully and affectionately shortening his name to "Ski." Frank liked it. He'd have it no other way.

There wasn't a lot of down time at Parker Ranch on the big Island of Hawaii where the brass had sent these Marines. Keeping fit and training for the next battle might save a man's life. From 0900 until taps, the sounds of pounding boots and barking voices filled the camp. In a rare break Frank sat at his so-called desk constructed of lumber acquired through "Marine methods" and struggled to write a letter to his wife.

They had met at Mike Lyman's in Los Angeles months before he shipped out. Like thousands of wartime newlyweds, Frank and Roxie had learned more about each other through V-Mail than time spent together. The Marines had honored him with the duty to lead men in a gruesome business, but what he wrote to a young wife embedded with her parents at their family hotel in a small Wisconsin shipbuilding town demanded more finesse. Finally, Frank began, "My Dearest Roxie."

That was as far as he got before Harry Edwards, his company captain, knocked on the tent post. "Colonel Murray wants to see you, Ski."

Frank understood the unspoken "now," pushed the letter aside, grabbed his garrison cap, and walked beside Edwards across the camp in a slight but steady drizzle.

It had been almost one month since the Sixth Regiment arrived at their new, desolate training area. After the seventy-four-hour hell of Tarawa, every one of the Marines had expected to return to New Zealand for rest and recuperation. Instead, the brass sent them to this remote spot for more training.

This wasn't the Hawaii of palm trees and grass-skirted hula dancers that families back in the States imagined. Saddled between the snow-covered volcanic peaks of Mauna Kea and Mauna Loa, this was just about the coldest corner of paradise. Hot, dry, dusty days flowed into bitter cold nights, when each Marine had only one coarse green woolen blanket for warmth.

Walking quietly past row upon row of pyramid tents, Ski interrupted the silence, "One of my boys wrote home that he finally figured out why they call this a rest camp. Because it's so far away from the rest of the world."

Their boondockers collected mud as they walked. Around them, enlisted men were taking advantage of the rare rainfall by hurrying outside with bars of soap to clean themselves and the rags they called uniforms. Gear hadn't caught up with them yet. They had been wearing the same dungarees since Tarawa, and despite numerous washings, the scent of death still lingered in the tattered fabric.

Instead of heading to Murray's Second Battalion encampment, Ski and Edwards veered toward Regimental Headquarters. Before entering, Ski looked at a crude plaque engraved on a fifty-gallon oil can lid hanging on a post.

CAMP TARAWA
In Honor of the Fallen
Marines killed on Tarawa: 2200
Marines wounded on Tarawa: 2100
Japs killed on Tarawa: 5000
All within 74 hours of fighting

A gust of damp, cool air moved into the pyramid tent with the two men—not enough to disrupt the haze of smoke that hung above the senior officers who sat or stood scattered, puffing away on pipes, cigarettes, and cigars. Behind a simple, tidy desk in their midst, a short man with a neatly trimmed cavalry-style mustache sat silent and straight-backed.

The wind did not ruffle the man behind the desk. Nothing ruffled Colonel James Riseley, the Sixth Marine Regiment's newly assigned leader—rigid, by the book, and a proper officer. His men referred to him as "Gentleman Jim."

Frank automatically assumed a position in front of the desk and snapped to attention. Save for the striking of a match, the reflexive spat of a tobacco leaf from a tongue, or the clearing of a throat, the room was quiet. Occasional sounds of camp life drifted in—a six-by-six transport truck backfired loudly, a jeep screeched to a halt nearby with its radio blaring, fresh Marine recruits in crisp dungarees marched past, double time, chanting,

The worms crawl in
The worms crawl out
The worms play pinochle on your snout....

and the bellowing of an exasperated drill sergeant pierced the air as he prodded the green boots with vulgarities and, "No! Your other left!"

Riseley glanced at his wristwatch and at exactly 0900 ordered, "At ease."

Clasping his hands behind his back and widening his stance, Frank stood in a minimally less rigid position.

Before Riseley spoke again, the noiseless room was entertained by the nearby jeep's radio playing Kay Kyser's "Who Wouldn't Love You?"

Frank fought back the smile that usually came to his lips when he heard that particular song. Back in San Diego, before he had shipped out to the Pacific, Roxie had sung the lyrics to him. "You're the answer to my every prayer, dah-link," she had crooned, affecting a poor Russian accent, "Who wouldn't love you, who wouldn't care?"

Frank stiffened. He couldn't let his mind wander to that place, not here, not now. "Therein madness lies," his married buddy Doc Webber often counseled.

Colonel Murray began the meeting. "Lieutenant, you're being put up for a Silver Star."

"A Silver Star?" An award for valor surprised him. "What for?"

"What for?" Murray replied. "For cleaning out that pillbox on Tarawa...."

"Single-handed," Edwards added.

Caught off-guard, Frank took a moment to scan the room of weathered faces—Bill Jones, John Easley, Bill Kengla, Ken McLeod. He wondered why all the regimental brass were present.

He drew a deep breath. "Thank you, Colonel Murray. The Japs had a pretty good spot, but there really wasn't much to it. I was only doing my job."

"Well, you did one helluva job," Edwards nodded. "That pillbox had all of I Company and half of your own platoon pinned down. And you took it out on your own."

"With all due respect, sirs, I don't deserve it.... I didn't do anything that any other Marine wouldn't have done."

"You couldn't have done what you did without deserving a Star," Murray stated. "If any other Marine would have done what you did, then any other Marine would be awarded the Star as well. So, you're being put up for it nonetheless."

"Well, thank you, sirs," Frank acquiesced, intuiting that something else had brought him there.

Riseley cleared his throat to speak. "Our regiment will be spearheading the next invasion, and it's been decided that we're going to form a Scout-Sniper Platoon." He took a cigar from a wooden box labeled "Flor de Murias" clipped the end, lit it, and savored the smoke in his mouth.

"Cigar, Lieutenant?" he offered. "Or should I call you Ski? That's what they call you around here, isn't it? Ski?"

"Yes sir," Frank said, accepting the cigar and putting it in his shirt pocket for later. "Don't mind if I do, sir. Thank you."

Riseley continued. "This unit will be a new breed of jungle fighter, modeled after British Commandos, specially trained in Black Death techniques. Living and working behind enemy lines possibly for days at a time, Silent Killing will be a better option than an M1. Scouting enemy locations, fortifications, and mapping them, doing whatever damage can be covertly done, and taking the fire to facilitate the advance of our line companies will be just one job. The other is acting as bodyguards of the command post." Riseley paused before adding, "Meaning me. The man chosen to organize, train, and lead the Scout-Snipers will report directly to me and my XO, Colonel McLeod."

Looking at the ash on his cigar instead of at Ski, Riseley now spoke rapid fire. "It's going to be a rugged job, and I need someone to lead the platoon. Someone like you. I'm new to the Sixth, but I've read through your fitness reports, and all your COs think highly of you. Very highly."

Riseley read from one report: "'An excellent young officer. Rugged. Particularly courageous under fire.' Colonel Kengla, after Guadalcanal."

Lieutenant Frank Tachovsky. *From the collection of Joseph Tachovsky*

Setting that one aside, he rifled through the stack and quoted from another, "'The service of this officer under enemy fire on Tarawa was outstanding. Excellent when the going gets tough. Excellent leader. Men like him....' Colonel McLeod." Looking up from another report, Riseley said, "Colonel Murray calls you rugged as well."

A grin slid across Ski's face before he could stop it, "I don't know about that, sir." In Marine Corps parlance, rugged meant tough. A rugged situation would be particularly dangerous, and a rugged person was one tough sonofabitch.

Setting the papers aside, Riseley looked up. "As Napoleon once said, 'In war it's the *man* who counts, not *men*.' Based upon your fitness reports and the recommendations of the battalion COs, I think you're the right man for the job. Are you the right man, Ski?"

Frank snapped to attention and barked, "Yes, sir. Thank you, sir."

"All right then," Riseley nodded his head. "Welcome aboard. You can choose the men you want from the entire regiment. Any questions?"

"No, sir. No questions."

"Dismissed." Riseley returned his gaze to the papers in front of him.

CHAPTER TWO

The Dumb Hayshaker

"I first met Ski in 1941. We were ready to board a ship
that was going to take us God-knows-where. We left San
Diego and ended up on Iceland. We saw it all together from
Iceland, New Zealand, Guadalcanal, Tarawa, Saipan, and
Tinian. Some of the best men I've known in my lifetime were
Marines, and Ski was a cut above the rest."

—Bill Knuppel

January 11, 1944
Parker Ranch

Stepping out of Regimental Headquarters, Ski glanced upward to the gray, overcast sky and let out the long breath he hadn't realized he'd been holding. Taking a slow step forward on the muddy ground, he started back to his tent and the letter to Roxie. But his new job took priority over finishing that compulsory daily ritual.

"A new breed of jungle fighter...." Riseley's words echoed in his mind.

Ski's mind raced...he would need a platoon sergeant, a true right-hand man, someone he could count on and trust when the going got tough. And it sure as hell would. The soft rain dampened Ski's uniform and chilled him. He checked on the cigar, still dry in his shirt pocket, and thought more about the task at hand.

A right-hand man he thought. Or men.

Ski first met Bill Knuppel and Bob Skeffington in July of 1941 while they were all stationed at Camp Baldurshagi, an outpost in the North

Atlantic. In June of that year President Roosevelt had finally given in to Winston Churchill's repeated pleas for assistance in Britain's war against Germany and sent the First Marine Brigade to Iceland. The hastily organized group of Marines, consisting mainly of the Sixth Regiment, replaced the British soldiers there, the same Brits that had been driven out of Dunkirk. Those troops were needed back home to prepare for Germany's anticipated cross-channel invasion.

On December 7, 1941, Knuppel, Skeffington, and Ski had been enjoying the swimming hall in Reykjavik where the Icelanders let the Marines use the pool on Sunday nights. As they were dressing and clowning around, Captain Raymond Murray (who would become Colonel Raymond Murray by 1944) entered the locker room. His look silenced the trio.

"We just got word that the Japs have bombed Pearl Harbor. They're attacking Wake, the Philippines, and all over the South Pacific. It looks like we're in for a fight. Semper Fi, boys."

Within four months the Marines on Iceland were replaced by Army troops and ordered to Camp Elliott in San Diego to begin training for war in the Pacific.

Every day off in California, Knuppel, Skeffington, and Ski would race north to Los Angeles to visit Skeffie's brother, who tended bar at Mike Lyman's. And each night off they'd creep back to camp at forty miles per hour, relying only on their parking lights because of wartime restrictions. Those restrictions, coupled with bellies full of booze, led to an abrupt, head-on meeting with a eucalyptus tree one night. Everyone in the car became a bloody mess—except for the diminutive Skeffington, who escaped unscathed, having passed out in the front passenger foot well. Those were simpler days.

Knuppel and Skeffington were assigned to the Second Battalion and Ski to the Third before shipping out. Their paths had crossed from time to time on Guadalcanal, New Zealand, and Tarawa. The Scout-Sniper platoon presented an opportunity for the trio to work together once more. Ski trusted these buddies and knew they shared his toughness and resourcefulness.

As he lifted his chin toward the clouds, the misting rain felt cool and invigorating on Ski's face. He changed his course and began walking toward the Second Battalion's camp. After a few inquiries, he located Knuppel's tent.

"You dumb Hayshaker!" Ski hollered inside.

Knuppel stopped his A-Page-A-Day Diary scribbling and stood. "Ski! Good to see you again. What brings you around?"

"Coupla things. Got something to drink? How's Skeff?"

"Didn't you hear?" Knuppel dug a half-full bottle of Four Roses and two tin cups out of his footlocker, filled the cups, and passed one to Ski, "Skeffie got sent Stateside. The bug bit him one good."

They clinked cups and Ski toasted, "To that little bastard. He always did have the luck of the Irish."

"I saw him before he shipped out," Knuppel took another sip, "and you know what that little shit said?"

Ski shook his head.

"He said, 'Thank God I'm goin' Stateside, 'cause I think those Japs are tryin' to kill me.'"

Ski chuckled, "Sound's like Skeff."

"He always had something to say about everything. Remember when we made port in Reykjavik? He yelled out to that motley crew of Limeys on the dock, 'To hell with the Queen!'"

"Yeah, and they yelled back, 'To hell with Shirley Temple!'"

"And remember that half mile of racks along the shore, all of 'em hanging with dried cod?"

"Who could forget that stink? We could smell it a mile out."

"Well, Skeffie gave me a nudge and whispered, 'Must be a girls' finishing school nearby.'"

"He's one damn funny little Irishman," Ski laughed. "On Iceland, he'd always threaten me that if I didn't marry Roxie, he would."

"She still sending all those boxes of goodies? I have dreams about that huge Christmas package she sent you in Iceland."

"That goddamn Skeff opened it while I was on a work detail. When I got back to our hut, that weasel had everything spread out on my cot, waving around a carton of Luckies saying 'Roxie forgot to send you cigarettes!'"

"What a grifter." Knuppel shook his head.

"Why in the hell did he ever start calling you the dumb Hayshaker?"

"That's a story."

"I got time," Ski wiggled his empty cup back and forth. "Must be a hole in it."

Knuppel poured more bourbon. "The name goes back to New Zealand. When Ol' Skeffie got me out of a tangle with an usherette."

"An usherette, no less."

"I gotta confess, Ski, I'd never had a piece of tail before in my life until New Zealand." Knuppel drank deeply. "One afternoon, I went to the opera house and there was this blonde usherette named Hazel. She's sashayin' up and down the aisle, up and down the aisle, hips working overtime, trying to get my attention, and naturally she does."

"Naturally."

"Then she starts giving me the ooo-la-la and smiling. Halfway through the movie, she sits down next to me and starts getting a little frisky, if you know what I mean. Well, one thing led to another, and she asked me to walk her home, so I walked her home. And, when we got there, she asked me up, so I went up. And then she asked me to spend the night. Well needless to say, a good time was had by all. That was my first piece of tail. At twenty-two."

"A late bloomer."

"Don't think I didn't make up for it in spades. Two weeks later, the next time I'm in Wellington, Hazel tells me, 'We've got a problem. I'm pregnant.'

"So here I am in my first tangle with a dolly, and I'm in doo-doo up to my knees. I'm sweating bullets and didn't know what to do. I wrote my Dad, I saw the chaplain, and finally I told Skeffie."

"What did he say?"

"'Farm boys…' He shook his head and then he says 'You should have come to me first. What's her address? I'll pay her a visit and see what I can do.'"

Knuppel emptied the bottle into their cups and continued, "You know what an operator Ol' Skeffie is, always working on some kind of angle. If anybody could do something about it, he could. So, I gave him her address, and he went to see Hazel. When he came back a few hours later, he looks at me and starts laughing.

"What gives, I ask, but he can't stop laughing.

"Finally, Skeffie said, 'I didn't raise you right, you poor dumb little Hayshaker! Didn't you just meet her two weeks ago?'

"I said yeah.

"'Well,' he said, 'Couldn't you tell that somebody else'd already plowed the field? She's noticeably pregnant!'

"How in the hell would I know that? I ask him, and Skeff puts his arm around me and says 'Did you just fall off the hay wagon? You can tell by her belly bump! She's showing, for Christ's sake! She's gotta be six months along.'

"When he stopped laughing, he told me not to worry, that he took care of it for me. And oh brother, did he ever. He told Hazel, 'If you bring this up to our CO or try to make any trouble for my buddy Bill, I'll have every damn Marine in Paekākāriki come in and swear that they spent the night with you.' Then he says, 'Next time take it easy, you dumb Hayshaker.' Can you believe Ol' Skeff?"

"To Skeff." Ski offered a final toast that drained the cups dry.

"Gee, it sure is good to see you again, Ski," Knuppel said. "But you didn't come over just to talk about old times. What brings you by?"

"I don't know how good you'll feel about it after what I have to say…"

"You got bad news?"

"Yes and no. It all depends upon how you take it. Gentleman Jim tagged me to form a Scout-Sniper Platoon for the Regiment. He told me

Sergeant Bill Knuppel. *Courtesy of the Knuppel family*

I've got the pick of anybody in the Sixth, and I pick you to be my platoon sergeant."

"But Ski, I'm only a buck sergeant, a three striper."

"That makes no difference to me," He pointed at Knuppel like a recruitment poster, "I want you! If you want it. This isn't going to be like the line companies, it's gonna be a rugged job, and I don't want you if you're not gonna be all in."

"Don't worry about me, Ski. I'm all in," Knuppel smiled, and the two shook hands, "It'll be my pleasure."

"Then let's get to work tomorrow. My tent at 0800. First job is drafting a notice to draw interest from the right men for the platoon. You go back to your diary scribbling, and I've got to finish off something for Roxie."

"Send her my regards."

As soon as Ski left, Knuppel returned to his diary. The smile quickly left his face. " . . . Over half my gear is gone, bed roll, sea bag, pack, helmet. Damn bunch of thieves around here. And as far as this camp goes, it's fit for a dog. When it's not raining, the dust is two feet thick. We haven't got any water at camp and no showers at all. Here we are in the dirtiest camp in the world with no water to wash. What a lash-up."

CHAPTER THREE

Mr. Kansas City

"If you want to live all your life, you can join the Army,
but if you became a USO soldier, I'd go over the hill to
'pass among them.' I'll not be disgraced by you joining
that outfit. One Marine eight ball is worth 150 dog-
faces—this is our opinion of them. I'd also steer clear of
the Navy. They've got too many rules and regulations for
my tastes—a deck is OK, but I'll do my fightin' on the
beach. Now, if you ain't got good sense and want to hog
all the fightin' with the 'death or glory' boys, well, you
know where to come."

—Don Evans's advice to his younger brother

January 12, 1944, 0900 Hours
Parker Ranch, M Company Encampment

Ski and Knuppel ignored liberty day, a Marine's one day off a week, which the enlisted men used to tend to personal tasks. Those who hadn't washed during the prior day's rain took a much-needed Navy bath using up to four helmets-full of cistern water. Some laundered their tattered uniforms—or stole somebody else's clean one left drying on a tent pole.

With Kona a little too far away for a day of diversion in the city, enlisted men leisurely read letters from home or gazed at pictures of wives and girlfriends left behind. More than one wolfishly ogled tattered pinups of Hollywood starlets like Dolores Moran, Elaine Shepard, and Maureen O'Hara.

If no mail arrived, they made the most of their time off playing cards, drinking Scottish products or other types of joy juice, and

Maureen O'Hara. Leatherneck Magazine, *September 1943*

listening to phonographs spin records. Buddy Williams's "When the Candle Lights Are Gleaming" and Vernon Dalhart's "Blue Ridge Mountain Home" provided a brief trip home. Many of even the hardest Marines found Deanna Durbin's "Beneath the Lights of Home" a little hard to take.

Having enjoyed a leisurely breakfast of "shoe leather" hotcakes, bacon, and powdered eggs, Private First Class Don Evans and two of his buddies lingered in M Company's mess tent. The trio sat quietly sorting packages, V-Mails, and letters into chronological order. Hal Moore, a wiry wrestler from Oklahoma, sat beside Evans; across the table from them, "Wild Bill" Emerick. A tough-looking club fighter out of Chicago, Emerick was the kind of guy who wouldn't take lightly the opinion that his mother was ugly—the sort of guy you wouldn't want to run into in a dark alley.

Emerick sporadically guffawed, reading a book of jokes his wife Eleanor had sent. Once in a while he broke the silence with, "Listen to this one…" But Evans and Moore had already started to chuckle before he could tell the joke. Not in anticipation, but because of the way their buddy spoke out of the right side of his mouth—a consequence of taking one too many right hooks—"from King Lewinsky," Emerick explained. "N' dontcha know, I beat him to a pulp," he'd boast. No one questioned his veracity.

Emerick's bruising appearance contrasted with that of Don Evans. In high school, the blue-eyed, larger-than-life Evans had been the star of

Plaza Theater Stages 'Beauty' Contest—
The Plaza Theater will hold a "Male Beauty Contest" tonight at 9 o'clock. The contestants will parade before the audience and the winner will be judged by the amount of applause he receives. Johnny O'Connor is shown here with Don Evans, center, who won the title of Mr. Kansas City last year, and George Brunker, right, who was runner-up. The management of the theater is still accepting entrants for the contest.

Don Evans (center) competes in the "Mr. Kansas City" contest. *Courtesy of Steve Evans*

every Southeast Knights' team and a heartthrob to the schoolgirls. He was built like a Greek god, with a naturally chiseled physique that had won him the "Mr. Kansas City" contest not once, but twice.

That title bore a certain irony now, when a clean-shaved face and neatly pressed clothes were about as far away as Kansas City.

Evans had turned down a football scholarship to the University of Kansas for the Marine Corps. Shortly after arriving at Boot Camp he wrote his parents, "The first twenty-one days is going to be hell if you can't take it, and several of 'em can't. Right now, we're only boots and scum. If you don't think too much and don't take anything too seriously, you can have a good time. These drill sergeants can't bother me, but I get a kick outta the other fellows' misery."

Evans's first taste of war came on Guadalcanal, mopping up. An inaccurate description; there was nothing janitorial about it.

On an anti-sniper patrol Evans, Moore, and Emerick had come across four Marines lying wounded on a dirt road, writhing on the ground where they had fallen. Strafing machine gun bullets were kicking up puffs of dirt and debris around the injured, as a torturous taunt. It was a common ploy of the Japanese not to immediately kill the injured, but to use them as bait.

With no regard for themselves, the three rushed to the aid of their comrades. The rescue was successful, but Evans was shot in the chest. The bullet narrowly missed his heart, penetrated his lung and exited near his belt line. As a jeep raced Evans's still body and the other wounded back to camp, his two buddies thought he was dead.

That night the skies released torrential rains while Japanese Zeros unleashed a storm of their own. Bombs and machine gun fire showed no respect for the field hospital where Evans had been taken.

The rainfall rapidly filled the dugout where Evans and other wounded were waiting for care. Their cries were unheard in the chaos. Mr. Kansas City managed to crawl from his stretcher and get help to save the others from drowning.

The following day Evans was evacuated by plane to a better-equipped Naval hospital in the New Hebrides. Less than two weeks later, he had made a miraculous recovery, but doctors told him that his fighting days were over. He was being sent home.

"Over?" the brash Jayhawk told the doctors, "I just got here."

To avoid a premature trip Stateside, Evans dressed himself and went AWOL. Stowing away on a transport vessel bound for Guadalcanal, he returned to his astonished buddies three weeks after they had carted him from battle.

Evans consoled his worried parents from the brig where he was sent for going AWOL: "It was considerate of the government to send you that telegram, but unnecessary as I ain't got no sores, goddammit. I gotta little red spot on my chest and lower back. I hope you folks didn't worry about that, as it was of a slight nature. So, everyone can stop prayin' for my quick recovery. It didn't kill me, goddammit."

He was also leniently fined five dollars a month in pay for a period of one month. During his time in the brig, the Corps gave Evans a Silver Star for his part in rescuing his fellow Marines and risking his life in the process.

Having served in the Corps together for almost two years and survived both Guadalcanal and Tarawa, Evans, Moore, and Emerick had formed an inseparable bond. The trio were as thick as thieves.

Mess men noisily clattered about, cleaning up after breakfast and preparing for lunch. Evans and Moore opened packages, read mail, and laughed each time Emerick chortled, "Here's another one…"

Besides letters from his folks, a copious number of fragrant letters and V-Mails lay in front of Evans. Dottie's smelled of lilacs and Elaine's of rosewater. Kathleen, melodramatic and silly, had sealed hers with a kiss. And Judy, a sawed-off little redhead, had written to him twice in the same day.

After reading and then crumpling a puzzling V-Mail from his mom, Evans opened a lilac-scented envelope. "Dearest Donny," the enclosed letter began,

> I was so glad to hear from you once again. It's been a good three months or more since your last letter, and I was awfully worried because I knew hell was popping over there, and you wouldn't be happy unless you were in the middle of it.
>
> At the present time I am in class, and the teacher just said that I might start taking notes at any time now to good advantage. Don't think I'll do that!
>
> I haven't heard from my brother Ross for more than three weeks. Mother got a letter on Christmas day from him but since then they haven't heard, either. As far as we know he is still in Sicily, but they have been shipping a lot of the boys

back to England in preparation for the new second front on the drive into Germany. Ross sent a Christmas box home that was quite interesting—twenty-two Italian chevrons, a wristwatch, a leather billfold from North Africa, some German cigars, a bullet, two blouses, and some lingerie. That's all I can think of at the present.

During the Christmas vacation I called your mother, and she said that she hadn't heard from you for some time. She had hopes that you were on your way home. So, naturally we had our hopes up too. But, no. You say it will be quite a spell before you'll be home.

My gosh, do you realize that you've been gone almost two years? And that some people back here would like to see you again? Namely, me, if you need an example.

Time's running short, best I should hurry. Haven't taken a single note this hour but I have received some awfully nasty looks.

Evidently you haven't been getting my mail because I know I have written several times since September 11. I guess you cover so much territory and jump around so much that you miss out on some of the mail.

With love, Dottie

Evans stared blankly at the page of bright blue cursive. Taking in a deep breath of the lilac-laced envelope, he exhaled mightily, and pondered the ceiling of the mess for a moment.

Looking at his mother's crushed V-Mail, he regretted his actions and attempted to smooth the wrinkled paper. Then, picking up a pen and a blank piece of V-Mail, Evans responded, but not to Dottie.

Dear Mom,

You know what I was looking for when I joined the Marine Corps, well I've had several solid years of it, and I've enjoyed every one of them. This war came at the most opportune time, and now I've found my calling. The Corps offers everything I've been looking for, and I've become a first class fighting man.

I've lost a lot of buddies along the way, but Hal Moore, Emerick, and me came thru the assault on Tarawa unscathed. The Japs said it would take a million men one hundred years to grab that island, but we Marines did it in three bloody days.

Thank Dottie for her nice letter, but aren't there any men back there at all? I've got too many women on the string that do too much wishful thinkin'. I'll have to sign up for four more years overseas duty just to escape 'em all. So, please don't tell any more gals to write me 'cause I won't be able to answer. I'm writing to Jean, Dottie, Judy, Kathleen, and Jeanette back home, one in La Jolla to whom I am betrothed, and a fiancée in New Zealand—a Maori girl, but oh my!

This Marine Corps versus Japan fight has the earmarks of a long & delightfully violent scrap, and I'm not about to miss out on any of it. I thoroughly enjoy a good healthy war, and the Marine Corps is no place for a married man.

Here's commentary on that lecture you gave me. I'm sure burned up over it and can't figger it out at all.

If you think I'm the sweet, clean, sensitive, sheltered, Sunday school lad that you think I am, why somebody is awful deluded. I've been livin', you know, and I've matured a little along the way. I've had about ten years of experience crammed into these last few years.

This war ain't being fought in church, not in this part of the world, anyhow. This jungle fighting don't follow the rules, and a pistol provides more comfort to me than a Bible. Your continual worrying and praying has got to come to an end.

And if you're going to do a lot of wishful thinking, count me out. What little enjoyment I partake in along the road is up to me. I'll enjoy life while I can. And as far as women go, those Maori gals are a lot cleaner than those in California. What do you want me to do, ask 'em for a medical certification before dating 'em?

Emerick says, "What my people don't know won't worry 'em, so I don't tell 'em much." I think he's got the right idea. So much for that.

Well, so this letter don't appear too austere, I'll add a belated Happy New Year.

Love, Don

Having overstayed their welcome in the mess, the three gathered their mail and headed to their tent to listen to a record Moore's little sister had sent, one of his favorites: Gene Autry's "Red River Valley."

"Dontcha know," Emerick read out of his joke book, "he's one of the three Polish cowboys, Gene Koo-yea, Gene Dobry, and Gene Autry."

CHAPTER FOUR

Borawski Done It

*"In the Marine Corps the preference was for people eigh-
teen to twenty years old because we just didn't have any
sense. Like I say, we was a crazy bunch. We was nuts.
Not many like us in the Marine Corps, I don't think."*

—Bob Smotts

January 12, 1944, Liberty Day
Parker Ranch, Shortly after Breakfast at A Company

During morning chow, four Marine privates overheard some corporal talking about a mythical place allegedly nearby. Listening intently to snippets of scuttlebutt going back and forth across the different dining tables, Walter Borawski latched onto a bit of news that their corporal's pal had heard from somebody who had a friend at headquarters, who had heard it on some colonel's radio. Borawski picked up certain key words—canned peaches, cigarettes, cigars, and liquor. The rumor had something to do with an Army supply depot near Kona, or maybe it was a Navy Officer's Club on the road to Hilo. He wasn't sure, but it didn't matter. It was liberty day, so the four decided they needed to go on a mission: *Operation booze run.*

The four of them began to scheme as they left the mess tent. Deep in thought, they walked past a jeep with its motor running. Three of the privates continued to walk on, but Borawski stopped dead in his tracks.

21

"So, what if we borrow the jeep?" That was his epiphany.

After all, it wasn't a Marine jeep; it was an Army captain's, so it was fair game. Acting purposefully, without a word, Borawski hopped in the driver's seat and hollered out to his buddies, "Let's go!"

"We'll be back quicker than a cat can lick his ass," Alfred Yunker, a Wisconsin farm boy, pledged to Bobbie Gene Smotts and Daniel Kenny as they all piled on board.

Glancing around cautiously, Borawski depressed the clutch, threw the stick shift into first gear, and let the clutch out. The vehicle lurched forward and stalled out. He tried again, and it bucked forward—not stalling out this time, but the herky-jerky getaway began to attract unwanted attention and wasn't as speedy as hoped.

"You do know how to drive, don't you?" Kenny goaded.

Borawski confessed he did not. Although he had committed various and sundry offenses in his hometown of "Sin City"—Utica, New York— stealing a car was not one of them.

"Move over," Kenny said, and the two traded places. The instant Kenny took the wheel, the spinning tires kicked up a cloud of dust, and the jeep shot off. Careening at breakneck speed, Kenny zigzagged furiously, avoiding numerous potholes in the bumpy dirt road. The jeep zoomed around blind curves as Smotts, Borawski, and Yunker laughed hysterically and held on for dear life.

As a tough little street urchin from Corktown, the Irish ghetto of Detroit, Daniel "Red" Kenny had grown up better versed in rolling drunks and stealing from hucksters than in his ABCs. He had graduated to armed robbery and begun running wild with the Irish gangs, excelling as a wheelman. The chippies of Corktown thought him handsome in a wicked way, with his shock of bright russet hair and a slightly scarred face. Handsome didn't help in the Marines, but the wicked ways did.

Seeing a slight hill in the road a hundred yards away, Kenny put the gas pedal to the floor. The privates gleefully whooped and hollered. The jeep hit the crest at full speed, all four tires left the ground, and everyone flew straight up out of their seats. Upon landing, Kenny quickly slammed on the brakes, drawing applause from his buddies.

Closing in on Hilo and noticing a group of buildings surrounded by a formidable fence, Kenny slowed to a crawl.

"That place's locked up tighter than a gnat's ass," Yunker observed with a degree of reverence. He gestured for Kenny to pull off the road and drive behind a clump of brush, then silently motioned for Borawski to follow him on a reconnaissance mission. They pretended to hitchhike while inconspicuously casing the facility.

"Dammit," Borawski muttered. An old Nash with two passengers drew close and slowed to a stop.

The man driving told them to get in.

Needing to scare off the unwelcome assistance, Yunker noticed a woman sitting in the front passenger seat. He draped himself on her door, leered through the open window, and sneered, "Nice."

The Nash sped off.

Free of witnesses, the pair soon reported back to Smotts and Kenny: No guards or sentries observed on foot patrol. One guard at the main gate on the east side. Barbed wire fencing and a coil of the spiked wire at the top. There had to be something worthwhile inside.

"This ain't gonna be a piece of cake." Borawski shook his head.

Smotts sat down on a coconut log and calmly lit a cigarette. "What if…" "How about…" "Why don't…" He listened to his buddies' hare-brained schemes and finished his lazy smoke before joining in the conversation.

"I was raised to be prepared." Smotts's eyes twinkled as he produced a pair of wire cutters. "I come by my expertise naturally as an Okie." Back home in Hominy, Smotts's grandfather had been rumored to be a horse thief and bank robber, a member of the notorious Oklahombres. "Like I say," Smotts said in his nasal twang, "I ain't no Boy Scout."

Like a two-bit surgeon in tattered dungarees, Smotts clipped the fence.

The search went on, peering through grimy windows of building after building. In many of them they saw crates and boxes stamped USN.

"Jackpot!" They smiled in unison. It was well known that the Navy traveled on its liver, so there had to be a liquor warehouse around somewhere. The hunt intensified.

The largest building, as big as a gymnasium, had windows too high to look inside and a door that was double-locked. This could be it. Wasting no time, Borawski picked the locks, a useful skill he had learned as a youth, and pushed the creaking door open.

No one said a word, just ogled the wondrous sight. A Shangri-La of booze. The rows and rows of crates stacked six feet high had labels like Calvert, Schenley, Hennessy, Teacher's, and Four Roses. Pabst Blue Ribbon lined one entire wall—enough booze to stock Naval Officers' Clubs throughout Hawaii. It was dumbfounding, salivating.

Ledgers and papers on a desk documented inventories of scotch, rye, bourbon, and gin.

"Somebody's gonna notice if a case or two is missing," Borawski muttered. "But a bottle or two from a bunch of different cases wouldn't be discovered for a long time."

Packing their dozens of single bottles into a couple of empty boxes, they placed the tampered cases at the bottom of a stack. Sneaking out of the stockyard, the four thieves resealed the fence for future use.

The Marines polished off a couple of bottles on their way back to camp, and Kenny drove off the road into a grove of palm trees to give Borawski a driving lesson. After mastering the clutch, Borawski slalomed in and out of trees to practice. Weaving to and fro, barely skimming past the leathery trunks, the jeep staggered back and forth sending bottles— and occasionally one of his pals—flying.

Borawski drove the rest of the way like a bat out of hell. Nearing Parker Ranch, he skidded off the road and down into a small gully. Planning for the future, the four camouflaged the jeep with foliage. With any luck it might not be found and prove useful again.

"And if they do find it," Smotts winked to his friends, "Who gives a damn? We'll just steal another one."

Left: Alfred Yunker. *Courtesy of Alfred Yunker, Jr.*
Center: Daniel Kenny. *Courtesy of Bob Smotts*
Right: Walter Borawski. *Courtesy of Richard Zuziak*

They buried bottles along the way back to their battalion and sketched the whereabouts on a hand-drawn map for recovery. Each carried a single inconspicuous bottle as they walked into camp.

Triumphantly entering their ten-man tent, the thieves were given a hero's welcome by the rest of their squad. When their tentmates asked where they had gotten the money to pay for the expensive liquor, normally twenty dollars a bottle, Smotts's eyes glimmered "I used Oklahoma cash." Everybody lapped up the booze like a bunch of starved kids.

"We're gonna get rip-roarin' soused!" were the last words Smotts said with clarity.

CHAPTER FIVE

Ellie, Tilly, Roxie, and Ruth

*"The sexual life of the camel is stranger
than anyone thinks."*

—*the first lines of Doc Webber's favorite limerick*

**January 12, 1944, Liberty Night, after Supper
Doc Webber's Tent, Parker Ranch**

Every evening of a liberty day, the Naval medical officer assigned to the Sixth Regiment hosted a poker night for his Marine buddies Edwards, Ski, and Lieutenant Joe Dulcich. Despite not being a member of the Corps, Lieutenant Jerry "Doc" Webber fit right in with his Leatherneck pals, who liked and respected the tough and even-keeled pediatrician from Michigan. He took the same risks in the field as any Marine and performed miracles on shattered bodies in the crudest of crude conditions. And he was funny as hell.

"For gallantry and intrepidity," Doc proclaimed as Ski entered the tent. The medical officer presented Ski with a tinfoil-covered tongue depressor in exchange for the package he had brought from his wife Roxie. Dulcich placed a tin cup of rye in Ski's other hand.

"May you be as successful at emptying our pockets as emptying that pillbox." Doc raised his cup. "Here's mud in your eye." All toasted, three with fingers crossed.

"Make sure y'all don't tell Roxie or she'll throw you a parade." Dulcich, the New Orleans artist, drawled and placed his drink on the jerry-built table. "Now let's go."

"Seven-card-stud." Doc started dealing and spinning stories. "The sexual life of the camel is stranger than anyone thinks. At the height of the mating season he tries to bugger the Sphinx. But the Sphinx's posterior orifice is packed with the sands of the Nile. Which accounts for the hump on the camel, and the Sphinx's inscrutable smile."

Cautious bids followed, along with ribbing about the award.

Doc repeated Dulcich's warning: "To echo the sentiments of our good friend from the great state of Louisiana, for Christ's sake, don't tell Roxie."

"Don't worry about that." Ski peered at his two down cards. "I made the mistake of telling her about malaria." Ski had come down with a case of the disease, which naturally worried his wife. "That's all I read about in her letters now. She's become an authority on it."

"I'm surprised at you, Ski," Edwards frowned. "To make such a tactical error. And you got a Star. Tsk, tsk."

"If Skipper hadn't spilled the beans, were ya gonna tell us?" Dulcich folded his hand.

"Someday." Ski exhibited and lit the cigar from Riseley. "From the Old Gent himself. You better pay attention to the game, or I'll be sending your money home to Roxie. Whose deal?"

During a break between hands, Doc excused himself to use the nearby latrine. His pals smiled at each other and waited in anticipation of the weekly routine.

Through the stillness of the camp, they listened as Doc offered one long, loud moan, followed by silence. Then came ten to fifteen seconds of brisk panting, and then quiet again. A tiny, faint falsetto scream slowly crescendoed to a loud, abrupt end.

A few more moments passed before they heard the sound of Doc clapping his hands together twice. Proudly he announced, "It's a boy!"

It never grew old.

Third Marine Battalion officers. Doc Webber is seated just right of center. Captain Edwards stands behind Doc's right shoulder. Ski is in the second row, second from the left. Dulcich stands in the back row, far right. *From the collection of Joseph Tachovsky*

They had been together since Guadalcanal and all had wives back in the States worried about them. Doc had been married the longest; his wife Ellie and their two daughters lived in Grand Rapids. The other three marriages were hasty war-jitter affairs.

Hordes of men rushed into marriage during the War, hurriedly getting the required Wassermann blood tests so they could marry their sweethearts before shipping out. Edwards, Ski, and Dulcich had all married in August of 1942. Edwards's wife Tilly lived in San Jose; Ski's Roxie in Wisconsin; and Joe's Ruth in New Orleans. The wives themselves had become a tightly knit group of friends, corresponding with each other on a regular basis, even traveling great distances to pay a visit.

"The Salty Sons of Sin," as Dulcich had labeled the group of men, had begun as five but now were only four. A fifth undrunk cup in honor of their lost buddy always sat on the table during their games. The group kept each other in good spirits. They had grown accustomed to the Spartan life of the Corps. But more important, they had a job to do. None of the men was necessarily homesick, but all would rather have been in the States with their loved ones.

With marital relations confined to pen and ink, and after sixteen months overseas and no rotation in sight, sex had become a distant memory for the husbands, so they stuck together for much needed moral support. They found it relatively easy to avoid the legalized brothels in Kona. The pretty Army nurses were a different matter. Ski wasn't the only one suffering recurring bouts of malaria contracted on Guadalcanal, and residual effects of dysentery from Tarawa also resulted in repeated visits to the infirmary.

Most of the nurses were skilled, professional, and aloof. But not all the caregivers emulated Florence Nightingale. Many "working girls" eagerly joined the military in hopes of cashing in on the abundance of sex-starved men. Hospitals proved a good hunting ground: sick boys were easily stirred. For those plying their more whorish skills on the job, meager military wages could be supplemented by hundreds of dollars a month—or maybe a wedding band on the left hand from some major or colonel.

The married officers steeled themselves to temptation, but the lure might be too great for some of the enlisted men. There was a story going around camp about precautions Colonel Riseley had taken.

As Doc said, "I heard Riseley warned others about how thousands of teenage guys might act with a feminine presence on Hawaii. The Old Gent arranged an informal meeting with the woman colonel in charge of the hospital.

"During their chat, Riseley mentioned that many of his boys hadn't even seen a girl in months and that her nurses would most certainly be a distraction. 'I'll do my best to keep an eye on my boys,' Riseley told his counterpart. 'And I think we'll both appreciate it if you keep your girls on a short rein.'"

"The woman colonel thought he didn't appreciate her nurses' smarts. 'Don't you worry,' she assured him and tapped a finger on her forehead, 'My girls have it up here.'"

Doc sat back, stiffened his spine like the Old Gent, lowered his voice, and wagged a finger. "'I don't care where your girls have got it,' Riseley had stated. 'My boys will find it.'"

Doing their best to avoid "it," the Salty Sons played cards, drank, wrote their wives often, golfed whenever possible, and only joked about sex.

"There was a young virgin named Alice," Doc began another limerick and gestured for Ski to open Roxie's package. "Who thought her vagina a chalice. One night sleeping nude, She awoke feeling lewd, And found in her chalice a phallus."

Edwards dealt out five cards to each man at the crowded table, carefully avoiding a cigar-filled ashtray, a Coleman lantern, cups filled with rye, and the various treats Roxie had sent. Without asking for permission, he eagerly grabbed a square tin and took a cookie. "The game," he said with a mouthful of marzipan, "is five-card draw."

Roxie's packages had become legendary. Her most recent Christmas package had contained socks that she had knitted for all of Ski's friends, along with cheeses, salami, mustard, nuts, cookies, a bottle of scotch, pickled herring, cigars, and a pair of slippers for Ski.

Edwards loved Roxie's cookies. "I'd really like to meet Roxie some time," he said as bets were made around the table. "She takes veeeery good care of me," he joked slyly.

If anybody else had made that wisecrack, Ski might have decked him, but there was no need for Ski to be jealous of his friend. The dashing Edwards was very much in love with his wife Tilly, an exotic beauty of Spanish descent. And Roxie was popular with all Ski's buddies. Besides the boxes of lavish treats that Ski shared with them, her letters would include "Hiya, Mac" for Edwards, "Take good care of Ski"—signed "Mrs. Ski"—for Doc, or "Tell Joe I just spoke with Ruth. She's an angel" for Dulcich.

With no electric lights in camp, the Coleman lantern allowed them to play past sunset. A cigar smoke haze grew inside the tent. The kitty in the center of the table grew as well. Hand after hand, the Christmas scotch emboldened the men's carefree wagering.

Edwards added two dollars to the kitty and took three cards for himself, Ski and Dulcich one each and anted up. Doc took two cards, raised his bet five dollars, calmly puffed on his cigar, and looked innocently upward. Edwards eyed him skeptically and threw in five. "It's a bluff."

"That's daddy's special boy," Doc said and smiled. Ski, adept at cards and a keen observer, had heard Doc use that same phrase a few hands earlier when Doc held the winning hand. So thinking it was no bluff, Ski folded, holding two tens. Dulcich was still in.

By the time the betting ended, the pot was enormous. Cards were shown. Both Edwards and Joe held nothing; a nine of spades was the high between the two of them.

"There was a young girl named Anheuser," Doc slapped down a deuce of clubs, "who said that no man could surprise her." He followed with the three. "But Pabst took a chance." Next came the four of clubs. "And Schlitzed in her pants." Then the five of clubs. "And now she's sadder Budweiser."

"Laughing boy!" Dulcich groaned as Doc showed his last card, the jack of diamonds.

"Poleshit!" Ski shouted in disgust at himself for folding for a bluff.

"I knew it. I knew it." Edwards handed the cards to Doc. "Your deal. What's it gonna be?"

"Five-card draw."

"Again?"

"You never bite the hand that pulls your pud," Doc answered coolly.

They continued to play until half an hour before lights out. Then, like clockwork, the game came to an abrupt halt; without a word, the deck of cards was stowed away for another week, the table cleared, the cups filled with a nightcap. Writing now took priority.

The Salty Sons knew that letters had to be written almost daily. Any lapse in correspondence would create either false hope or worry for Ellie, Tilly, Roxie, and Ruth. False hope because a lack of letters might mean a husband on his way home. Worry because something terrible might have happened. Each letterless day was filled with anxious anticipation or the dread of receiving that cablegram. The one that began with "DEEPLY REGRET TO INFORM YOU."

Doc opened his folder containing Red Cross stationery and began his letter with, "To Eleanor my sweet, and my darlings Lee and Chrissy."

Dulcich, who had received a Christmas package from Ruth containing a box of stationery oddly embossed with the U.S. Army insignia, shuddered in disgust each time he opened the box. Scribbling over the insignia, Dulcich scrawled, "Dear Ruth: I still can't believe that you could be so irresponsible...."

Edwards borrowed a piece of V-mail from Ski. "My Darling Tilly" was all he could write before the tip of the pen broke; he continued in pencil.

And Ski, as always, began his letter with "My Dearest Roxie..."

There are a few of your letters that need answering so here goes.

While we are all somewhat disappointed in our new training camp, all of us now appear in the best of moods thanks to those back home. My little wife is most thoughtful. I would kiss you if that were possible, but in the words of Akim Tamiroff, "Enough of this love making!" I must finish this letter before Taps.

Our gear has just caught up with us, and at last I have some clean things to wear.

Incidentally, I wore the socks you knit for me in this last campaign. However, I lost one of the socks in the recent shuffle—your Christmas socks were well timed. Of course, losses of such items are expected. I lost numerous things, but none as valued as the sock. I didn't lose the main item, though, myself. So, we done pretty well, huh?

In quite a few of your letters you asked many questions, all about malaria. Although it made me laugh, nicely, that while reading you began telling ME all about the disease. But I shall answer your questions regardless.

I am not sent home, Roxie, because I am a Marine, healthy and able to serve in that capacity. Frankly, I am sorry that I informed you that I had malaria. You can rest assured that we receive the best of medical attention possible and that we are well and able to fight, or we wouldn't be here.

Your trouble, Roxie, is that you married a Marine during war, and you are not taking it in stride. You can rest assured, darling, that I haven't had any more attacks of malaria. It's been ever so long since the last. I feel that for me the attacks are over.

Personally, if I come out of this war with only malaria, I feel I shall be very lucky. So does any other man out here, I am sure. So please desist in writing about malaria any more in your letters and don't worry any more on this score. If you didn't know what you were getting into when we were married, you do now, so try and be equal to the task. I don't want to say "I told you so," but remember that I did want to wait till this was over before we got married. I write this only because it appears necessary.

Spike Jones is coming over the radio from the jeep outside our tent, and "Der Fuehrer's Face" has taken me off of my soapbox.

Well, that is enough for now, my love. The guy may be right about "Man's love is of man's life a thing apart; 'Tis woman's whole existence." If so, I am apart from the biggest thing in my life, and I want so very much to be near.

It's really time to end this letter because it's getting so very close to Taps. So it is Goodnight once again, my love.

You have all my love forever.

Your husband, Frank

PS: Now don't you start calling me "Ski," I get enough of that around here.

The bugler playing "Taps" signaled lights out throughout the camp. Ski and his buddies hurriedly finished up, listening to the doleful music that seemed somehow a little longer and more dreamily bittersweet that night.

Lanterns were doused around camp. It felt good to hear the bugler blowing. After weeks in combat, when rest was never restful, the sound of "Taps" gave a feeling that all was secure. It was time to turn in and sleep well.

CHAPTER SIX

Sweet Dreams

"You're living with your nerves constantly frayed to the point where you're just trying to keep it together and not lose it. At night the barracks would sound like a nuthouse with all the screaming and hollering from the nightmares. Everybody had them. I don't know how anyone could not."

—Marvin Strombo

January 13, 1944, 0100 Hours
Parker Ranch, D Company Encampment

Lights out left every man in a different personal state. A few slept like babies, waking every once in a while, then falling back to sleep. Some slept like the dead, their bodies worn out and their minds shut down. But most battled with wartime experiences too powerful to give space for peaceful rest.

If he closed his eyes, he knew it would happen again.

Roscoe Mullins lay on his cot, uneasy in the blackness of the ten-man tent and trying to stay awake. Curled up for warmth beneath his coarse green woolen blanket, the sleepless private from West Virginia struggled to keep his eyes open and listened to the other members of his squad. Few of them slept quietly.

It had been months since he had had a good night's sleep.

Back home, he would be as tired as a two-dollar whore on nickel night. He could sleep like a log until his drunkard of an old man, a lumberjack and bootlegger by trade, spilled him out of bed at the crack of dawn to work him at felling trees until dusk.

Everything about the Marines fit Mullins. He loved to run, something he had learned on the obstacle course of logs and streams on Kayford Mountain. As one of ten kids in a poor family headed by a father even tougher than a drill instructor, he knew how to get by on the barest essentials. Growing up in the coal mining hills had prepared Mullins to expect little from life without a fight, and the Corps finished the process. Mullins enjoyed every minute of it. He worked hard, fought hard, and rarely broke a sweat. Until after lights out.

Most nights, Mullins would bolt out of bed to find himself standing in a cold sweat, shivering in the dark. No man could be trained to forget. For Mullins it was Tarawa and the Officers' Tomb.

Sometimes he could elude the torment if he drank himself to sleep. But if he fell asleep sober, the haunting dream ran over and over and over. He couldn't shake it.

Hour upon hour passed. Blinking in his fight to stay awake, Mullins was losing the battle, as always. His heavy eyes finally refused to snap back open. The soft, rhythmic white pulsing on the inside of his lids mimicked his heartbeat, gently lulling him to sleep.

Soon the peaceful pulsing segued into harsh white flashes that escalated into explosions. Once more, the nightmare began.

Whining and whistling mortars crescendoed into eruptions of sand. Fragments of debris and searing hot metal rained down from the sky. Maneuvering his way over the corpse-covered ground, Mullins passed hundreds of blackened bodies lying twisted and contorted where they had fallen. Their balloon-like stomachs pulsed as though alive, throbbing with the maggots that worked away inside.

A sudden loud popping sound like a firecracker made him cringe and turn, thinking a grenade had exploded. Instead, one of the heaving bellies had burst, spattering him with organs and blood. A swarm of plump flies, fat from gorging upon the dead, rapidly descended upon him and tried to enter his eyes, nose, and mouth. There were too many of them to shoo away, he had to rake them off his face as he pushed forward to escape.

Pausing thirty feet away from a large cement pillbox, he saw the barrel of a machine gun firing through a loophole; the peck-peck-pecking staccato cut Marines to shreds in short bursts of bluish-white flame.

"Get that woodpecker!" an officer's bellowed order drifted through the acrid haze.

Squinting up into the sun, Mullins watched the shadow of a Marine furiously kicking at an air vent on top of the pillbox until it finally broke loose. Other silhouettes quickly rushed to the man's side carrying tins of gasoline and emptied them into the vent, followed by a torch.

The immense explosion shook the ground and sent the pair of heavy steel doors that sealed the pillbox flying off. The billowing smoke cleared, and Mullins walked into the black haze.

The smell of burnt hair and roasted flesh, the sound of crackling fires, and the sight of a dozen charred Japanese officers greeted his numbed senses. A few of them had been blown to bits in the explosion, but most had already committed the ritual suicide of harakiri— disemboweling themselves.

Rummaging through the debris, he stumbled over a bloody mass, and turned over the remains of a shattered officer; the intestines oozed to the ground, and the hands still clutched at a short, ornate samurai sword embedded in the stomach. Beneath the gutted carcass, the brown eyes of a dead nurse stared blankly up at him. The officer had evidently put a bullet in her skull before slicing his own belly open.

Mullins heard a woman's voice whispering, "I don't want to die."

Wrenching his eyes away, he turned his attention toward the samurai sword. Coveting the ornate souvenir, he put one foot on the dead man's chest, grabbed hold of the sword's hilt, and yanked hard. As the blood-crusted blade slid out of the lifeless form, the gaping mouth emitted one last, foul exhale into Mullins's face.

He turned to leave, but a mass of fire blocked his exit.

A Marine with his torso aflame begged, "Kill me."

Mullins stood frozen, unable to lift his rifle. The fiery form slowly staggered across the smoking ground toward Mullins, with arms outstretched.

"Please kill me..." The Marine kept pleading as his burning flesh fell to the ground.

Powerless, Mullins closed his eyes, and the warmth on his cheeks increased.

The heat became suffocating.

Just as the human inferno was about to engulf Mullins, the voice shrieked directly into his ear, "KILL ME!"

Mullins sprang from bed as if jerked by a string. Disoriented, he stood frozen in the pitch-black tent gasping for breath, his skivvies and blanket soaked with sweat. The chilly air gradually roused him, and little by little the fierce thumping in his chest ebbed.

A hushed voice asked, "You okay, Roscoe?"

Mullins turned toward the only light in the dismal tent, the glowing red dot at the end of a cigarette, and recognized the voice of Marvin Strombo, his best buddy since boot camp.

They had little in common. The quiet, reserved Strombo came from a loving home in Dixon, Montana. He had joined the Marines because his older brother Oliver had led the way.

Despite their differences, the pair became fast friends and took care of each other through thick and thin. When soused-up, Strombo and Mullins acted as brothers would, practicing jujitsu or other hand-to-hand methods. The rough fight would escalate into a bloody drunken free-for-all, but the next morning they always walked to chow arm in arm laughing. Except for good buddies, it was rare for Marines to know each other's first names. And Mullins enjoyed knowing and saying, "Marvin J. Strombo."

"Welcome to paradise," Mullins replied, as he stripped himself of his wet underwear, put on his dungarees, and curled up again, using his poncho as a blanket for some warmth. Strombo ground the fading red stub of his cigarette out on the wooden decking under his rickety cot and rolled over, also not wanting to sleep, not wanting to dream.

It seemed as though only a minute had passed when reveille sounded.

Normally "You gotta get up! You gotta get up! You gotta get up in the morning" provided a rude awakening. But this day began unlike any other.

Before the war the Sixth Regiment's bugler had played the clarinet in Woody Herman's big band. Military life had tamed his jazzy stylings, but he was emboldened by his enchanting version of taps the night before and a little hungover from liberty day. So the bugler's common sense took another day off. Tired of playing reveille the conventional way, he had decided to jazz it up.

Dawn broke not with a brash bugle blaring, but with the smooth tones of a clarinet playing "Call to Post" before flowing into "You gotta get up in the morning." The clarinetist's improvisational riffs had men jumping out of bed and running out of tents into the cool dewy air. The enlisted men listening throughout the camp loved the outlandish interpretation. Many danced in their skivvies. When the impromptu show ended, the camp erupted in applause.

Cheerful conversations about the unconventional reveille buzzed as the men returned to their tents to dress for morning chow. Tussled blankets and cots were transformed into meticulous bunks for morning inspection. Everyone and everything had to be in its place and properly aligned for the surly corporal's daily scrutiny.

Despite the wet blanket, Mullins's bunk appeared crisp and shipshape. The soaked skivvies, pinned between his footlocker and the foot of his cot to dry out, were barely visible.

"'Tenshun!" came the command. The privates snapped to.

Walking between the rows of cots, the nitpicking corporal found some bit of fault with all. But he stopped at Mullins's cot. He had caught a glimpse of the damp underwear.

"Piss yourself again, Mullins?" he sneered, spitting out his frequent taunt. Unrelenting with all the privates, the abusive corporal took a sadistic joy in singling out Mullins and relished every opportunity to make an example of him. He didn't just chew him a new one, he chewed all the way around it until it fell to the ground.

No matter how much time he spent working over his Springfield with a toothbrush for inspections, Mullins had learned that a clean rifle was an impossibility. Fifty rifle push-ups would be the punishment. If his bunk or clothing didn't pass muster, the corporal marched the entire squad to a sandy area so his buddies could watch as the corporal tried to run him into the ground, having him double time in circles while holding his rifle at port arms.

Mullins never did him the favor of falling down.

Everyone hated the corporal. But there was nothing Mullins or any other private could do about it. Transferring out of a unit was a rarity in the Corps. Confrontations with a superior always turned out badly. In boot camp, Mullins made the mistake of punching out a sergeant. Even though the sergeant threw the first punch, Mullins was thrown in the brig; the sergeant was carried to the infirmary. A second altercation with another NCO might mean the Naval prison at Mare Island.

"Sweet dreams, Mullins?" The corporal tore the blanket off the cot and threw it onto the decking. After wiping his dirty boots on it, he ordered "Wash it," and left.

Left: Roscoe Mullins. *Courtesy of Roscoe Mullins;* Right: Marvin Strombo. *Courtesy of Marvin Strombo*

"I'm not shittin' you, Marvin J.," Mullins vowed through clenched teeth, "if I ever get the chance, and I can get away with it, I'm gonna kill that sonofabitch."

"Let's do our laundry and get some chow," Strombo said in his typical mild manner. "Then you can kill him."

CHAPTER SEVEN

I Got Me a New Boss

"Ski was one of the best. Those green dandy Louies just
out of school treated us like dogs, but Ski treated us like
men. We were a rambunctious bunch, and he put up
with a lot of bullshit from us, but we would have moved
Heaven and Earth for that man."

—*Roscoe Mullins*

Mullins and Strombo ate a quick breakfast before starting their laundry day system. They marched to another battalion's camp and searched for untended clotheslines. Mullins carried all their dirty laundry, leaving Strombo empty-handed. At opportune times, Strombo would pick the clean clothing other Marines had already washed and Mullins would leave their dirty clothes behind.

Bitching loudly about "goddamned" this or that, and joking about "wash, rinse, and repeat," the duo never looked like anything nefarious. To all appearances, they were just a couple of Marines doing their laundry.

Occasionally, they might have to make a hasty exit. If the rightful owners noticed what they were up to, Mullins and Strombo would artfully dodge around a corner, drop what they had pilfered, then turn around and walk calmly past the hot-in-pursuit owners. Returning to the same now unguarded clothesline, they would continue to "wash, rinse, and repeat."

Back at their barracks, the two got Mullins's bunk squared away in a jiffy and hurried back to the mess, arriving in time for another cup of tepid coffee. With only a few minutes before they had to report for duty, they sipped at tin cups of brown water and waited behind other Marines gathered in front of the bulletin board. Besides out-of-date papers or magazines sent from home, the bulletin board was the only source of news.

As Strombo and Mullins elbowed their way inch by inch to the front, they heard other Marines griping loudly, "He got a raw deal."

The jazzy bugler had been whisked away by the MPs as soon as he entered the mess for breakfast. The scuttlebutt was that he had received an immediate summary court martial. "To hell with them all," a private scoffed, on learning the news—then quickly added "sir" when he saw his corporal standing within earshot. But a sergeant from regimental headquarters set the record straight. The guy was getting off easy, sentenced to solitary confinement for seven days on rations of bread and water and his pay docked fifteen dollars for one month. Or so the sarge said.

The grousing began to ebb as Strombo and Mullins scanned the board for news from back home and the times of camp baseball games and boxing matches. Having been a ranch hand back in Montana, Strombo found his curiosity piqued by a flyer about a rodeo pitting the skills of American cowboys against the paniolos, local Hawaiian cowboys.

But all the men gathered around a news clipping that mentioned the dissolution of Marine Raider Battalions, a group of elite men trained to fight fire with fire.

At the onset of war in the Pacific, on Guadalcanal, Tulagi, and Gavatu, the Raiders had fought toe to toe with relentless enemies. Newspapers described Marines as bloodthirsty and cold-blooded killers. The Japanese didn't care if they lived or died, and the Raiders matched the enemy's ruthless attitude.

After six months of well-documented brutal battles, the formidable Imperial Army was on the run. "Uncommon valor was a common virtue," Admiral Nimitz declared, and an article proclaimed the Raiders to be "Super Men. Super Marines."

But the article also said, "Due to the changing nature of the war in the Pacific and with more large-scale assaults on well defended islands to come, the requirement of battalion-sized units of the Raiders has been negated."

Everyone grumbled about the announcement. Reading further, they learned that a forty-man platoon would take its place. A unit trained like the Raiders, but smaller and more agile, would be better suited for the battles to come.

Commentary swirled: "A fella'd be crazy!" "That'd be somethin'!" and "Just like the Black Raiders!"

A different bulletin caught Mullins's eye. He read intently the mimeographed sheet of paper that had been posted.

SOLICITING VOLUNTEERS FOR THE SCOUT AND SNIPER PLATOON

Purpose: This unit will be specially trained in scouting and patrolling behind enemy lines to obtain information concerning strength, disposition, and intentions of enemy forces; to disrupt enemy communications; to destroy enemy personnel. Men selected will advance one rank.

Requirements: You must be certified as an expert marksman and have combat experience.

Skills to be learned:

- Demolitions: use of dynamite, TNT, and primer cord.
- Map reading: using a compass and field glass to draw maps; sketching maps from memory. Estimating enemy strength. How to search terrain for enemy activity.
- Camouflage: silent surveillance, spider traps, silent communication, to move across various kinds of terrain without being detected.

- Silent Killing: Judo, jujitsu, the Biddle method of knife fighting.
- Patience: You will learn patience and control when assigned a mission of annihilating any enemy hindering our advance.

Submit your Record Book to First Lt. Tachovsky and Sgt. Knuppel, Scout-Sniper Platoon

"Marvin," Mullins nudged his buddy. "This could be my ticket out."

●   ●   ●

The word about the new Scout-Sniper Platoon began to spread throughout the Sixth Regiment and in every mess tent and Company Headquarters, from Waimea to Mauna Loa to Mauna Kea. Every Marine knew it would be an honor to be chosen. But not all felt up to the task.

From A Company, Smotts, Kenny, Borawski, and Yunker submitted their Record Books; Mullins and Strombo also applied, hoping to leave D Company and their sadistic corporal behind.

The greatest interest, however, came from within the Third Battalion, where many men knew Ski from serving with him on Guadalcanal.

Almost all of M Company huddled around the bulletin board. Evans proudly sported a beautiful Rock-Ola carbine slung over his shoulder. He had stolen an M1 Garand from some dogface and then traded the evidence to an unsuspecting swabbie for the brand-new carbine.

"Yo! Check it out," Emerick, who had jostled his way to the front of the crowd, yelled out to his buddies behind. "Ol' Ski's got himself a new job. He's got some big shoes to fill."

Working their way up next to Emerick, Evans and Moore studied the posting.

"Scout-Snipers…" Moore let out an envious whistle.

"I sure do miss the Ol' Boss," said Evans, who had the habit of calling anyone who outranked him Boss. "I don't got much faith in that worthless, loud-mouthed, illiterate Texan we got now."

"Why dontcha tell us how you really feel?" Emerick proclaimed loudly over the din of chattering Marines. "I don't envy Ski one bit."

"That's for sure," Moore nodded in agreement.

"Well, Ski's gonna need some help," Evans put his arms around his two buddies. "I don't know about you fellas, but I got me a new Boss."

CHAPTER EIGHT

A Full-Blooded Bunch

"There is a certain blend of courage, integrity, character and principle which has no satisfactory dictionary name but has been called different things at different times in different countries. Our American name for it is 'guts.'"

—*Bob Considine, co-author of* Thirty Seconds over Tokyo

January 16, 1944
Sixth Marine Regiment officer mess tent

Marines rarely left the platoon to which they were originally assigned. Buddies stuck together and took care of each other, quite often from boot camp until they were discharged from the Corps, growing to know intimate details of each other's families and homes, building an enduring brotherhood. More than one male baby born back home after the war would be named after a Marine buddy.

But this fledgling band of thieves would be unlike other platoons—made up of men from different outfits, most of whom had never met before.

Expertise with a rifle was only one prerequisite for being in the Scout-Sniper Platoon. Marines were notoriously good shots, which qualified about ninety percent. The big challenge was greater than handling a weapon. Ski needed men who could think on their feet, something that had been drilled out of them in the Corps. What he was looking for were guys who were independent thinkers—misfits in the regimentation of the armed service, and yet able to work together quickly, with the kind of camaraderie experienced in traditional platoons.

Over one hundred men applied.

Knuppel and Ski sat across from one another in the mess tent with a pile of Marine Record Books between them.

"Ski, why don't we just interview these guys?" Knuppel asked.

"No, not yet. For now, all I want to do is look at their records."

"What are we looking for exactly?" Knuppel picked up a sixth book, or a tenth. He had lost count.

"I want to see if they've been in fights or been thrown in the brig for drunkenness or being a brawler. You're not a good Marine until you've been thrown in the brig once or twice."

Knuppel nodded in agreement. "Gottcha. You want guys with office hours."

"Exactly. If a guy's spent any office hours for brawling that shows he's been in trouble and can handle himself." Ski put another book in front of Knuppel. "The guy that wins the fight is thrown in the brig, the other guy goes to the infirmary. The guy in the brig is the kind of guy we want."

"I got one with two tours. Private First Class Donald Lee Evans."

"Evans? From M Company? I know Ol' Don." Ski smiled as Knuppel paged through Evans's book. "He was damn near dead on the Canal, and he still managed to save guys from drowning in a dugout during one of those torrential storms. He's a Marine's Marine. I only know about one brig time. How did he earn the second stay?"

"He took a week off on New Zealand over a Maori girl," Knuppel answered.

"Bingo." Ski snapped his fingers. "We've got ourselves a corporal. Have you seen Joe Kyle's book?"

"Not yet. Why?"

"He and Valenciano were the only two guys in my old outfit worth their salt."

Knuppel ruffled through the remaining books. "I've got Valenciano's here, but no Kyle."

"Val's a keeper. But I'm surprised by Kyle. He and Evans are bud-dies…they went AWOL from that field hospital together…and he served brig time with Don…."

"Well, no Kyle."

"Too bad."

After reading through all the Record Books, Ski met with each man he considered fit for the job. He had a list of questions, some not quite traditional. The Marines were no different from folks back in the States. Protestants distrusted Catholics, Catholics loathed Jews, Native Ameri-cans were treated worse than dirt, the Irish hated Italians and vice versa.

But there would be no room for bigotry in this platoon. Working in small groups of two or three deep behind enemy lines, a Scout-Sniper's survival depended on the man next to him, regardless of race or religion.

"Jesus, Ski," Knuppel warned. "You can't change how people think."

"Maybe you can. It just takes time. With a line company you're assigned guys, and you gotta play the hand you're dealt. But we have the pick of the litter, and we don't need any goddamn bigots. We need *men*. If you're a bigot, you're not a man."

More than one Marine paused, fidgeted, and was shown the door when Ski looked the applicant in the eye and asked him this most impor-tant question: "In the field, there can be no hesitation, so there can be no doubt. You'll have somebody's back, and they'll have yours. If you've got a problem if that back is brown, red, or white, then this outfit isn't for you."

If they accepted Ski's perspective, he spoke on the level with them about the assignment. "Training is gonna be rugged. If, at any time, you change your mind and begin to doubt your choice, you can go back to your old outfit with no questions asked. I need every man to be all in." If he was pleased with the volunteer, he added the all-important question. "Are you all in?"

"Hell, yeah. I'm in!" was the correct response.

At the end of interviews, Knuppel hunted and pecked out forty names on an old, abused Smith Corona.

A portion of the Scout-Sniper Platoon on Hawaii. Standing, left to right: Richard Knoll, Francis Moynihan, Barney Wheeless, Daniel Kenny, Ira Causey, Albert Malanga, Don Evans, Bill Emerick, Bernie Jones. Seated: Otto Hebel, Al Yunker, John Zuziak, Lonnie Jackson, Hal Moore, Wayland Stevens, Keith Clark, Bill Knuppel. *From the collection of Joseph Tachovsky*

"What do you think of the boys, Bill?" Ski asked as he completed paperwork.

"I think we got what we wanted." Knuppel gave the typewriter a rest. "It looks like a full-blooded bunch. Very 'active' Marines."

Without the luxury of time to build the level of camaraderie that came from years of living, training, and fighting together, getting the men acquainted became a priority. *Esprit de corps* was a given, but these men were going to be working and fighting closely together behind enemy lines. It would be important for every man to know the man who watched his back. Forging an intimate bond—a bond that would last a lifetime— might save a life in battle.

The day before they were to report for duty to their new platoon, each Scout-Sniper received a note from his new CO. Knuppel delivered half the messages, and fellow sergeant and Scout-Sniper volunteer Vincent Slevin, an Iowa Hawkeye, delivered the note to the other half.

"What in the hell?!?" Moore puzzled as he stared at the note.

January 18
1700
20° 1' 23.0016" N
155° 40' 17.9796" W

"Lemme see," Evans snatched the note from Moore and compared the two. "They're the same…"

CHAPTER NINE

Old Dead Dog!

"Even though I've been in the Marine Corps six years, it still amazes me how well we do with little or nothing. Using Marine Methods, we quite often chisel, steal, and gather the materials and supplies that we need."

—Lieutenant Frank Tachovsky in a letter to his wife

January 18, 1944
Waimea, near Parker Ranch

Ski had learned from his Hungarian mother, widowed when he was fifteen, that people worked better if shown a kindness. In Beaver Falls, Pennsylvania, kindness was chicken paprikash, cabbage rolls, veal kidneys in a sour cream sauce, or dobos torta. In the Marines, it was booze.

The series of numbers and coordinates that Ski had given to his volunteers led to a specific location. By 1700 on the dot, a wild looking bunch had gathered in the lobby of the Waimea Hotel. Thirty-seven "wild barbarians," as Eleanor Roosevelt had branded all Marines, reported for duty sporting faded, torn, and ragged dungarees.

Including Ski, Knuppel, and Slevin, they tallied forty in number. This ragtag crew, raised in the Depression, came from the dust bowls of Oklahoma and Texas, the steel mills of Pennsylvania, the coal mines of West Virginia and Illinois, and big city ghettos. Those from the ghettos were the most rugged of all in the Corps. They had a particularly mean streak. A cruel streak. Although called Scout-Snipers, they had absolutely nothing in common with the kinder, littler Scouts back in the States.

Ski broke the strict rules prohibiting officers from fraternizing with enlisted men. To break the ice with his men before training began, he threw a party. He had intended to send his latest batch of poker winnings back to Roxie, including three hundred dollars from a lieutenant named Burbeth Whipple, who had the worst luck. But starting his new job trumped financing a trip to Chicago for Roxie to visit her cousin Gloria or treating her folks to Sunday supper at the Nightingale.

The hotel staff, skittish about having so many savage and unkempt Marines on the premises, laid out a spread fit for kings. During round after round of ice-cold beer, Private First Class Maurice Mehlin from New York sat at a slightly out-of-tune upright and entertained the men with a piano-playing shtick that rivaled Chico Marx's. When the tinkling ivories began the opening bars of Johnny Mercer's "Tangerine," Sergeant Slevin sidled up to Mehlin and began serenading the new platoon in a lilting baritone. In a little hotel in Waimea, the guys were hearing the voice folks in the Midwest paid to hear. Slevin had led a dance band famous for their risqué rendition of "The Sheik of Araby," coaching the audience to sing along at the end of each stanza the additional racy lyrics of "With no pants on!"

Feeding on a smattering of applause, Mehlin and Slevin welcomed requests. Slevin began to whistle the intro to "Who Wouldn't Love You?"

Ski, sitting on a windowsill, closed his eyes and smiled, remembering his first date with Roxie, a bus trip they took to Agua Caliente, the racetrack in Tijuana. And how they laughed like fools all the way back to San Diego having lost all their money. So hungry and without a cent, Roxie dug deep into her purse and giddily produced a linty piece of candy.

"After-dinner mint?" she offered.

"After what dinner?"

Ski laughed at the memory, leaned back—and plummeted from the wide-open hotel window to the ground. Knuppel saw his buddy suddenly disappear, rushed over, and peered down. "You okay?"

Feeling no pain, Ski casually put a cigarette to his lips and asked, "Got a match?" Knuppel tossed a book of them down. After enjoying his smoke, Ski struggled to his feet, brushed himself off, and looked at his watch. He told the still attentive Knuppel, "I think it's time we head back to camp."

The next day the party was over—all but the hangovers. And the work began.

For the first few days, the men worked at building their own camp, located on the northwest corner of Parker Ranch, far from the rest of the regiment. The Corps had generously provided ten-man tents. The Navy and Army, via Marine Methods, had supplied the wooden decking, cots, mattresses, and other creature comforts—even a few rocking chairs.

Needing something to hold helmets for the men's daily Navy baths, Private First Class Jesus Orozco from Santa Barbara stole an Army colonel's chicken coop—along with the chickens. Orozco, known as "the Ipana Kid," after the brand of toothpaste, because of his dazzling smile, scrubbed the wood clean and built the finest chickenshit helmet rack in all of Hawaii. "I'd steal anything that wasn't nailed down, unless I needed the nails," was Orozco's motto.

The chicken dinner was a bonus.

Borawski's stolen jeep, now painted in Marine colors, came out of storage. Unnamed members of the platoon employed the vehicle to abscond with bags of concrete, which Yunker used to build a fire pit out of collected rocks. And, of course, the jeep made a few more booze runs to Hilo. A baseball diamond was created just so the men could hide the pilfered booze under the oil-drum-lid bases. The acquired oil drums themselves were converted into windmill-driven washing machines.

Learning that a short-wave radio could pick up programs from the States, Ski sent Evans, Moore, and Emerick out to acquire one. They returned with a Hallicrafter, amplifier, and speakers.

Scuttlebutt painted the Scout-Snipers' camp as more like a social club than a Marine bivouac. Their growing reputation as prolific thieves earned them many nicknames, most of them unflattering. The brass referred to the unit as "the Skis" and turned a blind eye to their antics, but envious fellow Marines branded them "the 40 Thieves."

The Thieves trained hard, fought harder, and played even harder while they could. Whatever luxuries they acquired by whatever means, they deserved.

Each day at 0545, an hour before reveille, Ski woke the men bellowing, "Rise! Shine! Give God the glory...Jesus Christ, you gonna sleep all day?" They ran five miles as part of the daily routine. The sprint back to the main camp was a race to see who would be first to arrive at the mess tent. The rest of the regiment waited and cheered the Thieves to the finish line. Being the elite of the elite, the 40 Thieves had the privilege of being first in line for everything, from chow to movies to payday. There was a certain amount of swagger that went with having "Scout-Sniper" stenciled on your dungarees.

After breakfast, at 0800, Ski's encouraging "Old dead dog!" began all training sessions. The men thought it a curious phrase, didn't really know what it meant, but quickly understood what they were supposed to do when they heard it: get the lead out. Knuppel and Slevin adopted the phrase, and the men embraced it.

They endured the toughest training. Already-ragged uniforms were torn—and so was flesh—as the men crawled through barbed wire. Battered and bruised limbs carried them down rope ladders and up sheer cliffs. Fresh animal blood spurted on them as they sparred, scabbards off, with bayonet dummies. The sun burned their backs as they fired at surprise targets with every type of weapon, including some 1903 Springfields outfitted with state-of-the-art Unertl scopes. The rifles were accurate to an inch up to a thousand yards, and eight of the twelve that had been given to the Sixth Marines were issued to the Thieves.

They continued to master jujitsu and dirty fighting and took up knives—these with the scabbards on—for practice duels. They pulled no punches with each other. Everyone tried to win each sparring match, fighting as though comrades were the bitterest of enemies.

No one relished losing. Sparring often led to violent brawls. "Working together, we make each other better," Ski reminded his men when breaking up the fights.

The grind continued day after day from "Rise and Shine" to lights out.

Ski missed no opportunity to build tight bonds between the men. Tent assignments changed every two weeks, forging new relationships that might not have come about otherwise.

Learning about each other's lives beyond the Marines helped pass the time during the days of intense training, but it might also save a tentmate in battle.

The rotation exposed more platoon members to the individual eccentricities of fellow Marines like Private First Class Philip Johnson from Milwaukee, who dramatically threw out quotes and sound effects from his favorite radio shows. Johnson became known as an odd duck who spouted goofy lines in his tent, during training, or in the mess. On overnight jungle missions, as men drifted off to sleep, his Midwestern voice was heard quoting from the radio mystery show *Inner Sanctum*, "Pleasant dreams, hmmmm?" His timing raised laughs or eyebrows.

Tent rotation exposed everyone to *Lights Out*, Johnson's favorite radio show. In camp, after Slevin or Knuppel hollered, "Lights out!" and tired bodies crawled into their bunks, Johnson's guttural monotone could be heard whispering the opening line from the show, "It...is...later... than...you...think..." Eventually the entire camp whispered the line, almost in unison. Forty tired voices ending the day in a communal good-night wish.

Four squads began to take shape, each led by its own corporal. Martin Dyer from St. Louis, August "Fritz" Schieber—a no-nonsense German from Evansville, Indiana—and the gruff William Canipe from West Virginia joined Evans as squad leaders. Working together, the shuffling of personnel, and rigorous training molded the entire platoon into a tightly knit group. Even before the fighting began, the Scout-Snipers would know each other better than their own brothers.

One rare evening the platoon arrived back at camp early. Ski rewarded his men for their hard work by sharing some of his most recent goodies from home. Roxie's mom had sent a ham wrapped in red-wine-soaked cheesecloth, then tightly in foil. Roxie had sent two tins of home-made candies. And her dad's carefully packed bottle of Four Roses bourbon had arrived in perfect condition. The men devoured the ham and candies, and then one of them—sleep-deprived Mullins—had the idea of putting the liquor into an atomizer to ensure that every man got a taste of the precious booze. After many misty rounds, the alcoholic air had been savored to the last breath.

That night the men swapped stories around the firepit. Mullins bragged about learning to make moonshine, one hundred proof, before he learned to sign his name. Smotts discovered that he and Moore were neighbors back home: less than sixty miles separated their families in Oklahoma.

"Hey, Squirt," Emerick good naturedly ribbed Lonnie Jackson of Centralia, Washington, the shortest guy in the platoon. Jackson had wanted to be a Marine so badly that he had stretched himself by tying cinder blocks to his feet and hanging from a tree for a week to meet the height requirement. He could take a joke, but not about his height. Although he was half Emerick's size, the tougher-than-nails Jackson had the larger man pinned on the ground in a heartbeat and was pummeling him. Evans, impressed by Jackson's moxie, moderated an amicable ending to the fight.

"Never pick a fight you can't win," Evans advised his battered pal Emerick. Jackson and Evans became good buddies.

Borawski and Yunker argued about which one of them had the poorer upbringing: Borawski in the white ghettos of Utica or the penniless farm boy from Wisconsin.

"I went to funerals to steal the pennies off dead men's eyes," Borawski offered without emotion.

"We were so poor," Yunker countered, "that my mama used to cut holes in my pants pockets so I'd have something to play with."

Evans and Jackson. *Courtesy of Steve Evans*

Evans sat by himself, taking a brief timeout to write home.

Dear Folks,

Well, I'm back in camp again after a sojourn in the "boondocks," so I'll get to writin' again. I'm in a new outfit and got a new address, so make sure you make a note of it. I don't want any of Auntie Fawn's fruitcakes gettin' lost in the shuffle.

I'm now a corporal. I never could get out of the brig long enough to show those M Company people what I knew. This is the best outfit yet. It's the next best thing to the "Black Raiders," which is the American idea of what commandos oughta be.

Our lieutenant goes on beer parties with us and is always very friendly. He eats and sleeps and lives with us, and we can shoot the bull with him anytime because he's an ex-enlisted man. He don't think he's any better than any one of us.

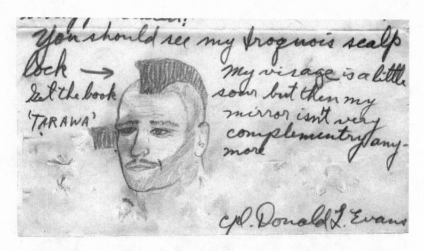

From Evans's letter to his parents. *Courtesy of Steve Evans*

Before I forget, all advice, motherly, well-meant, or otherwise in regard to anything I do, say, or think is strictly unappreciated.

You should see my Iroquois scalp look. My visage is a little sour, but then my mirror isn't very complimentary anymore.

Norman Duley came over for chow and brought Tommy Arello along. Norman & Tommy are OK. They're in the Army...I guess they're havin' a pretty good time of it. Those Army boys have to take a lot. That sitting, saluting, and standing at attention is a lot of malarkey.

I can't think of anything to say in a letter anymore. Everything interesting is censorable. How's everything at home? I've received all your packages except those with the pint bottles of "Joy Juice." (Bourbon preferred). I can't see paying twenty dollars a quart here.

Well, I'll quit for a while.

Your affectionate son, Cpl. Donald L. Evans.

●   ●   ●

Day after day, training continued, either in the field or in the classroom.

Intensive instruction on map reading was taught in a sideless tent known as "the classroom." Sergeant Slevin brought his knowledge and teaching skills to the lessons, introducing every member of the platoon to skills that could save his life, or end someone else's. Using field materials provided by Regimental Intelligence, he taught the men to read aerial photographs, use a compass to accurately locate targets for artillery and air strikes, pinpoint targets on a map in the darkness of night, mark locations at night (one man would lie on his stomach with a flashlight while others covered him with jackets to obscure the light), draw maps by hand, and sketch them from memory. Some of the volunteers may have had a sixth-grade education, but Slevin spoke to them in words they could understand, while demanding mastery of map reading and reconnaissance.

Strombo was attending Slevin's class one day, and it was quieter than Sunday School. Slevin stood behind a table, pointing to charts and maps tacked on a board as he lectured. As he turned to arrange the charts, a shirtless Marine entered the tent. Curious eyes turned toward him as he swayed his way into the open-air classroom.

"What the hell you lookin' at?" he slurred. The men in the front could smell booze and body stench from ten feet away. Strombo looked up from his study materials. It was his brother Oliver. When Oliver got soused on beer he'd be a happy drunk, but if it was whiskey he'd be nasty. Marvin could tell that it was whiskey—and that his brother was spoiling for a fight.

"Who's that asshole?" Private First Class Herbert McBride, a baby-faced Texan who had faked his birth certificate and enlisted at fifteen, whispered to Strombo.

Marvin shrugged and hurriedly switched spots with McBride to stay out of Oliver's sight. They got along as well as most brothers, but Marvin knew how to disappear when his brother was whiskey-drunk.

Oliver knocked over a chair, clumsily picked it up, and sat down. The class didn't appreciate the distraction.

"Get out, this isn't the mess tent." Slevin ordered. Oliver stayed put, slumped in the chair with his eyes closed. When he offered no response, Slevin waited for sixty seconds. He ignored Oliver and continued his instruction, using photographs obtained from carrier air strikes on an unnamed island.

"Today, we'll examine these military maps," Slevin said, using a Raider stiletto as a pointer, "study their parts, and learn more about their uses. To safely convey coordinates in a battle zone, you must know how to read a map, plot your location, and move in the right direction. If you can't navigate correctly, you risk getting lost—or worse, marking the wrong target." Slevin paused to change a map behind him.

"You don't know shit," Oliver sneered, muttering with his eyes still closed.

Slevin didn't hear him over the rustling of the maps. He went on, "Little was known about the Pacific prior to the war, and our crude maps are courtesy of *National Geographic*. You will note that aerial reconnaissance has provided further information which is noted in the margins of the map." Slevin paused a second time.

"He's dumber than a shit-house-rat," Oliver snickered audibly.

This time Slevin heard him. "What's that?"

"I said you are dumber than an aerial photo of a shit-house-rat." Oliver opened his eyes.

Slevin calmly came out from behind the table, stood over Oliver, and stared down at him. "Get the hell out of here."

Oliver sat impassively with his head down. To meet Slevin's stare, Oliver didn't lift his head, but he tilted his chair back. Drunken insolence made that move risky.

Slevin turned his order into an ultimatum "Get out...or I'll throw you out." Without waiting for a response, he kicked the chair, sending Oliver sprawling.

Spoiling for a fight but drunk as a skunk, Oliver stumbled and fell many times trying to get up. Slevin seized him by the scruff of the neck and lifted him to his feet. Oliver shrugged Slevin's hand off.

"Don't you touch me." Oliver and Slevin stood nose to nose. The entire class—except for Oliver's brother—rose out of their seats in unison.

The drunk invader clearly heard what was going on behind him, but he kept his unsteady gaze directed at Slevin.

"The door is this way," said Evans, grabbing Oliver's shoulder roughly from behind.

"I said don't touch..." Oliver made a fist to throw a punch but stopped short as he turned and his eyes met Evans's chest.

Slowly scanning Evans from his chest up to his face, Oliver reluctantly decided to leave. As he walked out, Oliver grumbled vulgarities and paused at the edge of the tent to offer a parting threat.

"I'm gonna get Marvin after you," he told Evans. "He'll kick your ass. I'll get Marvin after all of you." Marvin Strombo, the only Marine still in his chair, watched as his brother Oliver stumbled out and started on the hot and lonely walk back to his own regiment's camp.

Most of the Thieves wondered who this Marvin was that was gonna kick their asses.

●　　●　　●

As tentmates continued to be rotated, Strombo soon found himself sharing quarters with McBride. They sat on their bunks just before lights out, cleaning their Springfields. Walter Borawski and Roscoe Mullins sprawled lazily nearby, reading tattered dime novels.

"Godammit!" Mullins threw down an old worn out copy of *Spicy Detective*. "Some shit-head tore the climax out of every goddamn story!"

While Lonnie Jackson and others played poker—"I'll raise you ten"—Philip Johnson and Alfred Yunker straddled a cot playing a two-handed card game with a deck of only thirty-two cards.

Jackson stopped in mid-shuffle to watch Yunker deal four down cards and four up cards to Johnson and also to himself.

"What the hell you playin'?"

"Sheepshead, Squirt." Yunker's smart-ass smile was the only thing that kept him from suffering Emerick's fate. "My ol' German gramma taught me. She calls it Schafkopf."

"Why don't you just play poker?"

"The Shadow knows," Johnson replied in a radio-voice monotone, "that you can't get by in Wisconsin without knowing Sheepshead."

The cigarette in Jackson's lips bobbed up and down as he asked, "Who in the hell wants to go to Wisconsin?"

The sound of flipping cards mingled with quiet. McBride and Strombo broke the silence with periodic comments about nothing in particular.

"My name's Bert, short for Herbert," McBride casually mentioned, thinking Strombo might reciprocate.

He didn't.

The conversation grew stagnant as the rifle-cleaning continued.

"What's your first name?" McBride asked, to get the conversation going again.

Embarrassed, Strombo hesitated. "Marvin," he said quietly.

"Marvin." McBride's jaw dropped. "That Marvin?" The card games stopped. Dime novels were set aside.

A long pause lingered as eyes turned toward Strombo.

"So, you're Marvin?" Borawski said.

"Yup."

"He sure is," confirmed Mullins.

"Hmmm…" Borawski slowly nodded, with his lower lip out.

Eventually the card game resumed, and the dime novels reopened. Not another word was said until lights out.

"It…is…later…than…you…think…"

CHAPTER TEN

The Black Death

*"We was trained better than any other troops in the
service on how to kill in every conceivable method, ways
that you can't even fathom. We all carried piano wire
with two handles on it—you'd wrap it around their neck
and yank. Emerick called it a Mafia necktie."*

—Bob Smotts

Stealth was paramount.

The Thieves learned how to walk noiselessly, to communicate
intricate orders via sign language, to lie motionless in the dark for
hours—"playing possum," as Mullins called it—to listen carefully and
count the number of footfalls to determine how many enemy troops were
passing by. Most important, they learned to never return from a mission
by the same route that they had gone out on. Behind enemy lines the men
wore no jewelry of any kind, so no beam of light could make the metal
glisten and compromise their covert movement. Dog tags were wrapped
with tape to mute their jingling. A soft sniper cap, similar to a civil war
hat, replaced the cumbersome steel helmets that were the opposite of
stealth if dropped. Clunky boondockers were exchanged for sneakers.
Unfortunately for Hal Moore, his feet were too small for Marine-issued
sneakers.

These Marines had to be just as cunning and deceptive as the Japanese. They learned about listening posts, camouflage, and spider

traps—deep foxholes covered over by a lattice work of shrubbery designed to blend with the landscape. Lessons included disrupting Japanese communications with a simple straight pin. Severed communication wires could be easily found and repaired, but if a pin was driven through the wire and both ends of the pin clipped, the damage would be imperceptible.

Except for repelling the human waves of Japanese infantry in Banzai attacks on Tarawa and Guadalcanal, the Marines' prior killing had been accomplished from a distance with rifles, machine guns, and grenades. Scout-Sniper work would be more up close and personal. Firing a weapon would be their last option—so the men had to master a host of different techniques to cripple and kill quietly.

Basic equipment in this kind of combat included an array of razor-sharp knives for a variety of purposes. The Marine Corps' Ka-Bar, a seven-inch leather-handled utility knife, could be used to either kill or open C-Rations. Bayonets slid onto the barrel of a rifle effectively turned the firearm into a spear for thrusting at the enemy, deadly effective in hand-to-hand melees.

The "Raider Stiletto," designed for close-quarter fighting and named for the Marine Raiders, had a thin aquiline double-edged blade that made it one of the deadlier hand-held weapons. The Raider Stiletto's sole purpose was to kill quickly and quietly. The blade was so finely tooled that it could break if dropped on its tip. The Scout-Snipers learned to respect the delicacy of this elegant weapon.

The M1918 Trench Knife had a handle that doubled as brass knuckles. Another facet of the weapon was a metal pommel on the end of the grip. In savage one-on-one brawls, the heavy pommel could be used to crush skulls. Most also still carried a Boy Scout knife, a useful tool and an emergency weapon in a pinch. Mullins, with his backwoods skills, was very good with knives and a good tutor to his fellow fighters.

Back-alley tactics, which came naturally to the ghetto kids with that mean streak, were also taught and encouraged. Emerick's gruesome twist on the "Mafia necktie" was to substitute a section of rope for piano wire, roll that in glue, and then in crushed glass.

Colonel William Kengla, the CO of Ski's old battalion on Guadalcanal, paid a visit to his former lieutenant's platoon. Kengla, a protégé
of the legendary Marine Corps Colonel A. J. Biddle, had been sent specifically to coach the Thieves on the new "Biddle method" of knife and
bayonet fighting, using Biddle's *Do or Die* as a textbook.

Forget the Rule Book

SPORTSMANSHIP CAN BE IGNORED WHEN YOU'RE FIGHTING AXIS' BOYS

WAR is ugly business, and that's why American troops are mastering the deadly technique of so-called "dirty-fighting." The enemy asked for it and the enemy will get it.

The enemy, in fact, is already getting it, with United States Marines pacing the field in the employment of tactics they learned long before the German hordes opened up in 1939 and the imitating Japs climbed in two years later.

In training centers throughout the nation hundreds of thousands of Yankee fighters are learning what it means to kill or be killed when opposing forces clash at close quarters.

Raiders, Rangers, Commandos, Marine, Army, Navy—the fighting men of the service — have hurled back the gauntlet at the enemy and answered his challenge of dirty fighting with dirtier, deadlier methods.

America's first experience with the Hun came in World War I. America learned a valuable lesson. She learned another lesson in treachery and trickery from the Japs on December 7, 1941. Fortunately America had one branch that already knew the lessons and how to meet them.

The branch was the Marine Corps, whose men have been slugging it out with enemy forces in hand-to-hand struggle since it began, 167 years ago.

America, after that fateful December 7, cried out for a better, a mightier and if need be, a crueler battle machine. It must be a machine with men equipped to meet a foe and conquer him by individual power, to hit a Nip or a Nazi below the belt instead of above, unless above happened to be better. He must be alert to every trick.

GLOOMY FUTURE awaits this fallen foe as expert Major d'Eliseu jams rifle to throat, breaks right arm and bears down.

SOMETHING'S BREAKING, and it could be victim's neck. More pressure, plus hair yanking, will finish the job.

STRINGING PRISONERS to trees is an important job. And if they get unruly, jerks on the rope will break the neck.

JUDO DEFENSE against knife attack. Step in fast, grab the wrist and put on the pressure.

EX-GOVERNOR HOFFMAN of New Jersey, now a Major, gets the works as Major d'Eliscu applies a throat throttle.

SURE WAY to disarm a man is to wrest the rifle butt forward, breaking trigger finger. Note right elbow at the neck.

NEW WRINKLE in choking. The idea: slip up on enemy, loop rifle over the head, pull back sharply against windpipe.

DON'T SHOOT, mister. In fact, he can't. The major has taken charge, twisted the pistol inward and fractured a finger.

MARCH, 1943

Advice to Marines in training from the March 1943 *Leatherneck Magazine*: "Forget the Rule Book: Sportsmanship Can Be Ignored When You're Fighting Axis Boys." Leatherneck Magazine

In contrast to the old, classical style of bayonet fighting, the Biddle method incorporated movements derived from fencing. Instead of simply rushing in and trying to rip out an opponent's throat or thrusting the bayonet into his abdomen, then twisting and lifting to scramble your adversary's vital organs, the Thieves learned to use their rifle and bayonet in a more fluid manner, to parry and thrust, converting deadly bayonet fighting into an elegant and stylized art form.

"Kill with a smile" became the mantra of Kengla's classes.

The platoon took to Kengla's instruction, which broke up the monotony of their normal workday, with a passion. "Here's how you break a stranglehold," Kengla demonstrated on the much larger Evans, bringing him to his knees. "Now you can engage in a little play of your own," he added, employing a throat throttle.

"Dirty fighting," Emerick laughed.

"Call it that if you want to," Kengla replied. "Milquetoasts are squeamish about fighting fire with fire. Even against dirty fighters like the Japs and Nazis. It's either you or them. Gouge, kick 'em in the groin, yank off an ear. Do whatever is necessary to have it be them and not you."

"Now here's another. Straighten your hand. I call it the 'Japanese Fist.'" Kengla brought his hand down in a sharp blade-like manner stopping an inch above Evans's shoulder. "You can break a man's collarbone with that blow."

They were learning new tactics, but the men's practice scrimmages continued to be with their peers. The smaller Jackson took down the tall and muscular Evans more than once. Venancio "Val" Valenciano, from Kansas City and the only Native American in the platoon, worked even harder than most, for reasons only he knew. If he felt he had to prove himself, that wasn't necessary. None of his peers questioned his right and ability to be one of the forty.

Evans's Army buddies Norman Duley and Tom Arello made frequent visits to their old Southeast High teammate, often joining in training and sparring sessions on their days off. Ski kept a curious eye on their hard work and thought it a pity they weren't Marines.

Already seasoned combat warriors, each Scout-Sniper had made it through Tarawa, the worst and bloodiest battle to date in the Pacific. Now they were learning to use every dirty trick imaginable and shedding any inhibitions about using their new knowledge to save the civilization they remembered. The Thieves became well-schooled in "Black Death" techniques.

One night after a day's training and their evening chow, McBride and Marvin Strombo went to the movies together. The pair were looking forward to a night of light entertainment with a murder mystery. The billing featured *Ladies in Retirement* starring Ida Lupino and Louis Hayward, but the evening began with a short film depicting murder of a different sort. The ten-minute documentary, *The Good Earth Runs Red*, recounted Japanese atrocities upon the Chinese at Nanking in December of 1937—for motivational purposes. As if the Marines needed any more motivation. They already knew the Japanese were tenacious, cunning, and determined warriors. And they had heard the stories of their cruelty toward the people they conquered and took prisoner. But now Strombo and McBride saw the evidence.

Whatever cheerfulness Strombo and McBride had at the onset of the documentary drained away as the grainy black and white images flickered on the screen.

An emotionless voice narrated, "The scenes which follow are actual cases of civilians who were victims of brutality by Japanese soldiers."

A litany of graphic vignettes began. "This woman, captured by Japanese soldiers, was forced to wash their clothes by day and then raped from ten to twenty times each night. One evening two soldiers led her to an unoccupied house where they attempted to cut off her head." A doctor delicately manipulated the head of a woman, still alive: a section of her neck had been cut out, as a tree might be notched for felling.

Another head, which appeared more dead than alive, rested on a pillow, "This man, owner of a small sampan on the Yangtze River, was shot in the jaw by a Japanese soldier, who then poured gasoline over him and set him afire." The camera panned out to show his charred body in its entirety, "He died two days after this picture was taken."

Strombo knew McBride was young. McBride had bragged to everyone about faking his birth certificate to enlist. He wasn't eighteen, yet he always carried himself older than his years. And Strombo had never known his friend to be overly emotional. But as the movie continued, he noticed that McBride was growing increasingly agitated.

"This nineteen-year-old girl," the monotone voice spoke over the image of a swollen and battered face of a once-pretty young woman, "was pregnant with her first child. When captured by a Japanese soldier, she was stabbed over twenty times—face, body, stomach and legs—for resisting rape.

"Most horrible of all were the tortures inflicted upon children." A nurse held a limp, scarred lump of a body. "This small boy was thrown into a burning hut. And this boy"—the film showed a young face, badly swollen and mottled with blackened bruising—"was beaten with an iron bar and bayoneted when he told Japanese soldiers he wanted to go home."

The documentary lasted only ten minutes, but it had been a very upsetting ten minutes for both Strombo and McBride—more so for McBride. After numbly sitting through the main attraction, they left. Walking back to camp, McBride shook visibly. With teeth clenched, he talked to Strombo about getting even with the Japanese. From then on he rarely spoke of anything else. McBride told his buddies how he was going to make it right with the Japanese, how many he would kill, and the details of how he would do it.

"If I ever get the chance," he vowed, "I'll kill every last one of 'em."

Along with documentaries concerning the Imperial Army's sadism, veterans of Guadalcanal had observed the barbarity and savagery of their bitter enemy firsthand. Nothing sickened a Marine more than seeing the mutilated bodies of dead Marines: heads, hands, and feet cut off, severed genitals shoved into gaping mouths. In some instances, it was apparent that the mutilation had begun before death—to inflict a greater amount of pain and suffering.

The war in the Pacific had no rules. It was no holds barred.

The men talked often about what it would be like working deep within enemy territory. At any time, any one of them could be captured.

The concept of "no man left behind" did not apply to the Scout-Snipers. If a man was wounded to the point where he couldn't make it back on his own, trying to take him back might endanger the mission and the rest of the squad. They were told in no uncertain terms that if a man couldn't make it back on his own, he was to be left. That was something they accepted as part of the bargain.

One night after a day's work, the men talked about what they should do if the wounded couldn't take care of themselves and make it back.

Mullins spoke last. "I don't want to be left alive to be taken prisoner. I don't want any of you taken prisoner. That'd be worse than bein' dead."

Ski made a suggestion for the platoon to vote on. Around the circle of resigned faces, forty voices agreed they wouldn't leave the wounded alive. That's how they thought it should be.

CHAPTER ELEVEN

Pololu

"When you got a geisha, you had it made.
They are the best in the world."

—Roscoe Mullins

February 10, 1944
Scout-Sniper Encampment, Parker Ranch

"Ski!" Knuppel whispered.

The luminous dial on Ski's watch read 2330. "What is it?" came the wide-awake reply.

"It's Evans. The bug bit him one good again."

When Ski and Knuppel got to Evans's tent, the hulking corporal was shivering and sweating uncontrollably. Emerick knelt next to his delirious buddy. Evans's tentmates remained in their bunks awake with chins propped on hands, or sat with heads hanging respectfully, waiting like seagulls that circle above a dying gull on the ground until the inevitable, then fly away.

It had become a ritual, a sort of tribute to those who fought on Guadalcanal, to stay awake with a buddy for whom the battle continued with repeated attacks of malaria. No sooner would one recover than he'd be sick again. This was Evans's fourth episode.

Time and again the thrashing Evans threw his sweat-soaked blanket to the ground. Each time Emerick covered him back up and held him down until the shaking subsided into only the chattering of teeth. Emerick emptied a canteen into a t-shirt and wiped his buddy's brow and cheek. Somehow Evans was able to half smile.

That feeble smile meant more to Emerick than any letter from home. Every man in the platoon would do the same for any other. That's what buddies did—give a bath to a kid too weak to help himself; remove the wet boots and socks of a friend and clean the green rot off his feet after days in combat; hold the head of an injured comrade in your lap and tell him he's not going to die when he is. It was the kind of love that no mother, wife, or girlfriend could match.

"Who's on guard?" Ski asked.

"Borawski." Knuppel replied.

"Send him for Doc Webber." He then spoke to his men. "In the meantime, let's move Evans into my tent so you boys can get some sleep. Old dead dog."

Two others jumped out of their sacks and helped Knuppel and Emerick carry Evans, cot and all, into Ski's tent. They all wanted to wait until Doc arrived, but Ski ordered them to get some rest.

Ski recalled the first time that he had seen the effects of malaria. His tentmate on Guadalcanal, Pappy Morehead from Clinton, Mississippi, was a good-sized man like Evans. During one week of sweating, chills, and delirium, he was wasted to skin and bones. After Pappy returned from the infirmary, Ski didn't recognize him.

●   ●   ●

George "Pappy" Morehead, Joe Dulcich, and Ski had all graduated from the same Officer's Candidate Class. Along with Doc and Edwards, they comprised the Salty Sons of Sin. When Roxie moved to San Diego to be with her new husband before he shipped out, she met Dulcich and Pappy for the first time.

Roxie adored them both, but especially Pappy, an outsized moose of a man. Each time Pappy, a product of the genteel Deep South, spoke, his elegant drawl transformed him into Ashley Wilkes in Roxie's eyes. If not for Frank, she would have turned her charms on him, but Mrs. Ski was content with her Ski.

Ski's admiration for Pappy rivaled his wife's; Pappy was Ski's best and most respected friend.

The night before Ski shipped out, he and Roxie had wandered around San Diego. It was a tense night. With her husband leaving for war the next day, Roxie did her best to not cry.

Coming out of an ice cream parlor, they ran into Pappy. He had been drinking; in fact, he was well in his cups.

"You sure you don't have a sistah?" Pappy winked at Roxie. The three chatted a bit, and curfew drew near. Before they parted, Pappy asked sweetly, "Ski, may I have the honor of kissing yo' bride goodbye?"

Before Ski could answer, Roxie planted a kiss on Pappy's cheek, leaving a ghost print of red lips. She had been good about not crying, until then.

●   ●   ●

Doc arrived and took Evans's temperature, which stood at one hundred and six degrees, then sent Borawski back for a truck. Extracting a vial and syringe from his black bag, Doc administered a sedative. Evans's moist body shook madly as Doc replaced the wet blanket with Ski's dry one. Within minutes it was soaked as well, and Evans began to heave green slime. Doc rolled him over, onto his stomach. For now, that was all that could be done.

Doc and Ski, who hadn't seen each other for weeks, tried filling the time with a good bull session. Because of Evans's condition, they talked mostly about malaria.

"Nothing's changed. There really isn't a cure." Doc, too, had been infected on Guadalcanal. "And I've got no damn use for Atabrine. Quinine is the best. It kills the chill. But at least the recurrences become lighter each time. Thankfully for all of us who've been bit, eventually it goes away."

Quinine, an old Incan cure, was an effective treatment for malaria. If it was available. Which wasn't often. As hospitals ran out of the pills, corpsmen would administer the liquid by tearing a section of toilet paper, putting it in a man's hand and making a depression in the center. They'd measure out the quinine into the depression and quickly twist the corners of the paper together. The patient would have to swallow it before the paper dissolved and chase it down with a glass of water. If it wasn't swallowed fast enough, the quinine was so strong it burned like hell. When the hospitals ran out of quinine, the distant second-best medicine was Atabrine.

In the little time they had to chat, Doc showed Ski a recent picture of Ellie and the kids. Ski reciprocated with a cheesecake photo that Roxie had sent.

"It's nice to see someone with a good pair of legs," Doc joked.

"She calls 'em drivers…"

The truck arrived. Two of Doc's corpsmen helped Ski load the sedated Evans into the truck. As it sped off, Ski threw a helmet full of water from a lister bag onto the slimy spots on his decking, returned to his bunk, and lay awake. Rarely did he sleep at night.

Borawski, back on guard and dog-tired, stared at his watch intently as time ticked away to 0200. Marvin Strombo was next up to take the duty.

Lying sound asleep, Strombo dreamt he was home in Dixon. He could smell the bread baking and hear his momma's voice say, "Marvin, it's time to get up and go to school. Come on and eat your breakfast."

He felt a rude shove.

"C'mon Marine!" He opened his eyes, hoping to see his mother. Instead a Japanese night-stalker stood over him smiling. Looking around the room, he saw he was surrounded. Strombo felt like running away, but he was more afraid of what the Marines would do to him than he was of the Japanese. "Die, Marine, die!" The warrior's white teeth descended upon him in a terrifying smile. Swiftly curling his knees to

his chest, Strombo kicked as hard as he could. The enemy went flying, bounced off the tent post, and partially collapsed the tent. Grabbing the trench knife he always kept under his pillow, Strombo raced outside and plunged into the death-struggle. All around him he saw Marines and Japanese killing without mercy. He heard bayonets ripping into flesh, trench knives crushing skulls, and the gasps of the whimpering wounded about to die.

"Get him off me!" Someone tried to pull Strombo off the *night-stalker* he had pinned to the ground, but Strombo threw him aside. Strombo had Borawski pinned to the ground. Mullins tried to pull him off but got thrown aside for his effort.

"Marvin J. Strombo!" That was how his mother admonished him, but this wasn't her voice. "Marvin J., wake up!"

"Roscoe?" Strombo wondered if he was hearing Mullins's voice as he finally woke up—to find his knife inches from Borawski's throat. Strombo relaxed.

At last Borawski was able to escape and struggled to his feet bitching, "Jesus Christ! What the hell's wrong with you?" But as he looked Strombo up and down in shock and disgust, something in Borawski's brain clicked. The sneer left his face, replaced by a look of reverence. "You ARE Marvin."

The next night, Borawski tried to switch duty, but no other Thief accommodated him. Everyone in the platoon understood that Oliver knew his brother well.

●   ●   ●

One week later, Evans wrote home from the infirmary.

Dear Mom and Dad,

    Well, the "bug" bit me again. I got a 106 fever the other night, pretty good, huh? I had the heaves in the truck all the way to the hospital. I thought I'd throw my stomach out of joint. The next day the Doc said to me "How do you feel?" I told him I was feelin' kittenish. He said, "At least there's one good thing about your fever—you burned all the VD out of your system."

I've had the "bug" all week and have been ranging from 102 to 104 every afternoon. I got moved to a new ward, and boy what a nurse here! Looks just like Maureen O'Hara, so I'm suddenly feeling stronger!

I threw a chill last nite but only got up to 101. I got up and ate a lot of stuff and drank a coupla Cokes and felt a lot better, good enough to lose three dollars playing cards. I'll rejoin the boys tomorrow, so Doc says.

Thank Auntie Fawn for the fruitcake. I've got a quart of moonshine and almost a case of beer waiting for me back at camp, so when I get outta here, Evans will ride.

Your lovin' son, Don

Evans returned to the platoon on schedule and rejoined the training, albeit still a little weak. Day ground into day. From "Give God the glory" to "lights out" the 40 Thieves worked relentlessly, practicing Silent Killing until it became as second nature as brushing teeth. The only diversion might be a movie after evening chow, if they were in camp and not completely gassed from the day's rigors.

Long gone were those idle hours of liberty days spent lazily reading mail or listening to the phonograph. Their supposed one day off was no day at the beach—although it was usually spent at the beach, practicing landings with rubber boats.

The platoon had grown to dread the weekly camp visit by their colonel, James Riseley. After a briefing from Ski on the platoon's progress, Riseley's inspections were almost as nit-picking as those by Mullins and Strombo's sadistic corporal. If Riseley sent his XO McLeod, it was a different story. McLeod had been Ski's CO on Tarawa. McLeod's standards weren't as rigid, and Ski's briefing usually ended with McLeod carrying away a few of Roxie's treats.

The Thieves had informants at the regimental command post telling them who might be making the weekly inspection. If it was McLeod, they stayed put. But to escape Riseley's visits, the platoon woke at the usual 0545, tied their tents up tight, and set out on the thirty-five-mile run to a beach south of camp, near Hookena, under the pretense of practicing rubber boat landings.

On a normal workday, Ski sent squads on training missions in the Kohala Mountains either honing their skills as snipers or practicing survival tactics. Taking no rations and only one canteen, they learned water discipline and how to live off the land.

One such day, Ski showed Evans and fellow corporal William Canipe their objective through a pair of twenty-power binoculars. Twenty miles in the distance on the side of one peak was a barren patch of land. The two squads had four hours to reach that spot, laden with full combat packs. The distance seemed more challenging when they learned that the heavily jungled terrain through which they would travel received five hundred inches of rain a year.

Once there, they would signal that they had made it by spreading out a white sheet on the side of the mountain. That way Ski could tell if they achieved their goal even without his binoculars. From there they were to train in stealth and observation, reporting back to camp in one week.

Everyone made it to the designated area in less than the four hours allotted. While spreading the sheet to signal, Evans's group encountered a Chinese man who lived nearby. The chatty and informative man, who referred to Evans as "Yankee friend," showed him a tunnel through the mountain—a viaduct for water to wash sugar cane stalks on their journey down to the mill on the other side of the mountain.

The Marines and their new friend waded through the waist-deep water for a quarter of a mile. As they walked, the Chinese man told Evans of the bounty that lay on the other side. When they emerged from the darkness, the Waipio Valley lay before them. "See, my Yankee friend," the man spread his arms.

The verdant farmland of the Waipio Valley glistened in the sun. Little dirt roads lined with macadamia trees framed a picture of paradise. The men thought they had walked onto a movie set; the scenic waterfall was missing only one thing: Dorothy Lamour.

Modifying the directive to live off the land, the Thieves stole off the land. Besides huge China oranges, they pilfered armfuls of macadamia nuts, avocados, guava, papaya, and other fruit.

The hut-dwelling farm workers weren't thrilled. Afraid of the Marines, the farm workers threatened, "You better leave.... There's bubonic plague here! Rats everywhere!"

"Fanny's your aunt," Smotts said to Evans in response to the threat.

"It's bullshit," Evans agreed.

Emerick pulled down a China orange the size of a volleyball, peeled off the inch-thick hide and took a bite. Juicy nectar dripped off his chin onto his dungarees. "The pickins are good," he announced.

Mullins wandered into sugar cane fields, past a series of long chutes that carried twelve-foot stalks from the higher elevation down to the cane mill where they squeezed the liquid out and put it in barrels. Mullins grabbed a stalk, cut it, lay on his back and let the sweet juice drip down into his mouth.

The Marines' presence irritated the natives to no end.

Although Hawaii was a U.S. Territory, the boys had never felt farther away from home. Hawaiians were not only resentful of the Marine presence; often they looked more like their bitter enemies. And some of them were.

After Pearl Harbor was attacked in December of 1941, many Hawaiians expected the Empire of Japan to invade. A great number of loyal Japanese lived there, and they eagerly awaited the impending occupation. Although Imperial plans for the conquest of Hawaii were ended by the Allied victory at Midway, a good number of Japanese loyalists remained active on Hawaii. A network of spies operated despite FBI efforts, the military continually monitored the coast, and Marines remained on high alert against the possibility of Japanese infiltrators arriving by submarine.

The Chinese man told the Marines about three canyons north of Honokaa that had been cut out of the island creating natural fingerlike harbors. He lived in the closest canyon and mentioned that Japanese submarines often tied up to the low rock cliffs in the other two canyons and camped out there for days. The Japanese who lived in the village to the north would bring fruit, vegetables, and meat to the submarines and resupply them. According to him this went on weekly.

Walking north from the Waipio Valley, the Marines left their Chinese friend at his home. In the next two canyons the Thieves found garbage strewn about the ledges, indicating that Japanese submarines had indeed been there. Walking further, Evans, Canipe and their squads came upon the village of Pololu.

All military personnel had been restricted from Pololu because the entire population consisted of Japanese loyalists, and most of them were believed to be spies. When the Hawaiian Territorial Guard sent all the men from the village to an internment camp, the officials ran the Stars and Stripes up the flagpole and left—and immediately the women residents left behind took it down and replaced it with Japan's Rising Sun.

An elderly woman, a spy according to the Chinese man, ran the general store. She transmitted radio signals to Japanese submarines offshore and provided them with supplies and intelligence when they made port in the canyons. The FBI had set up a triangulation station near Pololu, monitoring transmissions and trying to locate the radio. They could pinpoint the location of the radio when the signal was sent, but by the time they arrived at that location the radio would be gone.

Besides the canteen each man carried, all the Thieves had a little money, some candy bars, and a pack or two of cigarettes. In Pololu there was an ice cream shop, beer…and more important, girls.

When the Thieves walked into the general store to look around, the elderly woman's eyes lit up. She quickly rounded up a bunch of pretty young Japanese women. Girlfriend types. Geishas, Mullins hoped. The boys began to socialize.

The girls tried to illicit information out of the Marines, but the boys were wise to their tactics. Seductively probing questions were answered with crazy fabrications. The Marines were having fun. After deflecting repeated attempts to learn why the Marines were on Hawaii and their next mission, Mullins noticed an ad on the wall.

> Many a wolf
> Is never let in
> Because of the hair
> On his
> Chinny-chin-chin.
> Burma-Shave

"Burma" Mullins blurted out.
"Now you've done it!" Evans exclaimed.

The girls of Pololu. *Courtesy of Richard Zuziak*

"We're gonna blow up a shaving cream plant!"

Living it up in this restricted Japanese village wasn't a bad way to "survive off the land" for a week. The boys knew their time in Pololu was highly illegal, but they didn't give a damn.

The boisterous Thieves concocted tales and impressed the girls with trinkets, Hershey bars, cigarettes, and sizable gratuities for delivering ice cream or beer. The girls reciprocated with traditional kindness.

In the midst of their "stealth and observation" training, it occurred to Smotts that the old woman had been acting oddly. So one time when she disappeared, he excused himself from his dutiful hostess to go to the restroom. On his way down the hallway he peered through a partially open storeroom door and watched the old woman remove a radio from beneath loose floorboards and then hurry out of the building. He lingered to watch her return and put the radio back.

After a few days of ice cream and girls, the boys were having the time of their lives. The girls were given American names such as Mildred, Grace and Evelyn. Mock military weddings were performed.

The mock marriage of "Evelyn" and Private First Class Carlos Lane. Orozco is left, and Emerick is partially blocked by Canipe. *Courtesy of Richard Zuziak*

Orozco, Lane, "Mom," Canipe, and Emerick. *Courtesy of Richard Zuziak*

The elderly woman took such good care of them that they began calling her "Mom."

Eventually the FBI got wind of Marines being in Pololu. Twenty Marines living it up in a town filled with girls could hardly be a secret for long. General Robert C. Richardson, Jr., military governor and head of Hawaiian Territorial Guard, who lived nearby, was informed of the situation. It wasn't difficult for him to locate the Thieves.

He found Evans, Smotts, and others in the ice cream shop and invited them to his house for lunch and a cup of coffee. Not men who would ever turn down a free meal, they took the general up on his offer. During the visit Richardson asked Evans if he was aware that Pololu was a restricted area and that no military were allowed in the town.

"Really?" Evans played dumb. "Boss, I had no idea…"

"That's sir, not boss, corporal," Richardson corrected. "What made you go into Pololu?" the general asked.

"Honestly," Evans leaned forward, "we came for the girls."

At the house of General Richardson. Moving clockwise around the table, starting in front of the refrigerator, are Valenciano, Smotts, Emerick, Evans, Orozco, and Private First Class Charles Fields. *Courtesy of Richard Zuziak*

Richardson took a picture of the group to show to Marine General Holland "Howlin' Mad" Smith, commander of the invasion force for the boys' next mission.

"You boys know that I'm going to have to tell your general about this..." he said. It was not a mild threat.

"Sir," Orozco smiled his Ipana smile, "If we'd known Pololu was off limits, we never woulda gone in."

"You see, sir," Smotts tried to play a different angle, "like I say, my birthday's comin' up in a few weeks. I'm gonna be nineteen, sir. It's all my fault, my buddies were just tryin' to do somethin' nice for me. Sorta havin' a little birthday party."

"Well, happy birthday, son," Richardson patted Smotts on the shoulder. "But you boys better head back to camp right now."

Leaving the luncheon, Evans asked Smotts, "You gotta birthday comin' up?"

"Next January."

Richardson made good on his threat and showed the picture to Howlin' Mad Smith. The general took copies of the photo to Colonel Riseley.

"Ski!" The order came down for the lieutenant to appear before Riseley at regimental headquarters.

Before he left, Ski called Evans in to make a report. Mr. Kansas City could sugar coat manure into candy. But there was enough solid information of value salted in with details about the girls and the parties and "Mom" to maybe buy a bit of leniency, if Ski played his cards right.

"That sounds like one helluva party," he said before dismissing Evans. "I'm sorry I couldn't join you boys."

Contact with the enemy always carried risks. Now Ski's men had created a dangerous situation that could result in brig time, possibly court-martials. On his way to a chewing out from his boss, Ski pondered his options. He was ready for the worst when he knocked on the wooden post of Riseley's tent.

"Enter." Ski walked in. General Holland Smith sat behind Colonel Riseley's desk, and Riseley stood at his side. Ski snapped to attention. Neither Riseley nor Smith said "at ease." Ski suspected he might learn how General Smith had earned his nickname: "Howlin' Mad."

"Look at this," Smith shoved a photograph across the desk. "Then explain it." The general's jaw twitched, and his hand remained flat on the desk with one fingertip on the picture, clearly indicating he did not expect Ski to fall out of attention and reach for the picture of Evans's squad at their least Marine-like.

There was no opportunity to respond. Smith's angry reprimand chewed up one side of Ski and down the other. Riseley stood by, not saying a word. Smith paused as though he might be through.

"Permission to speak, sir,"

"Permission granted," Smith said. "But I don't know what in the hell you can say."

"With all due respect, sir, my boys were doing their job."

Smith gave a sarcastic laugh. But his attitude changed as Ski continued. "The squad went into Pololu because they heard the FBI had

had difficulty in locating radio transmissions originating from Pololu. Transmissions that were being sent to Japanese submarines off the coast." With carefully metered calm, Ski told his superior officers where the FBI could find the transmitter, as well as how his boys had discovered that Japanese submarines were docking and resupplying near Pololu. It was possible Riseley smiled, just a little, as Ski fell into a respectful quiet.

Taking a moment to digest the information, Smith said, "I'll have that checked out. Your colonel will inform you of the punishment for you and your men. Dismissed."

The FBI found the radio; the canyons were mined; and the Thieves got off easy. In the Marine Corps it was generally assumed that one didn't get punished for the offense so much as for carelessness in having been caught. Their punishment in this case: guard duty, patrolling the officers' tents for one week.

It was a strange penalty. The officers' tents had the best booze in the whole camp. Having the Thieves patrol the officer's tents was like putting the fox in charge of the hen house. Patrolling back and forth all day in the blistering heat brought on a powerful thirst. The officers were away on duty, leaving no one and nothing around except the Thieves and the booze they protected.

Valenciano and Smotts, sweating profusely, walked into a tent to get out of the sun and sat down on the bunks. Smotts slumped over, elbows on knees, and noticed an open and almost full bottle under the bunk. He grabbed the find and shook it at Val.

Smotts's eyes glimmered. "Let's get rip-roaring' soused."

The bottle was passed back and forth until it was almost dry. Smotts then replaced the bottle under the bunk on its side, making it appear as if it had been emptied by being knocked over. Staggering out, Smotts and Val met other wobbling Thieves who had had similar ideas.

Orozco and Emerick were the only ones to get caught. The officers from the tent they patrolled returned from duty to find the wasted pair passed out on their bunks, clutching empty bottles like stuffed animals.

For punishment, Orozco and Emerick received one week in the brig on rations of bread and water.

Unfortunately for Orozco and Emerick, their brig time coincided with an appointment all their fellow Scout-Snipers had made to get their ears pierced, so they could wear a small gold ring in their left ear like Errol Flynn wore in swashbuckling movies. Orozco already had his ear pierced, but Emerick had missed his opportunity while sitting in the brig.

Emerick decided that he wasn't going to be left out. He'd pierce his own ear. Finding the necessary instruments, a long nail and a sizable rock, Emerick backed up to a fence post and put his ear flat against it. He gave the rock and nail to Orozco, who put the tip of the nail up to Emerick's ear.

"On three," Orozco began the count: "One…two…" and wham! Emerick's ear was pierced. Blood squirted everywhere. Not only was Emerick bleeding like a stuck pig, but the nail had sunk deep into the fence post. Orozco couldn't get it out. When the guards eventually responded to the cries for help, they laughed at the sight of the big lummox hanging by his ear. They left him there, tacked to a wooden pole for the amusement of the next men on duty. The Thieves were fearless, but that wasn't always the same as smart.

CHAPTER TWELVE

A Three-Day Pass

*"Do any human beings ever realize life while they live it—
every, every minute?"*

—*Thornton Wilder,* Our Town

March 1, 1944
Second Marine Division Parade Ground, Parker Ranch

The day Orozco and Emerick were released from the brig, an impressive ceremony took place. Admiral Chester Nimitz, commander in chief of the Pacific Fleet, paid a visit to give awards to those whose acts on Tarawa had been deemed above and beyond the call of duty. He decorated 171 men of the Second Marine Division, including Ski.

The cue for "Strike up the band!" was delivered, and the Marine Corps brass band launched into "Ruffles and Flourishes," followed by "Anchors Aweigh," to accompany Nimitz's climb up the stage steps. Navy and Marine officers on the podium wearing khakis or dress blues, greeted the admiral with salutes and handshakes depending on rank. Before Nimitz spoke, all in attendance stood at attention and saluted for "The Star-Spangled Banner."

A slight yet steady rain began to fall.

"Ski" and Admiral Nimitz. *From the collection of Joseph Tachovsky*

Privates were sent to find a raincape for Nimitz as he began, "We have assembled today to honor those among your number who have particularly distinguished themselves in battle against our enemy in the Pacific. The whole world knows of the gallant performance and achievement of the men who fought at Tarawa. Nothing can sufficiently express the nation's gratitude for the deeds of its sons in battle."

It's a nice ceremony, Ski thought. Despite the rain and his ambivalence about deserving an award, it felt good to be a part of the event. The pomp and ceremony reminded him of his first posting, as a private aboard the USS *Maryland* before the war. Grand events like this had been more common then.

Stiff at attention, he smiled inwardly, remembering his Old Mary buddies "Snerd" McIntyre, "Eyegor" Fay, "Shit-Sack" Rhode, and Frank "Goofy" Guthrie. Shit-Sack's nickname was well-deserved, but he was an accomplished photographer who chronicled the exploits of Goofy and

Ski, the two stars who helped the ship's football team win the Vanderbilt Cup in 1939. Neither of them could know it would be the last time they'd see each other. Frank Guthrie died on Wake Island.

Nimitz concluded, "…until our combined power has brought about the unconditional surrender of the Empire of Japan. I now present these awards in the name of the President of the United States who, were it possible, would have the keenest pleasure in pinning these medals on you personally."

Throughout the ceremony, the honored Marines stood in perfect formation in the rain. Nimitz progressed from Marine to Marine, decorating each man. On Ski's damp shirt he pinned the red-white-and-blue-ribboned Silver Star.

Along with his medal, each man received a flowery citation. The ceremony closed with "The Marines' Hymn." The ongoing war demanded that attention shift rapidly from formalities back to work. Ski changed into his dungarees, dropped the Silver Star in his footlocker, and hoped Roxie would remain oblivious of the day's event.

● ● ●

Ski rode his men hard through the first month of training. Japanese cruelty would be more merciless than anything he dished out. There was not one liberty day in four weeks. Nothing but "Old dead dog!" from 0545 to lights out—after which the Thieves were often rousted out of a sound sleep for night maneuvers. The rugged training served the purpose of discovering how much his men could take.

Four men from Dyer's squad had recently opted out, finding the training too rigorous. After those unfortunate departures, plus the unauthorized holiday his two squads had taken in Pololu, Ski recognized that his men needed a reward for their hard work. When the men were told that a two-day pass was being tacked onto their first liberty day, the camp erupted in cheers.

Before going on leave themselves, Ski and his sergeants met at regimental headquarters and drafted a second notice for volunteers.

"It's gonna be slim pickins this time around." Knuppel's words came haltingly as he hunted and pecked away.

"It's a little late in the game." Slevin added. "Most guys are pretty far along in training and well settled in with their own units."

"We've at least got to shake the tree and see what falls out. You done?" Ski asked. Knuppel handed him the announcement, which he had mimeographed. Handing several copies to each of his sergeants and keeping some for himself, Ski said, "We'll each hit a battalion, post these wherever you can, and then enjoy your time off. You deserve it."

●   ●   ●

Knuppel and Evans hitched a ride to Kona, sixty miles to the west, for their three-day holiday. After they were dropped off, they made inquiries as to the biggest and fanciest hotel in town and checked into the luxurious Kona Inn.

Evans flopped onto one of the soft double beds in their second-story room. Sinking into the comfort he sighed, "Boss, I'm gonna get disgustingly clean."

Feeling no need to rush, the two took their time, enjoying long, leisurely showers and shaves in the ample warm water of a sparkling bathroom. Changing into neatly pressed khakis and feeling like Rockefellers, they went down to the dining room and sat at a table set with crisp linens. They ordered a couple of beers before dinner, and Knuppel eagerly opened his menu while Evans scanned the room.

Many tables were occupied with officers, pilots mostly, who sat in groups. The Army Air Corps had been experiencing problems with pilots getting combat fatigue from flying too many missions, so they had fixed up some barracks outside of Kona into a makeshift resort. The pilots rested in comfort until their nerves calmed down to the point where they could get back in the air.

Knuppel prodded the waitress about the Army Air Corps diners, and she seemed to know a lot about them.

Quickly finishing his beer, Knuppel ordered more drinks and bantered with the waitress about what to have for dinner. Evans, cautiously nursing his bottle, gave Knuppel a poke as two nurses walked past. "Boss! That's her."

"Who?" Knuppel reluctantly let the waitress walk away.

"Maureen O'Hara."

"That's not Maureen O'Hara."

"She's the one from the infirmary that I told you about." Unable to take his eyes off her, Evans apparently found the look-alike more appealing than any dish on the menu. With dark auburn hair neatly tucked under her military cap, dimple-framed red lips, and eyes that glistened like emeralds, she hypnotized him. Raising his menu so he could unobtrusively track the two nurses all the way to their table, Evans stared hungrily in their direction as two bourbon and sodas were placed on the table.

"I decided we should live it up." Knuppel tried to get Evans's attention. "Don, if you're hungry, your menu's a little lower."

"Boss," Evans smiled, "I think those nurses look lonesome. I'm gonna see if we can get ourselves a date."

"You can see they're First Louies, right?"

"Yeah, all over."

"You better be careful, Don. You could get us in some deep shit."

"C'mon...afraid of a little girl, are you? Or are you still thinking about that chippie back in Minnesota? Old what's-her-name?"

"Helen."

"Yeah, I know. But I'm waiting for YOU to forget. It's time to stop livin' in the past." Evans leaned forward. "You see that redhead? I bet she's got eyes as green as the Missoura Valley."

"Is that the line you're gonna use?"

"Unless they're blue, then they're as shimmering as the Missoura River," Evans beamed.

"Jesus, Don."

"Well, she's mine. You can have the other one. Maybe her name's Helen, too. That'll make it easier when you get her in the sack." Evans

Don Evans. *Courtesy of Steve Evans*

whispered breathily, "Helen...oh yes, Helen...yes..."

Knuppel shook his head.

"Don't worry, Boss, there won't be any problems. I'm just gonna go over and talk to those pretty First Louies." On the hunt, Evans rose to his full six foot four, straightened his tie, and carried his highball to the nurses' table.

"Good evening, lieutenants," Evans greeted the two nurses. "Welcome to Kona." He motioned toward Knuppel, "My Boss over there and I would like to be your official tour guides to this lovely city."

The women, who knew the game, exchanged sidelong glances. They kept Evans standing for a while, laughing at his jokes, showing just enough interest. They offered him a chair, and he seized the advantage. He sat and motioned for a waiter. The lieutenants ordered scotch and waters, and when the drinks arrived he gallantly paid for them. Evans had the manners and gentle courtesy of a true ladies' man. From time to time the silver-tongued devil glanced over at Knuppel and gave him the high sign. Kansas City charm flowing, Evans peppered the conversation with honeyed words. When he used the line about the redhead's eyes, she smiled.

Goddammit, Knuppel thought, he's gonna get those girls. He's gonna get those nurses.

Evans left the table and walked back toward Knuppel grinning from ear to ear like he'd won a prize. "Well, Boss, you feelin' lucky? 'Cause I got us some nurses. The brunette, she's yours."

"Only if her name isn't Helen," Knuppel joked.

"Her name ain't Helen. Well, maybe it is. I actually didn't get their names," Evans shrugged. "We'll just have to improvise." Evans whispered breathily, "You…oh yes, You…yes…"

They both laughed, and Evans went on, "I've got the redhead. Her eyes are green, by the way. But they made some other dates for right now. So, they're gonna be leaving soon, but they'll get back in around midnight. I checked their room number, and they're just two doors down from us. My redhead said she'd knock on our door when they get back."

"Does that smell right to you?" Knuppel questioned.

"Hell, yeah! Why would they be blowin' smoke? We better get some supplies and stuff up in the room and be ready for them when they get back." Like the Boy Scouts, Scout-Snipers took pride in being prepared.

After dinner Evans and Knuppel walked around Kona, stopping at various shops and bars, buying the supplies of seduction—beer and a bottle of scotch. Returning to the hotel a few hours before midnight, Knuppel lay down to take a nap just in case his unnamed brunette happened to wander in. Evans paced around like a cat on hot coals.

Just before midnight, Knuppel awoke to an empty room. He heard a noise outside their open window, looked out, and saw Evans walking along on the ledge of the hotel, peering in the windows of other rooms.

"Jesus, Don. What in the hell are you doing?" Knuppel whispered.

"Seeing if those nurses are back."

With Kona under a blackout, no one saw Evans shuffling along the second-story ledge. He finished his voyeuristic mission and shuffled his way back inside. "Not yet," Evans reported.

"You know Don, there's a pretty good chance you got a line thrown at you tonight just to get you off the scent."

"No?" Evans paused and thought. "No. They meant it. She meant it. That pretty little redhead wouldn't be lyin' to me, Boss…after all we've meant to one another?"

"Well, I'm going back to sleep," Knuppel stretched. "Just keep me posted if a miracle occurs." Evans poured himself another glass of scotch—neat.

It was 0230 the next time Knuppel awoke. Evans was absent. Knuppel instinctively went over to the window. Evans was standing on the ledge once again. But this time he was peeping in the windows naked as a jaybird.

"Don, get the hell back in here!" ordered Knuppel in a whisper. Evans obediently wobbled his way back in. Knuppel would have grabbed for his friend's belt if he'd been wearing one. "You know, if you do that again, you might want to put on some pants, so they don't think you're being too forward."

By daylight, Evans had reluctantly given up.

"I guess you were right, Boss. They stood us up," Evans said dejectedly.

"Did you get any sleep at all, Don?"

"No."

"Well, cheer up for Christ's sake," Knuppel consoled. "There's plenty of fish in the sea for a good lookin' buck like you."

"I don't know about that." Evans sat deflated with his head down, then looked up at Knuppel. "There was just something about that little redhead…I don't know, Boss…something. Christ, I don't even know her name."

●   ●   ●

Having no plans for his three-day pass, Roscoe Mullins was lazing on his cot after breakfast with his eyes closed when Marvin Strombo silently crept in and tipped the wood and canvas bed over. Mullins flopped to the floor. Strombo laughed out loud.

"Marvin!" Mullins exclaimed good-naturedly from the wooden decking. "What in the hell do you want?"

"C'mon," Strombo extended his hand to help Mullins to his feet. "Get up, we're goin' to Kona!"

They quickly changed out of their tattered dungarees and into rumpled khakis before beginning the long march. The pair had trouble hitching a ride, and Strombo soon began to have second thoughts: "I'm not dressed up enough for goin' to town."

"Hell, we don't have to be dressed up, we just need some money," Mullins said. "And I got me twenty bucks. What about you?"

"Fifteen."

"Well then, we got plenty," Mullins reassured.

Trudging along toward Waimea where there was a paved road that ran to Kona, they kept hoping that one of the passing cars might heed their thumbs. Strombo asked, "Whaddya wanna do in Kona?"

"Well," Mullins said, "growin' up in the mountains, I never been around water in my life. The only beaches I seen so far, I was either bein' shot at, or practicin' bein' shot at. So, I think I just wanna strip down to my skivvies and lay on the shore and let the cool waves come and get me."

A car came roaring up behind them. An Army colonel raced by, leaving them choking in a cloud of dust.

"Goddamn dogface shit-head," Mullins muttered.

Arriving in Waimea, they noticed the same colonel's jeep outside of a store, untended, with the motor still running.

"Are you thinkin' what I'm thinkin'?" Mullins asked.

"Serves him right." Strombo replied. "Let's borrow it." They jumped in the jeep and raced toward Kona. The two buddies reached their destination by mid-afternoon, parked the jeep in a lot near the beaches of Honokohau Bay, and relaxed in the cool water for a few hours.

Just before sunset they walked into town, passing a large marina filled with luxury yachts. After they found a cheap hotel with two twin beds for two dollars a night, the famished Strombo asked the clerk about good, cheap places to eat. The clerk directed them to a bar that served fifty-cent burgers and twenty-five-cent Pabst. The place was packed with servicemen. Pouncing on the first open table, the pair ate and drank until curfew, but watched their cash.

The next morning bright and early, the two began a walking tour of Kona. On their promenade, Mullins and Strombo visited a coffee mill, went inside Mokuaikaua Church—the oldest Christian church in the Hawaiian Islands—and passed the Hulihe'e Palace.

"Says here this is some kind of museum, run by the Daughters of Hawaii. It used to be a governor's mansion. Won't cost anything to look." Strombo led the way. Mullins followed.

Continuing their sightseeing tour, they came across a long line of servicemen. Far ahead, over a block away, the queue disappeared around a corner.

Mullins whistled at the prodigious line, "Hey Marvin, what in the hell do you think this is?"

"Gotta be something good." They joined the shuffling line that slowly took them around a corner. The line ended at a house two blocks away where two MPs stood guard on the front porch. As the line grew shorter, everyone ahead became more anxious and antsy, prompting Mullins to elbow Strombo and nod toward the fidgety sailor ahead of him.

"Before we waste any more of our precious leave, could you tell us what we're waiting for?" Mullins asked the sailor.

The answer consisted of two words.

Mullins roared with laughter at the discovery. "It's a goddamn whore house!" Neither stepped out of line.

"This must be run by the other Daughters of Hawaii," Strombo said with mock seriousness.

As they neared the porch, the sailor turned around to advise the novices. "It costs two bucks to get in. Have your money in hand, ready to pay. And I tell you, they take you to a bed, and if you don't get your rocks off in good time, they'll kick your ass out the door. Two dollars. Two minutes."

●　●　●

For the officers' holiday, the Salty Sons were driven into Hilo by a private who drove the jeep like he was riding a bucking bronco. After getting settled into his hotel room in Hilo, and before heading out to sightsee with his buddies, Ski began the daily ritual that he had skipped too often of late.

> March 4, 1944
> My Dearest Roxie:
>   After a lapse of several days I am back with you again. Today we had an extended liberty day, and I used it as such. Four of us went to a town about sixty miles away. We had quite a bit of fun drinking and singing along the way. Joe, Captain Edwards and Doc are with me....

Pounding on the door, Doc put the letter on hold.

Edwards, Dulcich, Doc, and Ski looked forward to a few days of many little luxuries that they had been missing: cool drinks with State-side liquor served over ice; a working over in an honest-to-goodness barber chair instead of sitting on an old, wooden box and having some clumsy Marine chop away; large, comfortable beds in lieu of cots or foxholes; clean table linen; and sitting in a well cushioned seat in a cab, to name a few.

One cab driver told the Salty Sons that truck-driving Marines had been running cars off the roads. After one such incident, an MP had stopped to help the cabbie out of a ditch and bawled him out for driving on the wrong side of the road. He couldn't understand what the MP meant until he realized the Marines had previously been stationed in New Zealand, where traffic kept to the left. "You guys finally got it figured out," the cabbie told Ski and his friends, "but I'm still leery as hell about you Marines."

After a round of golf, the men went shopping for presents for their wives. Edwards bought Tilly a summery hat with a purse to match. Doc found a set of tableware perfect for picnics—six coasters, six napkin rings, and six placemats of woven fronds.

"Plannin' on two more kids when y'all get back home?" Dulcich ribbed the doctor.

For Ruth and Roxie, both Dulcich and Ski fell for antique, one-of-a-kind necklaces with matching earrings at exorbitant prices. Later they discovered that every man with a sweetheart back home had bought the very same unique jewelry.

Following dinner, a movie, and a native dancing show, which wasn't much, the Salty Sons returned to the hotel for cards, drinking, and fighting the Battle of Tarawa all over again.

Well in his cups, Doc entertained the others with his own version of the hula, which his three buddies thought to be far superior to any native Hawaiian's rendition.

The friends were gathered around a proper table for a change, cluttered with the traditional accouterments of bottles, ashtrays, treats from Roxie, five glasses filled with bourbon, and cards.

Ski raked in a sizable pot. There were moans from the others. Dulcich slid a flat, brown paper-wrapped package to his buddy. "Happy belated birthday, Ski."

"It's your birthday? How come you didn't say anything?" Edwards asked.

"I didn't even realize...Jesus, that was last month, the twenty-eighth. How did you know, Joe?"

"Roxie mentioned somethin' 'bout it to Ruth..."

"Well, happy birthday!" Doc laughed and cut off the unchewed half of his unlit cigar with a pocketknife and handed it to Ski, who graciously accepted.

"Open it up, Ski," Edwards urged.

He carefully sliced the tape and unfolded the brown paper. "My God, Joe. Did you do this? How in the hell could you draw a picture of Roxie?" Ski held up a charcoal sketch for all to see.

"I acquired a picture outta yo' footlocker. Happy birthday."

"Dulcich, you are some kinda artist...can I take a look at it, Ski?" Edwards gently took the portrait.

"That's what I did befo' the war," Dulcich drawled. "Didn't make much money at it. Made more in the WPA, paintin' signs fo' the Audubon

Zoo. Once in a while, tho', I'd get a po'trait job with one o' the landed families in the Ga'den District. I'd sign 'em all 'Joseph Benedict Dulcich.'"

"You've got quite a talent, Joe," Doc said, looking at the drawing Edwards had handed him. "If I gave you a picture of Ellie," Doc asked, "could you do a drawing for me? I'd pay you."

"One hundred and fifty," Dulcich paused, "bottles o' ferrous sulfate."

After the laughter subsided, Dulcich smiled. "Ol' Doc, I'll do it fo' nothin'."

Dulcich's drawing of Roxie. *From the collection of Joseph Tachovsky*

The gift made its way back into Ski's hands. "Thanks, Joe…" He stumbled, reaching for words as he gazed at the artwork, not knowing what else to say besides, "Thanks."

The card game was resumed, the battle reengaged.

"…Then this Jap comes out of a pillbox," Doc recounted "walkin' into our triage area, his hands clutching his stomach yellin', 'Me sick! Me sick!' And one of my corpsmen gets up."

"Tell me he didn't fall for it?" Edwards asked.

"Nope. He put a bullet through his skull. As he fell to the ground, two grenades fell out of his armpits and exploded. I put my boy up for a medal."

Cards were dealt, bets were lost and won. The bourbon having taken full effect, Ski's sunken eyes drifted back and forth from the portrait of Roxie to the fifth glass. "Pappy" was all he said.

"What about Pappy?" Dulcich asked.

"Roxie doesn't know." Quiet followed Ski's confession.

The evening of cards ground to a close, and the four staggered off to their rooms. Picking up where he had left off earlier in the day, Ski finished his letter.

> Before I left, a box from you arrived. It was similar to the last and contained a crock of cheese, some nuts, and a box of candy. The cheese is excellent. We enjoyed it on the ride into town.
>
> Answering your question, if I would get out of the way of "a dirty old mosquito," it's really just one of those things. While I miss you terribly, I couldn't intentionally attempt unorthodox methods in getting back to you. I wouldn't consider myself much of a man if I did that. Our turn will come, and then all of this will become just an unpleasant memory. I well know it isn't easy to take when you see other husbands and loved ones returning while we are still apart. There are a certain amount of bitter pills we must all swallow. It seems like we're getting our ration now.
>
> Well, it's getting late now, Roxie. Good night my love.
>
> All my love forever. Your husband, Frank

He paused, then added:

> P.S. In your letters you always inquire about Pappy. Well, Roxie, I won't be seeing Pappy anymore.

During the second day of the assault upon Tarawa, in the waning light of sunset, two tracked landing vehicles, LVTs, had maneuvered through a minefield toward shore. The first made it unharmed. With darkness descending, the second hit a mine and was completely destroyed, vaporized in an immense explosion. George "Pappy" Morehead was in that second LVT. His body was never recovered.

CHAPTER THIRTEEN

Red Sky at Night

*"Yesterday our platoon had a barbecue. We had
roasted pork, chicken, and beer, etc. My boys
had a pretty good time."*

—*Lieutenant Frank Tachovsky in a letter to his wife*

March 7, 1944, 0545 Hours
Scout-Sniper Platoon Encampment, Parker Ranch

The platoon's training was no less intense when they returned from
leave, but it didn't seem as rigorous. The men attacked each challenge
with renewed vigor.

"Rise! Shine! Give God the glory!" Ski bellowed the first morning
back, and it was business as usual. More getting up before reveille, more
"Old dead dog!," more daily five-mile runs, more sparring with scabbards on, more jujitsu, more Black Death.

Smaller men were required to go up against Emerick, Evans, and Orozco,
the platoon's larger guys, and it irked Emerick to no end that Jackson always
got the best of him. Emerick never uttered the word Squirt again. And when
Moore went up against Evans, the contest ended in a draw.

To date, the Marines' battles had not involved a civilian population, only enemy soldiers unwilling to surrender. Persuasive phrases
had been unnecessary. In April a new element was introduced into

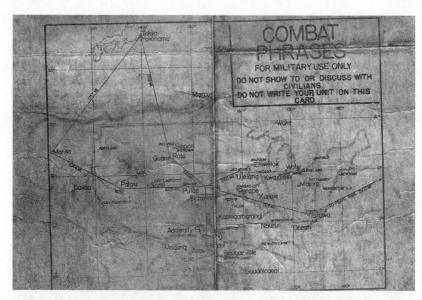

Map and list of Japanese phrases distributed to the 40 Thieves during their training. *From the collection of Joseph Tachovsky*

their daily regimen. A document the size of a postcard was distributed among the men. With the new list of key Japanese phrases and corresponding phonetic pronunciations, it quickly became apparent that the next mission would be different.

Scuttlebutt as to the target of their attack ran rampant. Most thought it could be Saipan, whose topography bore a striking similarity to Hawaii's. Saipan also had a Japanese-speaking civilian population. Others argued that Saipan was too far away, over a thousand miles from any U.S. installation. Speculation swirled.

The only thing the Marines knew for certain was that they could be sent anywhere, and they would be informed only after they were at sea and well underway.

Gathering around the fire pit at night to unwind became a pleasant end-of-the-day ritual. Atomizers of Joy Juice made the rounds. Letters were written and read in the waning daylight.

Evans opened one, unscented letter from home. A few photos fell out. He handed them to his frequently visiting buddies Arello and Duley.

"My Dearest Son," his mother had written.

> I've sure neglected you this last week. Seems like I am just swamped in work which really isn't as necessary as writing you. This big bond drive is on and I'm working on it. Gracie Allen, George Burns, and Dinah Shore put on a big stage show here in the auditorium last night.
>
> The radio news this morning said the war in Europe will be over this year but the struggle in the Pacific will be a long one. I can't bear to think of it.
>
> You left two years ago tomorrow, and it has been a very long two years for us here at home. Don't you ever get into a city where you can get a real photograph taken, one without whiskers and a freak haircut? Honey, you are going to ruin your beautiful hair by haggling it up in such an awful fashion all the time. You may lose that pretty wave.

Are you keeping well? Have you seen Tommy and Norman yet? Do you have any more attacks of that fever? I do pray that....

"Listen up!" Knuppel, flanked by two newcomers, walked into the midst of them. All eyes turned toward the new boots. "As you all know, recently four men opted out, and we posted for replacements."

"Good riddance to bad rubbish!" Emerick's opinion was greeted by raucous agreement from the Thieves who had stayed the course.

"No!" Knuppel quieted the men. "They're good Marines. This just wasn't for them. We interviewed up to a dozen men and took the cream of the crop. We've got two new volunteers joining us today. You gotta admire these two men for joining us so deep into our training."

Knuppel introduced the more grizzled of the two first: nineteen-year-old Private First Class Ira Causey. "He's from the bayous of Louisiana," Knuppel said. "Causey will be bunking with Strombo and Mullins."

Strombo nudged Mullins and coughed out, "Swamp Rat!"

Those near Strombo laughed. Causey heard the comment and smiled. Little did Strombo know that Causey took the moniker as a compliment.

Brows furrowed as Knuppel introduced the other recruit, an overgrown fresh-faced kid from Detroit: Private First Class Warren Tipton.

Smotts and Kenny were unenthused when Knuppel assigned the youngster to their tent.

Tipton immediately tried latching onto Smotts. "My uncle was a Marine fighter pilot and got shot down over Guadalcanal. That's when I decided to enlist and make the Japs pay."

"Go away, kid." Smotts cut him off, not wanting to be distracted from writing a letter to his girl back home, Alma Jean. "Red's from Detroit, go bother him."

Tipton followed the suggestion. "If the Tigers could get any hitting besides Wakefield and York, they could win the pennant, maybe even the World Series."

Staring blankly at the nuisance, Kenny rolled over and continued with a letter to his own sweetheart, Eve.

The silent treatment bounced Tipton back to Smotts. "Where are you from?"

"Who in the hell are you, and why can't you leave me alone?" Smotts glared.

"Tipton. Warren H."

"H as in hoo the hell cares."

"It's actually Hobart."

"Ho-bart!" Smotts laughed. "What the hell kind of name is Hobart?"

"It's my dad's name." Tipton smiled and shrugged.

"That's sweet." Smotts jabbed. "How old are you? You're just a kid."

Private First Class Warren Tipton. *Courtesy of Richard Zuziak*

"Seventeen. I'll be eighteen on June 15..."

"Good for you, Hobart." Smotts patted Tipton on his back, like burping a baby, roughly, and needled the kid, "That's what I'm gonna call you, Hobart. What do you think about that, Hobart?"

Tipton wanted to fit in, to be gung-ho, and prove himself. "I like it!" Smotts's insult had backfired.

•   •   •

Back in his own tent, Evans answered his mother's letter before lights out.

April 2, 1944

Dear Mom,

Just got back from some more "boondockin." It seems like we're always comin' and goin'.

You'll be happy to know the Boss gave me the word that I should shave off my beard. Last week he made me shave off my Mohawk.

I got your letter of March 1 today. I was glad to get the pictures. Them houn' dawgs sure is sweet. Spats is very muscular for such a little boy and Inky seems to be getting a gray mustache on her muzzle.

Mom, you've got a mother's viewpoint in regard to this war. If women had their way, nobody would have any fun. I think you're very wrong to deprive Babe of his right to get out and see the world. My kid brother would really enjoy this war, and he'd learn one helluva lot more than if he stayed for that last year of school. He will really be misplaced and unhappy with those less mature kids. He's no child, Mom, and you've got to let him live his own life.

It would be a pity to send Babe off to college. I'm genuinely happy this war got in the way of me going to college. It would've been a sad waste of time and money. I've aged ten years in this outfit and learned a helluva lot about everything in general. Do I make myself clear?

Arello and Duley stopped by again today. Duley's sick of fighting and can't see why the Marines are yelling for more. I told him to stop being such a dogface, it's embarrassing. They're coming over to spend five whole days with me.

I can't think of anything to say anymore. I got a letter from Grandma and one from Auntie Fawn.

Love, Don

The next day and the next, training intensified. "Old dead dog!" was accompanied by "EE-SO-Gay!" a Japanese combat phrase that roughly meant hurry up.

The two new recruits had to prove themselves physically every day—running everywhere, everything double time, training hard, night maneuvers, being out for days at a time. That was mandatory. The strenuous training had already taken its toll on four men. The veteran Thieves tried their best to break Causey and Tipton with little success.

By the end of April, as inspections and checklists increased, it became apparent that the Marines would be shipping out soon. With their next combat looming ahead, Ski sensed quiet anxiety growing in his men. He overheard Evans, Moore, Emerick, Knuppel, and others who had fought on Guadalcanal and Tarawa joke about the next battle in a resigned way, "The third time's the charm."

Before dawn broke, the order came from Sergeant Slevin: "Get your packs, and bring the rubber boats." The men thought they understood: it was another thirty-five-mile run to Hookena.

Ski led the way. Twenty minutes into the run, he veered off course and headed to a beach just a few miles away. Nearby a large pier jutted out into the ocean, and the cattle from Parker Ranch were being loaded onto boats. The farm boys among the Thieves stared in amazement as cattle swam to boats waiting offshore and were hoisted onboard.

The men were confused to have reached the beach by mid-morning but happy the hike had ended early. Accustomed to routine, they began settling in and inflating the boats.

"Boys," Ski interrupted, "forget what you're doing. We're having a barbecue!"

The men cheered.

Orders were given, with each squad assigned a specific event-related task. Evans's squad went out to hunt for dinner, another was sent to forage for fruit and other edibles, and yet another busied itself digging the

A map printed in *The Tarawa Boom-De-Ay*, the Parker Ranch camp newspaper. In the upper left-hand corner, cattle are being loaded onto a boat. Parker Ranch is at the center. *From the collection of Joseph Tachovsky*

barbecue pit. Ski gave Borawski's team a roll of bills to pay for as much beer as could be brought back from Waimea.

Strombo, whose squad had been assigned to prepare the pit, set to work digging a large, deep hole on the beach above the high tide mark, while others gathered tinder. Once the pit was dug, the men put a layer of wood at the bottom and started two large fires on either side of it. When Evans's squad came back with dinner, the coals would be ready.

Knuppel had joined Evans, whose squad had been allotted two hours to return with whatever game they could bag. These guys had been hunting together often on the island, and they knew where turkeys and peacocks could be found. The squad split up, and off they went.

Mullins wandered off on his own, to a place south of camp where he had often seen wild hogs rutting. There was one hog that had particularly piqued his interest, a big, feisty black one. The elusive hog wouldn't let anyone get close, but Mullins saw him among some other pigs about six hundred yards away, just a little out of range. He took aim and fired. A cloud of dust popped at the hog's feet, and he jumped in the air. "Dammit," Mullins cussed to himself, for not getting closer before taking the shot. Before Mullins could get another shot off, all the hogs vanished.

No one had any luck in the hunt. Knuppel shot two peacocks and Evans a twenty-pound turkey, but the birds were so lice-ridden they were left behind. Stymied, with time running out, they faced more than embarrassment if they returned empty-handed.

Emerick had noticed a pig farm a few miles down the road, not far north along the beach. Pork sounded like good eating to the crew.

For a moment or two they discussed targeting the farm, well aware they could get into a lot of trouble if caught. Stealing domesticated animals was strictly forbidden—just like going into Pololu. But they weren't going back without dinner.

"What the hell!" Knuppel approved the plan.

Evans, Johnson, and Knuppel got to the farm before the others and crouched in the nearby brush, scheming how to steal a pig. Evans plotted how they could corner the pig and put a field jacket over its head to muffle the squeals. While those three planned, Emerick, Smotts, Valenciano, and Orozco bolted into action. The four jumped the fence and chased chickens, skewering them onto their bayonets, two or three per rifle. They got that done quickly, and surprisingly quietly. Nobody from the farm appeared.

The pig wasn't as easy. Evans, Johnson, and Knuppel chased one all over the pen. Repeated dives to grab the prey ended with face plants in mud, straw, and dung. The quest for stealth ended immediately as a squealing pig became a siren in the farmyard sounding RED ALERT. Amid the mayhem, the poultry thieves went back in for round two and skewered several more chickens.

At last Evans subdued the pig, then struggled to get out of the pen with the kicking dinner tightly wrapped in his jacket. Astride the fence and filthy, Evans paused when the Japanese man who owned the farm came out to check on the ruckus. Seeing the mud-covered Marines absconding with one of his pigs, the farmer stood paralyzed with his mouth agape. He stared at the Thieves, scared to death.

"Get the hell out of here!" Evans's order to his buddies was also obeyed by the farmer, who ran away.

The Marines fled, carrying the pig kicking and squealing. A few hundred yards down the road, Evans cut its windpipe to put an end to the noise. Back to the beach the gang trotted with the pig and chickens in tow.

"Where'd you boys get so lucky?" Ski asked.

"Do you really want to know, Boss?" Evans answered.

Ski shook his head.

Evans and Knuppel waded waist-deep out into the ocean to clean themselves and butcher the pig while others plucked and gutted the chickens.

Borawski returned from Waimea laden with cases of beer and soda. With a knowing wink, he gave Ski back all the cash he had been given. Other men piled pineapples, coconuts, bananas, oranges, and macadamia nuts on the beach. The barbecue was taking shape.

Strombo had the coals beside the pit good and hot. Half the coals were kicked down onto the tinder and banana leaves laid on them. A lattice of green wood went in next, on top of the leaves, and after that the pig, garnished with sliced pineapples, followed by another layer of banana leaves and then the chickens. More banana leaves covered the chickens first one way and then the other, so that sand wouldn't sift down onto the meat. The last of the coals were kicked down on top of the banana leaves, and then it was all covered with about a foot of sand.

A deep hole was dug closer to the water line for the soda and beer. The ocean water could just reach the hole, trickling in and keeping the drinks nice and cool.

Orozco, reminiscing about the barbecues his grandfather had in Santa Barbara, remembered one of his unique sauces made of coconut milk, bananas, and sugar cane juice. He scavenged for the ingredients and improvised.

It would be five or six hours before the barbecue was ready. The men relaxed, sitting around in small groups, shooting the breeze. Some stripped down and went swimming or drank beer. Strombo and Mullins went out in rubber boats to ride the breakers in.

The 40 Thieves taking it easy. *From the collection of Joseph Tachovsky*

Evans challenged everyone to foot races on the beach, and Valenciano almost beat him, once. Orozco body surfed. Marines competed to see who could throw a rock the farthest or played a version of horseshoes, seeing who could get a coconut the closest to a Ka-Bar stuck in the sand.

Ski lay shirtless on the sand looking up at the sky and listening to the sound of his men enjoying themselves. Knuppel, fresh from a swim in the ocean, wandered over and quietly sat next to him.

"You did good, Ski."

"The boys deserved a break." He added confidentially, "Besides, it could be any day now."

A few more moments passed before Knuppel asked the question that had been puzzling him for months. "Ski, What's this 'Old dead dog!' business all about?"

"Well, Hayshaker," he explained. "It's something I picked up from my father-in-law. George is a real character and says the damnedest things. He's an old Navy man, sailed around the world in Teddy Roosevelt's Great White Fleet. He tells a story about making port in Singapore, and anytime the Chinese dockworkers heard the Americans holler out, 'Let's go, let's go!' the sailors would scurry about, and the Chinese laughed. It happened all the time. Eventually, George asked one of the dockworkers what was so funny about 'Let's go, let's go!' They told him the words sounded like 'Old dead dog!' in Mandarin, and they found it funny that old dead dogs made the sailors work faster. George says 'Old dead dog!' all the time, and I liked it. One time on the Canal I blurted it out. It kinda stuck."

Knuppel chuckled, lay down, and closed his eyes against the warm sun.

Ski saw movement in the underbrush. An islander appeared to be surveying the scene.

"The Marines who stole your pig went that-a-way." Johnson yelled at the farmer. Others laughed.

Ski understood what his men had done, and he gestured for the man to join him, away from the beach. He admired the courage of the Japanese man for walking into his group of trained killers. "It sounds like some Marines made off with your pig, and I understand that we might all look the same to you. So if your pig was taken without permission, I'd like to make that up to you and reimburse you on behalf of the United States Marine Corps."

As the apprehensive farmer thought about it, Ski tried to lighten the moment. "I guess you'll be relieved when we're gone. How much do you want for the pig?"

On the beach his men watched, worrying not about being caught, but that their barbecue might be in jeopardy. Those closest saw Ski count out thirty dollars from his pocket, extend it to the farmer, then shake on the deal.

The sun was close to setting when the pit was opened. The warm air filled with the smell of roasting meats. Ka-Bars served as knife and fork to fill liner-less helmets with as much food as anyone wanted.

"Boy, what a feast!" Knuppel's eyes lit up at the sight of meat so tender it fell off the bone. The face meat was the best.

Strombo, his mouth full, told Mullins about the time he had visited his brother when Oliver was working at the copper mine in Butte. "Before I enlisted, he took me to a place called Pork Chop John's. I thought that was good, but Jesus, this pig roast!"

"My Christ!" Knuppel reveled in the bounty, but then shook his head. "But if we'd gotten caught stealing that pig. Boy oh boy, we'd have gotten in a whole hell of a lot of trouble."

"Now, Boss, Ski paid that farmer for the pig," Evans corrected his buddy. "So truth being told, we really didn't steal the pig…just the chickens."

The sun began to squish into a blood-orange oval as the feast ended. Twilight hung in the sky, and small fires still burned on each side of the pit. It would have to be lights out soon, but there was still a little bit of the day left.

The lieutenant and his two sergeants sat on the beach in silence watching the dying sun bleed streaks of crimson.

"Red sky at night…" Slevin began the old mariner's rhyme.

"…sailor's delight," Knuppel answered.

Ski nodded and had a thought, "You know what's missing? What would be nice for the boys, Vince?"

"What's that?"

Ski asked Slevin if he could give a command performance of "The Sheik of Araby" for the men. Slevin had sung at many of the "opportunity programs" that were held before the evening movies, when men were encouraged to showcase their various talents. But so far, although it was much talked about, none of the men had ever seen his famous bawdy rendition of "The Sheik of Araby."

Slevin, Orozco, Mehlin, and a few others who were musically inclined sometimes got together back at camp for some impromptu sessions performing for their own pleasure, but "The Sheik of Araby" had not been part of their repertoire.

"Give me a few minutes," Slevin said.

The ragtag band gathered some improvised percussion instruments and huddled together away from the rest of the platoon. While they laughed and rehearsed, "With no pants on!" Mullins goaded Private First Class Otto Hebel to put on an opportunity program of his own.

Hebel had been born in Kreimbach, Germany, and German was his native tongue. His family had emigrated to the United States in 1927 during Hitler's rise to power. Hebel did a perfect imitation of the Führer, transforming himself by slicking back his hair with pig grease from dinner and drawing a mustache above his lip with charred wood. Throughout his schtick, his buddies howled with delight.

"...*gute Deutsche, folgen me undt stadtfahrten, undt gutenfahrten, undt fahrten-fahrten outen zee hinders!*" Hebel concluded his performance by raising his hand in triumph and goose-stepping off stage to cheers of "*Sieg Hebel!*"

With perfect timing, Slevin declared that the a cappella version of "The Sheik of Araby" was now ready. "Spike Jones ain't got nothin' on us."

With the red sky having faded and the ocean as their backdrop, Slevin and his band of Thieves performed. A rhythmic Arabian pulsing began. Slevin crooned,

> I'm the Sheik of Araby
> Your love belongs to me
> At night when you're asleep
> Yes baby, into your tent I'll creep

"With no pants on!" the band of Thieves sang.

> The stars that shine above
> They'll light our way to love
> You'll rule this land with me
> Yeah, I'm the Sheik of Araby

The band signaled for the rest of the platoon to join in, "With no pants on!"

> Well I'm the Sheik of Araby
> Yes your love, your love belongs to me
> Whoa at night when you're asleep
> Into your tent I'll creep

"With no pants on!" all the Thieves yelled.

The stars that shine above
Honey, don't you know they'll light our way to love
You'll rule this land with only me
I'm the Sheik

"Yes, Yes, Yes!"

I'm the Sheik

"Yes, Yes, Yes!"

I'm the Sheik of Araby.

"With no pants on!"

AHA!

By the end of the song, the whole platoon was on its feet, and when Slevin ended with "AHA!" everyone dropped his pants.

It was dark now. The men laughed as they pulled up their pants, finished their beers, and kicked the fires into the pit, throwing sand on top. The platoon settled in for the night.

There they were, a bunch of roughnecks lying on a secluded little strip of beach in Hawaii, watching the sun set, having gorged on delicious food, beer, and a band to boot. What a time.

For one brief moment, nobody remembered that a war was going on somewhere else in the world.

CHAPTER FOURTEEN

Arello and Duley

"If they ever black your eyes, put me wise.
If they ever cook your goose, turn me loose.
If they ever put a bullet through your brain, I'll complain.
It's friendship, friendship, just a perfect blendship.
When other friendships have been forgit,
Ours will still be it."

—Cole Porter, *"Friendship"*

May 18, 1944
Scout-Sniper Platoon Encampment, Parker Ranch

At 0545, some men were still sleeping, but most were looking at their watches. There were no shouts of "Rise, and shine, and give God the glory." Those awake saw Sergeants Slevin and Knuppel sitting, waiting.

"What gives, Boss?" Evans asked.

Before either sergeant could reply, a jeep sped into camp and came to a screeching halt. Ski jumped out, a serious look on his face. "We got the word. We're moving out tomorrow. Tell the boys to mount-out."

Marines were always ready at a moment's notice, and they had twenty-four hours to get aboard ship and move out. At the crack of dawn on May 19, the 40 Thieves boarded ships and left Parker Ranch, sailing to the other side of Hawaii for a week of maneuvers and practice landings on adjacent unoccupied islands.

From the onset, the maneuvers did not go as planned. They uncovered several errors that would have resulted in loss of time, equipment, and personnel in combat. At 1505 on the second day of the practice landings, while the men were loading mortars and ammunition onto landing craft, a large fireball erupted into the sky. The first eruption was followed by larger and louder explosions. With twenty-nine ships and landing craft tied up beam to beam at six adjacent piers, the disaster quickly escalated.

Black smoke billowed upward, and the smell of burning fuel and gunpowder filled the air. More shattering booms marked the spread of the fire to five more ships. Men were propelled into the ocean. Burning debris landed everywhere, even on the Thieves who were watching from shore. Cries for help rose above the chaos as wounded men floundered in the burning water.

As the fires raged, vessels trying to vacate the area ran into firefighting ships maneuvering toward the inferno. The bottleneck added to the chaos. Many small explosions sprayed the area with shrapnel. High-octane fuels stored on deck of many of the boats ignited, adding to the blasts.

As the disaster stretched over six hours, injured Marines and sailors floundered in the water. Some of the Thieves swam out to help. The firefighting ships tried to subdue the flames, but to no avail. When the smoke finally cleared, six landing craft had been destroyed, almost two hundred men killed, and hundreds more wounded.

Rehearsals ended abruptly. General Holland Smith ordered the convoy to set sail for Pearl Harbor. Once safely in port, the men received one last liberty before shipping out.

Although granted liberty, few of the Thieves had any money. Only half went ashore. The rest stood on deck wondering how they could manage one last fling. Knuppel had heard some scuttlebutt that the Red Cross would lend servicemen money under certain circumstances. As platoon sergeant, he decided to pay them a visit.

Always persuasive, Knuppel explained the final liberty to the lady at the desk and told her sincere stories about the hard work of his men. She listened politely, wrote down his name, rank, and serial number, and nonchalantly asked for his father's name, phone number and address.

Somehow he got fifty bucks out of them. He didn't know the Red Cross would call his father in Minnesota the next day to ask for repayment.

Knuppel distributed the money as equally as possible among the guys left behind who wanted to go ashore, and they took off in groups. Evans and Knuppel, who had seven dollars between them, started off for nowhere in particular until it occurred to Don that his high school buddies Arello and Duley might be at the Army's Schofield Barracks.

"Even if we can't find 'em," Evans said, "there's bound to be a slop chute with cheap beer, and cheaper women."

They hitchhiked to the barracks, got there around 1030, and found Duley sprawled on his bunk.

"Don!" Duley sat up, surprised. "We heard you shipped out."

"Not yet, but soon. Where's Tommy?"

Duley thought Arello might be on KP, and the three headed toward the Mess Hall. Arello was unhappily scrubbing pot after pot, but he beamed at the sight of Evans. By paying some other private five bucks he was able to switch shifts and be done by 1330. To kill the time, Duley took his Marine pals swimming at the Schofield pool.

Knuppel and Evans exchanged disgusted glances about the swimming pool. "We're treated worse than a dog and you Army guys have a swimming pool?" Evans said to his hometown buddy Duley. To his Marine buddy he added under his breath, "Dogfaces."

At 1330 on the dot the trio headed back to the barracks to collect Arello and find the nearest slop chute. Beer, a good bull session, and reminiscing about the good old times at Southeast High was the plan for the day. The friends did a very workmanlike job of downing the cheap beer and had a great time. Hour upon hour the bull flew. Arello mentioned the Alaskan island of Kiska only in passing. But Evans and Knuppel picked up the bone and ran with it.

"Kiska. Jesus Christ," Knuppel sneered. "The Marine Corps would never do such a dishonorable thing to their men." The previous August, the Army had landed a large force to retake the island from the Japanese—who, it turned out, had already abandoned it.

"Thirty thousand dogfaces…" Evans began.

"Watch it!" Arello warned.

"Excuse me." Evans begged and continued. "Thirty thousand ARMY soldiers to invade an island occupied by, let's see, I forget, how many Japs?"

"None," Duley reluctantly replied, as the Marines burst into laughter.

"It's not our damn fault the Japs took a powder. You forgettin' Attu?" Arello shouted over Evans and Knuppel.

"Attu?!?" Knuppel scoffed. "Jeezus Key-rist…"

"Too bad you boys didn't get any huntin' in." Evans gave Arello a shove.

"I don't know where we're headed," Knuppel piped in, "but you can bet your ass there's gonna be plenty of good hunting."

"It won't be no damned Kiska," Evans poked. "You wanna see Kiska? I'll show you Kiska!" Using no hands, Evans took the long neck beer bottle into his mouth, lifted his head back and drained the bottle dry.

"Now that's Kiska!" Knuppel laughed.

"Yeah, yeah. I've heard enough about Kiska. Four more beers here!" Duley hollered to the bartender.

"Goddammit," Evans said, "I know the Corps would never put us on such a disgraceful island. What an embarrassment."

"Marines don't play that way." Knuppel drained his bottle, "No siree."

"Quit your braggin'. You've been luckier so far, but we'll get our share of huntin' soon enough," Arello cut in.

"You can bet your boots there's gonna be plenty of Japs for everybody where we're goin'." Knuppel ordered more beer. "You should join us."

"Jesus Christ, you spend enough time in our camp, you're almost as good as Marines," Evans quipped.

"Whaddaya mean 'almost'?" Arello and Duley asked in unison.

Evans replied by whistling, "A-Hunting We Will Go." They kept up the razzing and the drinking for hour after hour after hour.

At 2030 Evans asked drunkenly, "Why don't you come along for the ride? We're leaving in the morning."

"What are you, crazy? Or drunk?" Arello said.

"Drunk? I've never been drunk in my life. Crazy, well..." Evans slurred his words.

"If you guys want some action you should join up with us," Knuppel prodded.

"Tommy, Norman." Evans tone turned somber. "I'm begging you, don't be dogfaces for the rest of your life."

Arello and Duley shook their heads and smiled, not looking at each other.

"I bet you one month's pay I kill more Japs than both of you combined." Evans kept it up. "That's twenty-five dollars for each of you dogface boys. And I tell you what, I'll give you odds. You two ante up just twelve-fifty each. Do the math 'cause I can't right now."

"I can only do simple math. One, two, three," Arello counted the bottles and called out, "Four more beers!"

The four of them kept drinking until their money ran as dry as the empties, and it grew near 2200, the designated time when Evans and Knuppel had to be back aboard ship. As they stumbled back to Arello and Duley's barracks, Evans and Knuppel whispered "The Marines' Hymn" in their ears.

As they reached the barracks, all the razzing and the pressure paid off.

"Semper Fi!" Arello shouted. Duley agreed. In unison they shouted, "We're in!"

They told a few of their closest Army buddies what they were doing— they didn't want anyone to think that they were going AWOL out of cowardice. Their sun-tan Army khakis were similar to Marine uniforms, except for red braid on their caps and Seventh Army patches on their shoulders. Evans and Knuppel took out their Boy Scout knives and went to work, one on Arello's uniform and the other on Duley's, clumsily cutting the braid and patches off. Afraid their friends wouldn't look "raggedy-assed" enough, they rubbed dirt onto the clean khakis, making them look a little more like Marines. One last finishing touch added to the disguise. Knuppel and Evans took Marine Corps emblems off their own shirt collars and put them on the Army hats. With Arello and Duley transformed into Marines, they left Schofield Barracks for the ship.

Getting the two recruits past sentries monitoring the gangplank might be tricky. But as the hour marking the end of liberty approached, a lot of besotted traffic stumbled on board. The four waited until a larger group of rowdy Marines distracted the sentries. Evans took the point, with Arello and Duley close behind, and Knuppel brought up the rear. They marched up the plank, just four more drunken Marines. Evans pretended to vomit to distract the sentries, allowing Knuppel to push Arello and Duley past the duty officer unquestioned. It went off smoothly. Two new Scout-Snipers had boarded the ship in a matter of moments. Knuppel and Evans beamed with pride. Absconding with two Army soldiers outdid Borawski's jeep, the pig, and any amount of booze and sundries the platoon had stolen to date.

Evans requisitioned bunks near his for Arello and Duley, and the three went to sleep that night with big Kansas City grins on their faces. With the acquisition of the two new "Marines," the Thieves were forty-strong once again.

On May 30, 1944, the Sixth Marine Regiment set sail from Hawaii. Over five hundred war ships—light and heavy cruisers, escort carriers, destroyers, aircraft carriers, submarines, and battleships of all kinds—formed the most impressive armada ever assembled. All the vessels circled and protected the armada's most precious cargo: the troop transports carrying the invasion force of Marines. Among them, the USS *Bolivar*, which held the 40 Thieves.

CHAPTER FIFTEEN

A Pact and a Premonition

*"Courage is not the absence of fear, but rather the judg-
ment that something else is more important than one's
fear. The timid presume it is lack of fear that allows the
brave to act when the timid do not. But to take action
when one is not afraid is easy. To refrain when afraid is
also easy. To take action regardless of fear is brave."*

—*Ambrose Redmoon*

June 1, 1944
At sea, aboard the USS *Bolivar*

The men grew accustomed to life aboard the overcrowded transport.
Hundreds of Marines were packed aboard the *Bolivar* like sardines
in a tin can, facing the agony of waiting for the inevitable once more.
Playing cards, cleaning weapons, sharpening bayonets, calisthenics,
and rope climbing kept them occupied. They would eat, sleep, and do
it all over again the next day, and the next.

Gambling...rolling dice...they did anything to help time move along.
If anyone had a harmonica, men gathered and sang along if they knew the
words, otherwise they'd just listen. Orozco, who had a wonderful tenor
voice, sang Spanish ballads such as "Amigo Mio" and "Señorita."

Shortly after leaving Hawaii, the men received the last mail they
would see for possibly months. They read on the sun-drenched deck
or in their clammy, crowded bunks and then dashed off a quick letter

to friends and family. Evans's V-Mail was ferried to Hawaii for posting back to the States, along with thousands of others.

Dear Folks,

Well, we're at sea and headin' for a right smart shootin' match. I'll bet that makes you all happy as hell. Now, you people stand by that radio, you hear? And save the write ups for us.

Tommy Arello, Duley, and me have been in our sacks all day talking over old times. They've turned out to be pretty good Marines. I guess we'll be together quite a while. Tell Mrs. Arello and Mrs. Duley that, if they hear anything to the contrary, Tommy and Norman are both OK.

They can give Hawaii back to the wild hogs for all of us. When we came from Tarawa the people were deathly afraid of us and considered us a bunch of professional killers. And the dogfaces had the kindness to lay out our camp way back in the lava beds and cactus sixty-eight miles from Hilo. All we could do was "beat our chops."

We've got a cute little PFC in our platoon who is seventeen years old, and his birthday is in a coupla weeks. He's having the time of his life and learning more than he ever would in high school. It's a cryin' shame that Babe, as big and brawny as he'll ever be, has to stay home and miss this swell war.

Tom and Norman send their love. Norman is as big as a barn and heavily muscled. He's about 195 lbs. This will be the last letter for a long time, so tell our public to send us a publitudiness amount of Pogey Bait. It'll come in okay thru the mail. Wrap it good, tho. I can't think of anything else, so I'll end.

Love, Don, Tommy, and Norman

Blue skies smiled on the Marines, along with smooth sailing and pleasantly warm weather. Men sprawled on the deck and sunned themselves during idle moments between training and meals, which became an all-day adventure. With hundreds of Marines plus the crew of the ship, the mess lines aboard the transport ship seemed endless. Everyone swore they saw men lining up for the next meal right after finishing their first. Serving two meals a day—one from sunrise until noon and the other from noon to sunset—the mess hall was working twenty-four hours a day.

After three days at sea, Knuppel found Evans, Arello, and Duley on deck.

"Sooner or later," Knuppel began, "Ski's gonna find out about our two volunteers. I guess I should tell him, before he hears it from somebody else."

"You don't think he'll send us back, do you?" Arello was worried.

"Where would he send us... overboard?" Duley shrugged.

"Tell the Boss he can thank me later." Evans smiled.

"I'm sure he will." Knuppel found his way through the narrow passageways to Ski's compartment. The door was ajar, and he was on his bunk playing a game of solitaire. Knuppel knocked.

"Hayshaker! What brings you by? Drink?" Ski offered his half-full bottle of Four Roses.

"Thanks," Knuppel smiled and took a sip. "Ski, remember back in January when you came to me with your news about leading the Scout-Snipers?"

Ski nodded and took a sip as well.

"Red four on black five," Knuppel kibitzed. "Well, this time I've got some news for you, good or bad depending on how you take it."

"Take a load off, Bill." Ski offered a chair and the bottle once more. "What's the good news? And I underscore the word 'good'."

"I won't beat around the bush; we picked up a couple volunteers back in Honolulu."

Knuppel knew Ski to be unflappable, always calm and collected. Nothing ever seemed to faze him. On the rare occasions when he got angry, Ski wouldn't say a word. He just became a bad kind of quiet.

The game of solitaire went on, quietly. The silent treatment made Knuppel wonder if he should begin to worry, but the pause only seemed long to him.

"Could you run that by me again?"

Knuppel refreshed Ski's memory about Evans's two Army friends who had become a fixture around the 40 Thieves' camp. He went on to tell how he and Evans persuaded the two high school friends to leave the Army and fill the two vacant spots in the platoon. The card game stopped. Knuppel fidgeted.

Ski laid down three cards, "They'll fit right in. I always thought they'd make damn fine Marines. Tell them we're honored to have them among us."

Knuppel let out a sigh of relief. "They were worried. I'll let them know." Knuppel pointed to the King of Spades, "Black king moves over, and Ace of Hearts moves up."

"Good. You do that." Ski sat back. "But Bill, I'd like you to do two favors for me."

"What's that?"

"One, let me play my card game myself," Ski smiled. "And two, just between you and me, you never came to my room, and you never told me anything about this. Do you understand?"

"Understood." Knuppel stood up to leave. Before he could go, Ski stopped him; his face, serious. "And Bill, you take care of those men. That's an order. You make sure that those guys are armed when we hit the beach. No, this is Don's handiwork. You tell Don to make sure of that."

"Yes, Ski," Knuppel nodded and stopped himself from saying "Red deuce plays on black trey."

•　　•　　•

Before evening chow, the ship's loudspeakers blared, "Now hear this, now hear this!" Broadcasts could be either routine—announcing a change in mealtimes—or urgent—warning of approaching Japanese Zeros. "All Marines check your weapons for missing rifle serial number one, three, eight, two, one..." In his quarters Ski smiled. When another rifle went missing the next day, he laughed to himself, Don's been busy.

While they were at sea, the target of their attack was disclosed to the troops: the Marianas—over one thousand miles from the nearest U.S. installation, deep within Japanese territory, and surrounded by enemy

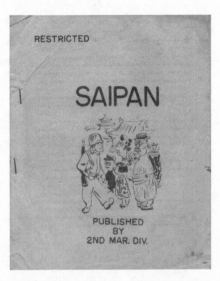

Material distributed to the 40 Thieves aboard the USS *Bolivar*. *Courtesy of Joseph Tachovsky*

bases and airfields. This bold action would be the riskiest move yet of the savage war in the Pacific.

Every Marine received a thorough briefing on the plan of attack and attended staff exercises, lectures, and classes; photographs, charts, relief maps, terrain models, and other materials had been prepared and distributed to all units. Among them was a small booklet.

Corporal Martin Dyer from St. Louis sat alone, sunning on deck and leafing through the pages of the pamphlet. It wasn't unusual for Dyer to keep to himself. Though Dyer wasn't his squad leader, Strombo had grown to know the loner quite well. Since leaving Hilo, the pair had occupied bunks next to each other and struck up a friendship. After lights out and hearing Johnson muttering from somewhere in the dark hold of the ship, "It...is...later...than...you...think..." the pair would chit-chat well into the night.

"This seat taken?" Strombo sat down next to Dyer, not waiting for a reply.

"Look at this shit," Dyer tossed the booklet to Strombo. "The cover makes it look like we're going on some type of goddamn holiday."

Strombo read aloud in dramatic fashion, "For the first time, Marines will be operating in territory that has been part of the Japanese Empire for twenty-five years. So far, our battles have been fought to reclaim Allied territory and combat has been in relatively unpopulated, wild parts of the Pacific. From the sweaty jungles of the Solomons to the sandy beaches of Tarawa, the local populations, if any, wore grass skirts or loin cloths and willingly helped the Marines oust the occupation forces of Japan."

"Cut to the chase, Strombo."

"Don't kill civilians."

"Go back to the chase." Dyer closed his eyes. "What's it say?"

"It says that some of the civilians are natives of Spanish descent, Chamorros. They might be friendly to us. Let's see. 'As we move closer to the Japanese mainland and encounter more civilians, what happens on Saipan may determine whether or not other Japanese civilians decide to fight or not to fight. If we can convince these civilians that we are doing our best to observe international law and not cause unnecessary harm, most of them will not take up arms against us.'"

"That'd be nice," Dyer said, with his eyes still closed.

Strombo assumed his dramatic voice again, "Our humanitarian actions on Saipan will give us, and through us, all Americans a reputation of fair play for generations to come."

Dyer opened his eyes and applauded. "Bravo!"

"What the hell?" Strombo was dumbstruck as he read further. "This is disappointing."

"What?" Dyer asked.

"They're saying we're not supposed to pillage!"

"Pillage? What the hell is pillage? Sounds like something we need more of in our diet. Four out of five doctors recommend adding more pillage to our diets for a healthier digestive tract."

"It means stealing. We're not supposed to steal. Listen to this, 'Most Japanese civilians, according to our standards, are very poor. What few possessions they have are treasured by them.'"

"What about us? We're poor..." Dyer put in.

Strombo read on, "International law, military law, and the laws that we are all used to in our own homes forbid thievery, which is nothing short of robbery of people who cannot defend themselves. Remember what we said earlier in this booklet. Our success on Saipan and beyond will depend on whether or not we can play fair by the civilian population."

"Give me that thing." Dyer grabbed the booklet. "All right, maybe I won't steal. Does it say anything in here about the girls being pretty?" He read silently, then suddenly stopped in astonishment. "I don't believe this, it says the natives, all of them, have VD, gonorrhea and/or syphilis! Jesus Christ, what a lash-up. They must be a frisky bunch if they all have VD."

"I wonder if they're saying that just so we don't screw the girls," Strombo speculated.

"I wish they would have told me this stuff before I enlisted," Dyer shrugged. "Listen to this, besides the VD we'd get from screwing the native dollies, here's what else we can look forward to: Dysentery, again. Yaws, which are festering sores... doesn't that sound pleasant. Pink eye. And schisto... schisto-something or other," Dyer read, "an infestation of blood flukes, that is contracted from bathing in infected water. The larvae come from certain infected snails and infect men through the skin. Once inside the body, the larvae develop into worms which live in the blood vessels for years. Female worms release thousands of eggs which are passed out of the body via bodily functions."

"Jesus Christ! That's disgusting... and I'm used to disgusting," Strombo lamented.

"Here's a bonus," Dyer went on. "There won't be malaria. Instead they've got different mosquitoes that carry this thing called Dengue. And get this, it's worse than malaria. I've had malaria…how could anything be worse?"

"A regular Roman Holiday." Strombo shook his head.

•   •   •

On June 6, 1944, while the 40 Thieves anchored in Eniwetok for final maneuvers, the Allies invaded Europe, landing on the beaches of Normandy.

In a radio address to the American people on D-Day, President Roosevelt offered a prayer at this pivotal moment in history. Stateside, a nation gathered around radios with bowed heads. Aboard the USS *Bolivar*, Marines crowded around loudspeakers above and below deck.

> My Fellow Americans: Last night, troops of the United States and our Allies crossed the English Channel in another and greater operation. It has come to pass with success thus far.
>
> And so, in this poignant hour, I ask you to join with me in prayer.
>
> Almighty God: Our sons, pride of our nation, this day have set upon a mighty endeavor, a struggle to preserve our Republic, our religion, and our civilization, and to set free a suffering humanity.
>
> They will need Thy blessings. Their road will be long and hard. For the enemy is strong. He may hurl back our forces. Success may not come with rushing speed, but we shall return again and again; and we know that by Thy grace, and by the righteousness of our cause, our sons will triumph.
>
> They will be sore tried, by night and by day, without rest— until the victory is won. The darkness will be rent by noise and flame. Men's souls will be shaken with the violence of war.
>
> For these men are lately drawn from the ways of peace. They fight not for the lust of conquest. They fight to liberate.

They fight to let justice arise, and tolerance and goodwill among all Thy people. They yearn but for the end of battle, for their return to the haven of home.

Some will never return. Embrace these, Father, and receive them, Thy heroic servants, into Thy kingdom.

And for us at home—fathers, mothers, children, wives, sisters, and brothers of brave men overseas, whose thoughts and prayers are ever with them—help us, Almighty God, to rededicate ourselves in renewed faith in Thee in this hour of great sacrifice.

And let our hearts be stout, to wait out the long travail, to bear sorrows that may come, to impart our courage unto our sons wheresoever they may be.

And, O Lord, give us faith. Give us faith in Thee; faith in our sons; faith in each other; faith in our united crusade. Let not the keenness of our spirit ever be dulled. Let not the impacts of temporary events, of temporal matters of but fleeting moment—let not these deter us in our unconquerable purpose.

With Thy blessing, we shall prevail over our enemy. Help us to conquer the apostles of greed and racial arrogances. Lead us to the saving of our country, and with our sister nations into a world unity that will spell a sure peace—a peace invulnerable to the schemings of unworthy men. And a peace that will let all people of the world live in freedom.

Thy will be done, Almighty God. Amen.

Smotts and Kenny sat topside with Tipton, who muttered. "Amen,"...then asked, "I wonder if there'll be a prayer for us?"

"If there were, would it do any good?" Kenny shrugged. "Just a bunch of words."

"Hobart, there ain't no God where we're goin'," Smotts added. "Besides, it's too late for me to repent upon anything. No amount of prayin's gonna save me now. I'll be judged on the things I done, not with some prayer. But everybody to his own."

The possibility of death weighed heavily on the minds of all. While in port, the men had an opportunity to write one more letter home. One more letter, which might be the last.

June 8, 1944

My Dearest Roxie

This is a very appropriate day to write—a far more appropriate day to be with you, today being your birthday.

At present, I don't know exactly when this will be mailed, definitely sometime after D-Day on our next island. You will receive it late enough to not worry too much as the worst will most likely be over. Knowing you are worrying and will continue to do so, this might be some alleviation to you knowing that I am in combat. I am not writing home as I seem to feel it will be easier on Mother if she doesn't know.

I received quite a bit of mail from you before leaving Hawaii. If my morale needed any boosting that certainly did the trick. I am very grateful for your consistent writing. Previous to our leaving Hawaii there were lapses in my writing due to our training program under which circumstances it wasn't possible to write as often as I would have liked. You can rest assured you are always in my thoughts, and my next letter to you will be written as soon as possible.

I find this letter difficult to write under the atmosphere of going into combat. I debated long in deciding to write but concluded it was better than not writing at all. You will worry, so you might just as well know what you are worrying about. I am in excellent health and sporting a nice tan.

This will be a belated but sincere Happy Birthday, darling. Know that you fill my thoughts. For now, I leave you, but only in writing.

As always, you have all my love forever.

Your husband, Frank

P.S. I carry your picture with me at all times.

Roxie. *Courtesy of Joseph Tachovsky*

Ski carried a small brown leather wallet with him into every battle. Inside, along with the photo of Roxie, was a letter folded up behind it. The letter, which Roxie had written to her husband before he shipped out for Guadalcanal, was well worn from numerous readings. As the ships set sail from Eniwetok on June 11, Ski read the letter one more time.

My Darling

You've only been gone but a little while and you'll be back at 12:00. But today you took most of your things back to camp with you and although I've been pushing the thought that you will soon be gone out of my mind, today makes everything so definite. But I'm just going to slip this note in your khaki uniform pocket and when you find it, it will be to tell you again, I love you.

I hardly know what to say to a husband who is going away to war except God bless you, and every breath I take is a prayer for you.

All these past weeks have been very happy weeks for me…I think I made you happy too. And we'll have so many happy ones after this is all over. I suppose it's selfish of me to begrudge and to hate every hour we're parted, but since I married a Marine it is only fitting that I should make everything I do a compliment to you.

I'm going to stop writing now. This isn't the easiest letter I've ever written but before I do, Dear heart, I'm going to say again I think I'm the proudest and the luckiest girl in the whole world—you've made me so...and Frank, I believe so much in you that I don't think there is anything that you couldn't do. I wish we hadn't been pressed for money—I would have liked to give you something to remember the day. But I give you my love...and now...God bless you, and take care of yourself, my wonderful husband, and come home soon.

All my love, your Wife

Roxie

X that's for my Lieutenant

X that's for my Dear heart

X that's for my Husband

X that's on general principles & because you have the nicest eyes in the world

•   •   •

Aboard the *Bolivar* on June 14, Colonel Riseley gathered his key personnel, from sergeants to colonels, and his Scout-Snipers together for a final briefing held topside because of the large number of men. Despite the slight breeze created by the ship's traveling at ten knots, the men sweated profusely in the heat.

"Tomorrow, we'll be striking into the heart of the Empire of Japan, the first link in the chain of home islands that will take us to Tokyo. Some of you," Riseley nodded to Ski, Knuppel and Slevin, "may be interested to know that the Spanish first called these islands 'Las Islas de los Ladrones,' The Islands of Thieves."

"Our Regiment has the honor of spearheading the invasion on this island of thieves, Saipan."

"I'm not going to sugarcoat this for you, we're in for a fight," cautioned Riseley. "These brown buggers are scrappy. They aren't quitters, they're warriors."

"Tomorrow night," Colonel Murray concurred, "we can expect one helluva Banzai. So dig in. They're going to throw everything they've got at us, including the kitchen sink."

The men knew Murray's comment was no joke. Riseley, who referred to a map throughout the briefing, added, "The days ahead will be rugged ones. It won't be easy. Unlike Tarawa, this is not a flat atoll. The island itself will be as tough an enemy as the Japanese. But we Marines have learned never to be afraid of taking a calculated risk, especially where the stakes are great. And the stakes will be great.

"By capturing the Marianas, not only will we sever the lines of communication between Tokyo and its bases farther west in the Pacific, but we'll also take possession of the two finest airfields in the Pacific, putting Tokyo within striking range of our B-29s. Hopefully after this the Air Corps can finish this thing off, and we can all go home.

"Of most importance, I want to remind everyone the trees will have ears, Jap ears," Riseley told. "Moving forward, we're all going to be on a first name basis, make sure all your men are aware of this. From now on, I'm just Jim."

The formalities of military life completely disappeared in jungle warfare: officers went by first names, code names, or nicknames and insignia of rank were never worn. It would be signing a death warrant to address an officer by his rank, or even with "sir." Japanese snipers were adept at killing officers.

Riseley went on. "Like Tarawa, we'll take the island by storm. General Smith estimates that this will take three days. I think you men will agree, this seems overly optimistic, but that is our goal. Once he establishes his command post at Charan Kanoa, that'll give you, Ski, the green light to turn your boys loose. I'll digress for a moment to share with you

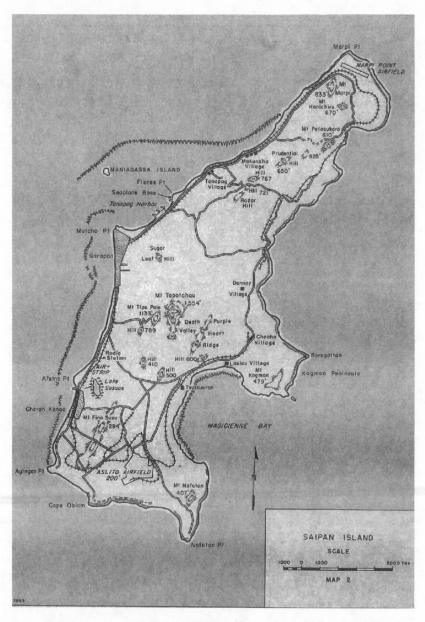

Map of Saipan. *From* Saipan: The Beginning of the End, *written by Major Carl Hoffman for the Marine Corps*

a statement from General Saitō, commander of the troops on Saipan. He vowed that if we tried to invade, he'd 'Drive the American Devils back into the sea.'" The Marines listening to Riseley scoffed in mumbled commentary.

"Since we're devils," Riseley spoke over his men, "let's give 'em hell.

"Last, and most important, I want you men to know that this is a great honor for me to serve with you in writing a new and glorious chapter for the Corps and the Old Pogey Bait Sixth. I have the utmost confidence in all of you that victory will be ours."

A late evening meal was called, but the lines were thin. The Salty Sons lingered in the Officers' Mess and didn't eat much. Not much was said—no levity, no declarations of "It's a boy!" no re-reading letters from home, no card games. Being together one last time before battle, hearing a buddy's voice, or exchanging a glance meant more than anything.

"Marzipan?" Ski unwrapped a piece of foil, proudly producing treats from Roxie. Edwards's eyes smiled. Ski, Doc, Edwards, and Dulcich munched while sipping a cup of hot coffee, quite possibly the last for some time.

The group dispersed one by one. Ski and Edwards, finding themselves alone, moved topside. Standing at the railing savoring cigars, they watched the fading sun disappear behind swaths of gathering clouds, streaking the sky with hues of deep blue.

"That's a scene only Mother Nature can paint," Edwards said, staring out at the blackening Pacific. "Roxie's been good to us over the years," he added. "Tell her, 'Skipper says thanks.'" Smoking together but alone in their thoughts, the two stood shoulder to shoulder. Finishing his cigar first, Edwards straightened to leave. "I'd really like to meet Roxie someday...and tell her in person," he flicked his butt into the churning wake below.

"She'd like that," Ski smiled. "She'd like that a lot." His cigar followed Edwards's.

Darkening clouds loomed over the horizon. There was no red sky that night. With the moon obscured, the armada cut silently through the sea, edging ever closer to Saipan.

Aboard the *Bolivar* that night, no one slept.

Three levels below deck the men lay wide awake, whispering to each other, mumbling prayers, or clacking rosaries—crowded together in bunks stacked five feet high, the canvas hammocks spaced so closely together that nobody could roll over without jostling those above or below.

Johnson and Yunker had their bunks one on top of the other.

"I sure hate living aboard this tub," Johnson said to Yunker on the bed below.

"Smells like a dance hall. All armpits and feet."

"I'm happy as hell to be getting off this iron pig and breathe some fresh air," Johnson rolled on his side.

"Even if it is 90 percent lead."

Johnson did not answer immediately. "Well, I don't care how many Japs there are, just so long as we get off this goddamned boat." Then he was quiet.

Having played countless games of Sheepshead with his Wisconsin buddy, Johnson brought up a topic both wanted to discuss, but found difficult to broach. "If the third time's the Charm for me and I don't make it home, would you visit my folks? Tell 'em…"

"I'd be honored." Yunker quickly cut him off. For a change he had no wiseacre response.

"Thanks. You can count on me, too," Johnson reached down his right hand, and the two shook on their pact.

•   •   •

For Martin Dyer and Marvin Strombo, the night before the invasion of Saipan began like every other night. The two waited until all the lights went out and then talked in whispers about nothing much. Through the darkness Strombo watched Dyer cover his head with the blanket, so that just a little bit of his face could be seen.

Dyer brought up a difficult topic. He wasn't necessarily ashamed, just a little reticent to talk about fear. "Some guys can handle fear, and some can't. All of life is managing fear, fear of the unknown—whether you're a little kid afraid of what's in the closet and under the bed or an old man afraid of his own mortality."

Dyer told Strombo about his first time in battle, on Guadalcanal, "I was a tough kid, and I thought nothing could scare me. But I shamed myself on the Canal. I didn't perform too good. I got scared. Fear got the best of me, and I froze. I almost got other guys killed." Dyer grew quiet.

Strombo broke the silence, "We all get scared, I got scared before Tarawa."

"Yeah, but I acted like a coward," Dyer confided. "I did all right on Tarawa, and I'll do better on Saipan."

"Just because you're scared, doesn't mean you're a coward," Strombo said. "Lots of guys get scared. You'd be crazy not to be scared a little, I guess."

"I won't be scared," Dyer stated, then said quietly to himself, "There's nothing to be afraid of anymore, and I won't be a coward."

Strombo broke the pregnant pause. "Everybody knows my name's Marvin. What's yours?"

"Martin Russell Junior. The old man's Martin Senior, so my family calls me Russell. Dyer paused a few moments. "You know, it's my birthday."

"How come you didn't say something? Happy birthday."

"I'm twenty-one. And that's all she wrote... You know what bothers me, Marvin?"

"Besides all those Chamorro girls with syphilis?" Strombo joked.

"Not that." Dyer did not laugh. "No. It bothers me that after everything I've gone through—boot camp, the Canal, Tarawa, and training on Hawaii—that I won't be around to enjoy it when this is all over."

"Whaddya mean?" Strombo asked. "You gettin' leave?"

But it wasn't that. Although Dyer was a first generation American, he was still Irish enough to believe in second sight and premonitions.

He had felt the cold hand of Death on his shoulder. He shared with Strombo his waking dream of a white cross bearing his name in a cemetery on Saipan.

"Don't think like that," Strombo said firmly. "You don't know that; you couldn't know that."

"No, Strombo, I do. I just do. I'll be buried on Saipan."

"It's gonna be rugged, but..."

Dyer cut him off, "No, I'm not gonna make it. Saipan is as far as I go."

●　　●　　●

In Tokyo, Emperor Hirohito, Prime Minister Hideki Tojo, and Foreign Minister Mamoru Shigemitsu met with the leaders of the Imperial forces. During the meeting they concluded that the Marianas would be the first line of defense of their homeland. That being determined, they assumed the Americans might attempt an attack on the Marianas as early as July. Hirohito ordered an immediate fortification of defenses on those islands and plans were put into action to increase troop strength.

They were too late.

Hell began on June 15, 1944.

CHAPTER SIXTEEN

Red Sky at Morning

"Every time you go into battle, you don't know how you'll react, even if you've done it before. It's always different. You're different. You just don't know who you are anymore. War is a nasty and cruel business with man at his worst. But once you're in it, you have to go all the way. There's no looking back."

—Frank Tachovsky

June 15, 1944, 0330 Hours
Aboard the USS *Bolivar*, Offshore from Saipan

In the dank darkness of the cramped troop hold, restless eyes clamped shut in hope that churning minds might fall asleep. Hour upon hour dragged by in the dead silence that didn't induce sleep. Thoughts of home or prayers or resignation to their fate kept the men awake.

Until "Now hear this! Now hear this!" blared over the intercom. "First ashore will be first served in the galley..."

Though they didn't know when they might have their next hot meal, the condemned man's breakfast of steak and eggs could not entice the men to eat. The veterans knew that a full stomach slowed a man and would make it more difficult for the corpsmen to patch up stomach wounds if he got hit during the landing. All opted for just a cup of luke-warm coffee—except for Causey and Tipton, who eyed the steak and eggs hungrily. Sergeant Knuppel told the pair of green boots to go easy on the chow, "That's an order." They obeyed. Some Thieves in the galley joked and placed wagers on how many Japanese they would kill. Others, stone-faced, kept to themselves. Despite the suntans they had acquired in Hawaii, the Thieves looked grizzled after two weeks aboard ship—rugged and unshaven with salt-stained dungarees. The relaxing pig roast felt as far away as home.

Bombardment of Saipan had begun over three days before the armada arrived. Before dawn on June 15 it intensified, as Navy ships carrying Marines and Army troops converged on the island. Blinkers on signal decks flashed messages back and forth. General quarters sounded. Loudspeakers droned the call to action: "All hands battle stations! Marines, man your debarkation stations!" Flashes of artillery illuminated the twilight of dawn, revealing a cloudless sky. Ski and two squads would be going in first, before dawn. Knuppel and the rest would follow with Colonel Riseley and the Regimental Brass at 0900.

One of Corporal Fritz Schieber's men, Private First Class Paul Lewis, watched the first wave make their way down the Jacob's Ladder—not the biblical connection between Heaven and Earth, but a Marine's connection from Earth to Hell via the bobbing Higgins boat below. Lewis was a seasoned veteran of Guadalcanal and Tarawa, and visions of the carnage on both islands flashed through his mind, but he quickly shook off the flashbacks and listened to the latest scuttlebutt from those waiting on deck: "The Japs took a powder for sure…" Lewis knew this would be no Kiska.

How can Ski do it, Lewis wondered almost aloud, if I had a wife back home… A chill ran down his spine. What if there's no tomorrow? Lewis was startled back to the present by someone yelling up from the Higgins boat below.

"Hey!" Dyer hollered from the boat, not to Lewis but to the Marine next to him. "Strombo! It's been a pleasant ocean cruise!"

"Now for the Roman Holiday!" Strombo replied, giving a salute.

The landing craft pushed off the *Bolivar*. The task that had been assigned to Ski and his vanguard of Thieves was to eliminate enemy pillboxes on Red Beach Two and Three, which were strategically located to hinder the invasion force scheduled to land at 0830. By 0930, according to Howlin' Mad Smith's plan, the beachhead would be fortified, and his Marines should have pushed one mile inland.

The fire-support ships USS *California*, *Halsey Powell* and *Coghlan* laid down salvo after salvo—an incessant thunderous barrage—as the landing craft bobbed and bucked through surf toward shore. Smotts, Kenny, and Tipton stood, resting their eighty-pound packs against the ribs of its gunwale, watching red streaks in the sky reach toward Saipan. Every time the *California* fired its fourteen-inch guns, she lurched back in the waves.

It was misery to wait, because waiting meant thinking. No good came from that. Breathing heavily, his eyes grown wide, the overgrown kid from Detroit who was aiming to avenge his uncle's death appeared overwhelmed. So Kenny distracted Tipton with a shove. "Nice way to spend your birthday, ain't it, Hobart? Think all these fireworks are for you?"

Tipton nervously tossed an unsmoked cigarette over the Higgins boat's side and smiled weakly to acknowledge Kenny's remarks. Standing nearly shoulder to shoulder with these seasoned Marines, Tipton felt unprepared. He was digging deep for the courage to stand behind his commitment to revenge. In a month of working with the platoon Tipton had gained confidence in his muscles, his reactions, and his decision-making. He had been ready to carry a pack into battle. But this was real. He couldn't let them see how scared he was. All his platoon buddies joked about death, but they never talked about having your gut tied in knots.

As the landing craft drew closer to Saipan's shore, Kenny thought Tipton's last cup of coffee might be coming up with the boat's next smash into a wave. His own first ride into combat felt like a lifetime ago. Kenny watched the kid's lips mumble a line or two of prayer, but the veteran had more faith in being trained as a Marine and surrounded by Marines than in God's protecting him in the days ahead. Still he knew that no amount of training at Parker Ranch had prepared the kid for what was to come.

As dawn broke, the red sky of morning backlit the ominous black peaks of Tipo Pale, Mount Tapotchau, and the other rocky hills that

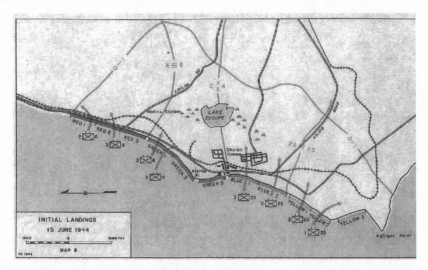

The American landings on Saipan. *From* Saipan: The Beginning of the End, *written by Major Carl Hoffman for the Marine Corps*

formed Saipan's jagged backbone. The island smoked and simmered after absorbing shell after shell after shell of unrelenting bombardment.

Nearing shore, the coxswain interrupted his steersmanship to alert the men, "Get down!" Smotts, Kenny, and Tipton crouched in the bottom of the landing craft, and within moments bullets pinged off the landing ramp and zipped past where their heads had been. The noise peppering the Higgins boat sounded like popcorn popping. The pair of Browning machine guns behind the coxswain opened up, strafing the shoreline with short bursts.

Ski had briefed his men that their landing might be relatively unopposed. "Saitō won't tip his hand until more are ashore."

The Higgins boat hadn't quite made it to the shore when the coxswain hollered again over the gunfire, "I ain't goin' any farther!" The ramp didn't go down.

"Old dead dog!" Ski bellowed. Everyone bailed over the side.

Tipton and Kenny landed in chest-deep water. Kenny looked sideways to see if his green buddy had made the jump. He had. For Tipton's sake and his own, Kenny hoped that the kid had it in him. From now on, they had to rely on each other.

Off to the other side, Kenny saw Smotts sink below the surf. When he didn't pop back up right away, Kenny thought his buddy had had his ticket punched for good. But Smotts had simply plummeted into one of the many deep shell-holes created by the artillery barrage and—weighed down with his rifle, ammunition, knives, bandoliers and grenades—fallen like a rock. He managed to save himself from drowning by crawling out on his hands and knees.

Ski's first wave of Thieves landed during a lull in the Naval barrage. The rattling of small arms replaced the thunderous booms, and the sudden shift in volume had an eerie effect.

Hitting the beach was a relief. There was no more time to be alone with thoughts. It was time to act.

The Thieves rapidly established a position behind a three-foot-high coconut-log wall, which buttressed a road that ran from Charan Kanoa in the south to the capital city of Garapan in the north. Several well-placed pillboxes were scattered across the beach inside the wall. With "Old dead dog!" and curt directions from Ski, the Marines began their work. The blasts of satchel charges punctuated the eerie silence as one pillbox after another was eliminated. Tipton rallied, relied on his training, and scored his first success, silencing one of the pillboxes with a muffled explosion. A few Japanese ran out of hiding to engage the invaders, but they were quickly gunned down.

As the Thieves chipped away, eliminating beachhead resistance, more and more Marines were ferried toward shore. Contrary tides and an unanticipated reef took the landing craft hundreds of yards north of their target beaches, making the Thieves' work only half effective.

Wary Marines setting foot on the beach wondered if the Imperial Army had indeed taken a powder. But the enemy was only waiting patiently: as soon as General Saitō determined that enough American Devils had amassed, the creepy quiet ended, and hell broke loose.

The familiar sound of artillery filled the air, hundreds of deafening freight trains woofing overhead without end. Smoke and debris obliterated morning sunshine. Whining and whistling mortars crescendoed into eruptions of sand mixed with metal and flesh. Constant machine gun fire now kept Ski's group pinned down behind the coconut log wall. Smotts glanced down the line of crouching Marines and saw one stick his head over the wall. In a moment he was dead, his helmet riddled with bullets.

Long streaks of American red tracers flew inland, and Japanese white-blue streamed out. The noise never slowed or stopped. A cacophony of high-pitched screeching accompanied the rumbling of thunder overpowering ears, bodies, minds. Wounded Marines lay where they fell, the beach painted red as their blood soaked the sand. Cries of "Corpsman!" competed to be heard over the deafening symphony of sounds.

A blast from a mortar left Tipton and Smotts safe in the newly created shell hole. A corpsman ran past toward a group of injured as another mortar struck the sand with a growling roar. The concussion blew out Smotts's right ear. His watch flew off his wrist in pieces.

Searing hot shrapnel tore into the running corpsman, slicing his arm off at the collarbone. His legs turned to jelly and crumbled under him. His severed arm fell out of the sky and landed between Smotts and Tipton. Smotts picked it up, remembering his own initiation in war. His first gunnery sergeant had picked up a hand torn from a Japanese soldier and waved it at him. "The Japs are saying hello," the crusty old gunny had told him. Smotts ad-libbed for Tipton's baptism, "Welcome to the war, Hobart. Someone wants to shake your hand Happy Birthday."

Tipton's first taste of war was the acrid flavor in his mouth after he threw up. Smotts tossed the arm aside.

The collapsed corpsman writhed wildly and screamed a terrible howl. Smotts tried to help, to pull him out of the line of fire, but he couldn't get near. A hailstorm of mortars rained down. One of them ended the corpsman's suffering. Again Tipton felt his stomach betraying him. He wiped the vomit from his chin and wondered, How? Why? He thought he would never forget the smell of air filled with sulfur, fuel, and burning flesh. Smotts calmly lit a cigarette and said, "You think too much, Hobart. Now ain't the time to worry. If it's a-comin', it's a-comin'." Something in Tipton clicked. Don't think. Do. In a moment, the kid grew up—or at least tried to.

The Japanese shot down on the Marines from mountains and ridges. Every square yard of the beaches had been taped out by the Japanese with red range-marking flags to make their mortar and artillery more accurate, and deadly. Shells that didn't find a target created geysers of water; those that hit landing craft sent up billows of oily black smoke. Fragments of metal and bones whirred and tore into bodies, killing and maiming.

Looking back out to sea, Marines watched landing craft drive into deep shell holes and turn turtle, pinning comrades beneath to drown. Under endless fire, cluttered with shattered equipment and a dangerous crowding of troops, the narrow beachhead became too congested for an orderly debarkation of men. Mounting casualties littering the beach became an obstacle course for the living. Bodies mottled the shoreline, slowly blackening in the searing tropical heat. By 0900 the waters lapping the shore had turned a ruddy red. The beach had become a bloody mess. Yet the Marines kept landing.

Aboard the *Bolivar*, Knuppel readied the rest of the platoon for the journey to shore. Lewis's mind drifted, "They're dying like flies."

Shoving off from the *Bolivar* at 0910, two Higgins boats containing the rest of the Thieves, Riseley, and the Battalion COs neared their landing area. Mullins sat next to a stoop-shouldered and grim Causey in one of the wildly lurching boats.

"Spit quick or die," Mullins counseled. The Louisiana boot tried but couldn't; his mouth had turned to cotton.

"Here." Mullins handed Causey a plug of chewing tobacco. "Nobody knows how long their luck'll last, so there's no point in thinkin' about it. But I'll tell you one thing that's for damn sure... we know what's expected of us, so we better get it done. You train, and you train, and you think you know it all, but when you hit the beach, you realize you

The Scout-Sniper Platoon landing on Saipan: Ski is far left. John Zuziak is center, looking at the camera. In the foreground Evans rests his head on his hand. *Courtesy of Richard Zuziak*

don't know shit. School's just begun. Stick close." Mullins looked toward the smoking island, at Marines struggling to make it to shore alive. "If you wanted to live forever, you shoulda been a dogface."

Lewis overheard Mullins's comment. "Live forever," he repeated to himself. "In ten minutes, I could be dead. I don't want to die." He felt like screaming. His mind raced, "I've gotta get out of here…gotta get out of here…"

Rumbling onto Red Two, the landing craft's ramps went down.

Through the din, Mullins heard Knuppel's voice cry out "Old dead dog!" from the other Higgins boat. Mullins clutched Causey's arm, and the pair raced down the ramp. Pocked sand made it difficult to walk, let alone run. Four or five steps were taken before falling, sending those behind stumbling and sprawling as well. Sometimes a corpse tripped the living running for their lives. Whistling mortars zeroed in on the new arrivals. Each blood-curdling screech grew louder and louder before erupting in thunderclaps that made the ground swell and quake.

Everyone in both vessels hit the beach, sprinting directly into the relentless gunfire, except Lewis. He stayed behind, frozen.

After being yelled at repeatedly by the coxswain to "Get the hell out!" Lewis tentatively entered the bloody circus. The Higgins boat he had just left retreated into the water just twenty yards when it was destroyed by a direct hit, sending smoke and debris into the sky. Had he stayed onboard, Lewis's bones and flesh would have been part of what was flying through the air. He ran.

A shell landed near Knuppel and sent him sprawling to the ground. After the smoke settled, he tried to look around, but sand in his eyes made everything blurry. Rubbing his eyes with his sleeve, Knuppel heard a familiar voice cry out "corpsman!" Turning his head, he recognized Colonel Murray and thought he could see both legs torn open by shrapnel. Behind the colonel lay two of his lieutenants, decapitated.

Knuppel felt certain that Murray was in bad shape. He stayed low and scurried toward the colonel. Another shell burst closer, knocking him back to the ground. Now unable to get up, Knuppel flailed in the sand, feeling warm blood on his face. His eyes would not open. "My eyes!" He heard the pain and fear of his own words, keeping an arm plastered over his face.

"Your eyes are okay," a voice reassured. "They're just filled with sand." A corpsmen rolled Knuppel onto his back and cleaned blood from his face. Holding Knuppel's eyes open, the corpsman flushed them with water from a canteen, "It'll hurt like a sonofabitch, but you're fine." With assistance, Knuppel reached the wall.

Able to see again, he watched the corpsman join another and help Colonel Murray, propping him against a jeep and temporarily bandaging his legs. The colonel began to bark out orders to those nearby. Riseley hurried to the scene, wondering how Murray could even stand.

"You're losing too much blood," he told Murray.

"I'm fine."

"You've caught too much shrapnel. You need to be evacuated. Now."

"I said I'm fine!" Murray snapped at Riseley—just as a bullet ricocheted off the jeep and into Murray's hip.

"My God, this is bad," said a corpsmen to Murray, who was bleeding profusely.

Knuppel heard Riseley trying to convince Murray. "Raymond, you can't command this way...not in your condition. Just look at you! There's hardly an inch of your uniform left." Murray wouldn't listen to reason, and Riseley finally lost patience. "Corpsmen! Get this man on an Amtrac immediately!"

Murray fought the four corpsmen who came to evacuate him. Breaking away for a moment, he collapsed, then gave in to their assistance.

Over the entire beach Navy corpsmen braved enemy fire to help the wounded and dying. Marines marveled at their saviors, who performed foxhole surgery with rudimentary tools while the battle raged. The grateful Marines knew all too well that the Japanese showed corpsmen no mercy, targeting and killing them to prevent the saving of lives.

Photo of Navy corpsmen on Guadalcanal. Lieutenant Jerry "Doc" Webber, U.S. Navy, is seated center. Twelve of the nineteen corpsmen pictured with Doc would be killed or wounded in combat. Four hundred fourteen corpsmen were killed on Saipan. *From the collection of Joseph Tachovsky*

Despite the violent bombardment, loss of leaders, and heavy casualties, wave after wave of Marines continued to hit the beach. Time stood still. The deafening shelling continued to hum—an unrelenting, primal whistle that overwhelmed the senses, rumbling through the sand, growing louder and louder with each salvo. Nerves were stretched to the breaking point.

But no one wanted to be that guy. The one who lost it. It took great concentration not to go insane. In the whistling and pounding, Lewis reached his limit. At first he ran from the Higgins boat into the nearest shell hole, laughing quietly to himself that he hadn't been blown up. Evans, nearby, heard the laughter grow louder and change to repeated muffled pleas of, "Just get it over with." Before anyone could get to Lewis, he bolted to race in circles around the beach, running as hard as he could, hollering and screaming.

Arello and Duley tackled the crazed Lewis and dragged him into their trench. On his hands and knees, he tried to escape by burrowing with his bare hands deep into the sand.

"Boss!" Evans called out.

Knuppel and Ski hurried over in answer to the call. "Lewis...Lewis." Ski tried to get through.

"He's gone berserk, Boss," Evans poured water on Lewis's face, making sure he took a drink.

Lewis calmed down. "I'm okay," he said, but he wasn't speaking to the men around him.

"What do we do with him now?" Knuppel spoke as though Lewis wasn't there.

"Shoulda let him run." Arello suggested.

"On the Canal, Tarawa, he was a damn good Marine." Ski replied. "He just can't take it anymore."

"But what do we do with him?" Knuppel asked again. "Jesus, just look at him. We can't have the guys see him like this." Lewis was horribly changed, his jaw clenched tight to keep his teeth from chattering, a haunted look in his eyes, a thousand-yard stare that could spook anyone.

Lewis had gone through hell at Guadalcanal and Tarawa and endured the toughest training to reach this point, but this was no time for sentiment. "If he can't make it on his own, leave him." There was nothing more to be said, and no time to waste thinking about it. Ski nodded to Knuppel, who understood.

●   ●   ●

At 1000, Riseley began to fortify a shell hole near the water's edge of Red Two. Dozens of Japanese infiltrated from the north just as entrenching tools began digging his temporary headquarters. The enemy sliced through a staging area for the wounded, with Riseley's command post directly in their path.

"Any word from Ski?" Riseley asked his XO, McLeod.

"No, Jim."

"Ski!" Riseley hollered.

A young boot named Albert Hauske, near Riseley's shell hole, heard the call and jumped in.

"Yes sir!" Hauske reported.

"Who in the hell are you?" Riseley questioned. "And don't call me sir! How green are you?"

"As green as they come, si…" Hauske stopped himself short.

"I'm not looking for you, I need Ski."

"I am Ski, Albert Hauske, junior language offi…"

"Alright, then," Riseley interrupted. "You're Ski Two. I want Ski One."

Just then Ski strode into the shell hole. "Yes, Jim."

"What's your status?"

"One man down. Lewis."

"Japs are coming from the north." Riseley said. Ski needed no instructions. He left running, yelling out "Moore! Mullins! Old dead dog!"

"Who was that, um, Jim?" Hauske asked. "He walked right through those bullets like he was walking in a park."

"He's the leader of my Scout-Snipers...I take it this is your first combat?"

Hauske nodded in the affirmative.

"At first it's a natural reaction to duck," Riseley handed an entrenching tool to Hauske. "But when the bullets are zinging all around you, there's no point in ducking."

"Why's that?"

"You're never going to hear the one that gets you. With that bit of sage advice, get to work and start digging, Ski Two."

Moore's Browning Automatic Rifle and Mullins's Unertl-scoped Springfield swiftly eliminated the infiltration from the north. At 1045 Riseley ordered the command post to be moved two hundred yards inland.

"Old dead dog!" Ski gave the word and led his 40 Thieves over the log wall toward the Japanese. Lewis purposely lagged behind, pretending to fiddle with his Reising submachine gun, acting as though the bolt had seized up.

"It's jammed. Rusted," he said to Strombo as he passed by.

"Here's mine," Strombo replied, knowing there was nothing wrong with the Reising. "I'll take yours. You can't stay here. Now c'mon, follow me." The swap was made.

Lewis followed reluctantly, leaving the corpse-strewn beach and running inland. Compelled to look back, he stopped and turned. His feet were planted on Saipan, but his mind returned to Tarawa and images of thousands of bodies baked, blackened, and bloated in the sun.

Tarawa was where he had learned what happens to a man after he's shot and killed in the Pacific. Lewis had watched the process: within a few short hours in the searing tropical heat, a man's body turned completely black because all the oxygen had left his blood; after eight hours, flies crawled inside the body, breeding; slowly the body would swell, completely filling with maggots. Bellies heaved as though alive. Clothes burst at the seams.

"C'mon!" Strombo yelled again. Lewis shook his head, trying to clear his mind, and followed.

The platoon pushed into a coconut grove, a few hundred yards inland.

"Secure the area!" Ski ordered. As Kenny sprayed the tops of coconut trees with machine gun fire, Smotts and Tipton watched the ground beneath.

"Got one!" Tipton yelled as he noticed blood dripping on the ground. More men fired into the foliage until a body fell.

They peppered a larger tree with gunfire, and though no body fell, a few drops of blood spattered the ground. Another barrage of bullets proved as futile. Japanese snipers often wrapped themselves in binding and tied themselves into a tree with a rope. If hit, the binding kept them from bleeding out too rapidly, and the rope held their bodies above the canopy. Marines could waste bullets and time, not knowing if they had killed their enemy.

Smotts employed a different tactic. Each of the Thieves carried primer cord and three one-pound blocks of TNT. If the tree had been smaller, wrapping the primer cord around the base of the tree would have done the trick. But the size of this tree required TNT. Smotts took his crimper and dug a hole into one of his white, chalky blocks. Inserting a cap, he tied in the fuse and primer cord and stuck the block into the base of the tree. Lighting the cord, Smotts and Tipton dove for cover. The base of the tree shattered as it smashed to the ground. Wading through the debris, they found a Japanese sniper's body crushed, tied to one of the heavy limbs. It was a teenage girl.

With the area secured, Riseley, McLeod, intelligence officers, corpsmen, and other regimental support staff moved up and re-established the command post. From it, they could see the peaks of Tapotchau and Tipo Pale looming in the distance.

"Knuppel!" Ski called, and his sergeant reported. "Put two squads around the CP…the Old Gent wants us to check out what's ahead. Send Evans and his boys toward Tipo Pale and Dyer's toward Tapotchau. If anybody hits anything hot, send a runner back."

Tipo Pale, the closer of the two mountains, at less than four thousand yards away, had a road twisting down its side. Evans's squad had closed within one thousand yards when an opportunity presented itself.

"Look at those bastards ridin' like hell," Mullins pointed at Japanese troops streaming down the side of Tipo Pale headed toward the beach, peddling on bicycles.

"Check it out, Boss," Evans noted to Knuppel. "They're bottle-neckin' when they come to that curve." About halfway down, the soldiers had to execute a U-turn. To maneuver the hairpin curve, they had to stop, get off their bicycles, and carry them around the severe bend in the trail.

"Mullins, how far?" Knuppel asked.

"Maybe nine hundred yards."

Evans and Mullins carried Unertl Scoped '03 Springfields. The two began firing alternately, picking off the Japanese one by one.

"Just like a carnival game." Mullins smiled, slid the bolt, and loaded another cartridge.

Evans and Mullins continued firing in methodical succession. Round after round snapped from the Springfields. Silently, the enemy soldiers tumbled from the mountain.

"What the hell's wrong with 'em?" Mullins mumbled to himself. Finally, the enemy stopped coming. It was the only time the Unertl scopes were used in battle. By the next day moisture had accumulated inside, rendering the Unertls useless.

With perimeter defenses set, Riseley established communications with his battalion commanders. The news was not good: half his officers were either dead or wounded; the Second Battalion command post had received a direct hit from a Japanese mortar shell, injuring the major who had replaced Colonel Murray; the Third Battalion's leader, Colonel Easley, had been wounded as well; and Riseley could not find out who had assumed his command. As Colonel Jones's First Battalion ferried toward Red Two with reinforcements, a dead enemy tank near the water's edge suddenly came to life, opened fire, and scored several 57mm hits on Jones's unit. Casualties skyrocketed.

The Thieves, placed every ten to fifteen yards around the perimeter to guard Riseley and the CP, listened to the roar of battle and fidgeted from the adrenaline. Strombo looked to his left and made eye contact with Johnson, who motioned for a cigarette. Strombo ran over, lit up two Luckies, and gave Johnson one.

"Thanks," Johnson inhaled deeply. "And now we bring you... *Suspense.*"

Throughout the day of the landing on Saipan, the Japanese fought back violently in fits and starts. In one uncoordinated thrust, when three Japanese tanks rumbled toward Marine lines, bazookamen easily destroyed two before exhausting their ammunition, but the third tank eluded destruction. Then the Japanese spied the Sixth Regiment's command post and changed course, churning closer and closer toward their prey.

Rattling to within one hundred yards of the Thieves' defensive perimeter, the tank's intense machine gun fire sent everyone diving for cover. Borawski crouched behind rocks firing his rifle in vain; the bullets ricocheted harmlessly off the tank. Johnson concentrated his fire on the open pistol port which hurriedly snapped shut. Knuppel made a run at the tank with a grenade, but a spattering barrage kept him at bay. The tank had everyone helplessly pinned down as it clattered onward. Lacking a bazooka, the Marines could do nothing to stop it.

Yunker thought this was it; his time had come to meet his maker. Not knowing a prayer, he made the sign of the cross and muttered, "Spectacles, testicles, wallet, and watch."

Standing outside his tent, Riseley watched the threat grow near. "Where in the hell is Ski?" the colonel fumed out loud. Ski had taken off running at the first sight of the approaching tank. Knowing that a bazooka team had bivouacked close by, he had run as hard and as fast as he could, trying to locate them. With precious moments ticking away, finally, out of breath, he spotted a group of Marines huddled around the stovepipe-shaped weapon. He picked up his pace.

"I need your bazooka team now!" Ski commanded the green lieutenant in charge.

"Who the hell are you?" the young officer replied, in a huff, "and why should I give you my men?"

"I don't have time to argue, I need that damned thing now!" Ski seized the bazooka and said to a private carrying the rockets, "Come on!"

The addled private hesitated until Ski yelled, "Old dead dog! Let's go!" Responding instinctively to being hollered at, the private bolted to his feet. Ski took off running, with the private at his heels.

Ski raced toward Riseley and McLeod with the private trailing behind. By the time he got back, the tank had closed to within fifty yards of his platoon's front line and slowed. Maneuvering between the Third Battalion Headquarters on one side and the Sixth Regiment command post on the other, the Japanese were alternately strafing both targets with fire from the tank's two 7.7mm machine guns, sending the Americans scattering for cover behind shattered stumps and logs.

"Who in the hell is that?" Yunker watched in amazement as a solitary figure ran out toward the withering fire.

The men in the tank spotted the threat and slowly began to turn its sights. The turret pivoted, both guns cutting an arc of exploding dirt toward Ski.

"Old dead dog!" he barked at the private who trailed behind. "Fire this damn thing. Now!" The private scrambled to Ski's side as the puffs of dirt neared and slid a rocket down the tube. Ski pulled the trigger. Nothing. It was a common problem—wires needed to be reconnected for firing. The tank gunners raised their sights to intersect at Ski's chest. But before they could fire, the private connected the wires. "Now!" Ski fired the bazooka.

The rocket smashed into the turret, creating a little puff of smoke, and the tank stopped immediately. Everyone wondered if it had worked. By outward appearances, there was no evidence of damage. Inside, however, a devastating concussive force entered the tank through a pinhole created by the shell, and the force of the explosion traveled forward. There was no shrapnel to wound those trapped inside, just a massive concussive force—blowing out ear drums and eyes and tearing Japanese bodies to bits from the inside out.

After a few minutes, the hatch beneath the tank opened, and a Japanese soldier spilled onto the ground. Dazed and bleeding from his ears, he began running toward Riseley. Ski charged out to tackle him, but the soldier hadn't made it more than ten yards before a hail of bullets from Yunker, Borawski, and Johnson cut him down.

By nightfall, the beachhead had been tenuously secured, and defensive perimeters established for the night. The landing had gone badly, with a casualty rate nearing thirty percent. Riseley worried that Saitō's vow to "Drive the American Devils back into the sea" might come true.

Shortly before dusk, a forward patrol of Thieves observed large groups of Japanese streaming down from the hills outside of Garapan onto the coastal flats well to the north of the Sixth Regiment's lines and reported the movement to Riseley.

"Ski!" Riseley hollered. "Seventy-five yards ahead of our front lines, there is a small ridge. That will be the Japs' way of approach. Before the ridge are a series of trenches that lead up the mountain. Take your men and position yourself in those trenches. When the Banzai hits, if our lines don't hold, you need to stay there and hold them off, so our forces can evacuate."

When Ski relayed the orders to his men, Smotts explained to Tipton, "We're the sacrificial sheep."

A gray moon hung low in the sky, barely shining through a murky, stagnant haze that reeked of chemicals, smoke, and rotting bodies. In the dark, every one of the 40 Thieves—with the single exception of the shell-shocked Lewis, who had stayed behind at the command post— grimly dug into the trenches and waited.

CHAPTER SEVENTEEN

The Kitchen Sink

"There was always a lot of anticipation but never any surprises. You knew what to expect—that at any time you could be dead. So there was no point thinkin' about it, you just went right into it and what comes, comes and what will be, will be. You'd just as soon get it over with, because you knew that sooner or later it's comin'. All of us thought that death would be our only way out."

—Roscoe Mullins

June 15, 1944, 2100 Hours
Red Beach 1, Saipan

Huddled in trenches in groups of threes and fours, the Thieves waited. One man stayed awake and kept watch while the others tried to sleep. Hands gripping rifles slowly began to swell from multiple mosquito bites. The caramel-smelling USMC-issued "No-Bite" insect repellent seemed to attract rather than repel.

In the trench occupied by Smotts, Kenny, Moore, and Tipton, no one slept. Not only could they hear the chattering Japanese in the distance, but Moore was trembling and sweating profusely. The only veteran of Guadalcanal among them was suffering from a malaria relapse, which was making him shudder and throw up a putrid green slime. One of the most fearless Thieves, the tough Okie was rendered useless, a liability for the team. Smotts used a poncho as a bib around Moore's neck.

"Those rascals out there are workin' themselves up," Smotts commented.

"I don't give a damn if they come or not," Moore managed. "If they do, I'm done. I'd just as soon get it over with."

Japanese voices screamed in the distance "Die, Marine, Die!" and "Kill, kill, kill!"

"I gotta get some sleep," Moore uttered. But no one slept. They kept an eye on their buddy as he continued to sweat and quiver, his chattering teeth adding more noise to the distant Japanese. The waiting stretched out.

The first Japanese assault took place at 2200. The enemy were probing and searching for a weak spot in the hope that the Marines might fire and reveal their position. But the Marines held their fire and repulsed the attempt with grenades. The Japanese withdrew.

As the uneasy night wore on, sleepless Marines fidgeted in the darkness, anticipating the frenzied Banzai. Tipton listened to the enemy's shrieks in the distance and knew he would never forget that sound—or the sight of the shivering Moore.

"He's in bad shape." Tipton's hands quivered in an imitation of the St. Vitus's dance.

Smotts offered reassurance. "He's gonna be alright. We've seen it before. A smoke helps calm the nerves," he suggested, offering a cigarette. "But light up under your poncho, or it'll be your day in the barrel."

"Thanks. You sure he's gonna be okay?"

"Like I say, we've seen it before."

Hours passed with the Marines repelling a rapid series of exploratory jabs. With each attack the Marines braced themselves, thinking that this might be the one. Not yet.

Finally at 0300, an eerie bugle call in the distance sounded "Charge!" Swarms of Japanese lurched forward, shrieking and brandishing swords that glistened in the pale gray moonlight.

Riseley quickly radioed for illumination shells, and within moments Naval artillery littered the sky with parachute flares revealing the horde of flesh pressing forward, waving flags, and madly yelling, "Drink Marine Blood!" and "Banzai!"

Having heard that the Japanese Army employed the cruel tactic of using civilians to mask their advance could hardly prepare a Marine for facing women and children in the line of fire. Not wanting to kill the human shields, the Marines initially held their fire as hundreds of people, all on foot, advanced slowly in waves, taunting them to shoot just a few rounds and reveal their machine gun placements. As the swelling enemy edged closer and closer, cresting yards away from the Marines' lines, they could wait no longer. Orders were given, and the killing began.

All placements began shooting at once, spewing a sheet of red flame. The machine guns, locked on the forward protective line, crossed fire. The women and children fell one on top of another and began stacking up like cordwood. Their bodies were trampled by Japanese troops. There seemed to be no end to the crazed and determined onslaught.

The Japanese who survived the barrage were kept at bay with grenades. And for those who kept coming, the gruesome business of hand-to-hand fighting began—killing without mercy. Ka-Bars slashed at flesh. Rifle butts smashed into jaws. Thumbs gouged out eyes. Barbaric sounds filled the air. The gasps of the whimpering wounded and the savage cries of the victor could be heard.

After almost three relentless hours of butchery, at 0545 the Japanese overwhelmed two Marine artillery positions near the beach, forcing the crew members back.

As the enemy rampage continued, Riseley feared that Saitō's forces had won. He plugged gaps with diminishing troops as best he could until the gloomy dawn silhouetted five hulking shapes rumbling along the beach. The Second Tank Battalion, which had landed on the southern Green Beaches late the day before, had dispatched five M4 Shermans. The tanks' timely arrival swung the balance back in favor of the Marines.

The Banzai slowly wilted and ebbed. What little light filtered through the smoke-filled sky revealed a grisly scene of human carnage. Over seven hundred enemy bodies littered the blood-soaked ground, slowly stiffening in the searing heat.

Evans's squad had left after dawn, mopping up. The sharp crack of sporadic gunfire could be heard as they wandered among the torn and twisted heaps and dispatched the groaning enemy still alive amid the dead. Feeble calls for "corpsman" signaled hope for finding fallen but still surviving Marines.

Of the eight thousand landing troops who stormed Saipan, 35 percent lay dead on the beaches or had been evacuated with severe wounds to hospital ships. If any Marine had managed to get any sleep on board ship the night before landing, there had been precious little chance since, and there would be no opportunity in the near future.

●   ●   ●

Sitting behind his folding-table desk, Riseley consulted with Ski. On one of many maps he pointed to an area southeast of Red Beach Three, between Afetna Point and Lake Susupe. Ski referred to a smaller map he kept in his breast pocket.

"The Japs have set up a line of defense keeping us from consolidating the beachhead. Scout it. If your boys can't take it out, then I want to know how to get it done."

With Evans out on patrol, Ski huddled with his remaining corporals, each with a similar map. The rest of the platoon sat in their squad groups, trying to eavesdrop on their lieutenant's orders. While ears trained one way, their eyes were riveted on another—Lewis. He sat alone, away from his comrades, and his sallow, haunted look generated commentary. Whispered words of "What the hell's wrong with him?" "He's scared shitless," and "Coward" were uttered by more than one.

Before the war Ski had led men on basketball courts and football fields. In Officers' School he had learned to lead men in combat—studying a textbook titled *The Art of War* with sixty other candidates and finishing third in his class. The art of military command had evolved technologically since the sixth century B.C., when the Chinese general Sun Tzu wrote that book, but the basic tenets remained the same: "If you know the enemy and know yourself, you need not fear the outcome of a hundred battles."

"Fear makes men restless" Sun Tzu wrote. Ski learned that fear was an enemy greater than any opposing force. The Marines had translated this teaching into modern language: "Men are prey to certain emotions, the strongest of them is fear. If fear hits a man in your unit, it can be more fatal than a bullet. Fear disrupts group action and in combat, the danger is that it becomes a distraction, thereby making a unit vulnerable to an alert enemy. Whenever you have a member of a group who falls prey to fear, the bond of camaraderie is jeopardized. Remove the rotten apples from the group barrel. As a leader, you must never falter to take swift and ruthless action, all with a studied purpose."

Lewis had become a burden and unwanted distraction. Ski spoke to Riseley about removing his rotten apple, but the Colonel had more pressing matters than dealing with one shell-shocked Marine. "He's your problem," Riseley responded.

Dyer's squad got the call to move out toward the Japanese line of defense on Red Beach Three. He spaced his men at ten- to fifteen-yard intervals, with Smotts on point, and his squad silently marched off.

Emerging from a dense mosquito-infested jungle, Dyer and his men came to the edge of a field of waist-high salt grass. Demolished buildings stood amidst the grass. Dyer signaled for his men to halt and break from single file to form a skirmish line. They advanced into the salt grass with every third man walking backwards, scanning the terrain.

In front of Kenny, the grass rustled. Before he could motion to the group, an enemy soldier popped up, ready to throw a grenade. Kenny immediately pumped two rapid blasts from his shotgun, sending the Japanese sailing through the air, flying five yards backwards. The grenade exploded without leaving the enemy's hand.

Directly in front of the Marines, a brief burst of machine gun fire sent a barrage of bullets pecking through the grass.

Everyone hit the ground. Lying pressed against the earth, they listened. The clattering of bayonets being fixed and jabbering voices could be heard a short distance ahead. Dyer sent Smotts to scout the Japanese position. He crawled forward and reported back within minutes.

"Forty yards dead ahead," Smotts whispered, "there's about a dozen of those rascals in a jury-rigged dugout. Maybe more. They got some small arms, grenades, a coupla light machine guns, and we're lookin' straight down the throat of a woodpecker."

Dyer directed Borawski and Yunker to circle around the earthen shelter on the left side, take up a position behind it, and be ready to cut down any Japanese who might try to flee. His orders to the rest were, "Crawl to the right." Dyer stayed put, gave his men time to get in position, and threw a grenade off to the left of the enemy position. When the machine gun began peck-peck-pecking in the wrong direction, Dyer opened fire. His men on the right threw two grenades directly into the dugout.

Dyer stopped firing when the explosions erupted. The Thieves rushed in. All eight of the Japanese inside appeared to have been killed by the shrapnel. While Smotts and Kenny dismantled the woodpecker, Tipton spied a slight movement out of the corner of his eye. A "dead" man was reaching for his rifle. Tipton put two bullets into him. Any more than two shots, and the kid from Detroit wouldn't have heard three more "corpses" coming to life. One held a hand grenade, but three more bullets stopped him before he pulled the pin. The other two fled—into Borawski and Yunker's waiting bayonets.

The bodies and the packs of the dead were searched for information and diaries. There was no time to collect souvenirs. Smotts rolled one of the Japanese over and rummaged through his pack. What in the hell are they doin' with all this cologne, he wondered, taking a whiff from an open bottle. Going from corpse to corpse inhaling deeply, he at last exclaimed, "That's it!" He turned to Tipton, pulling him close to one of the dead bodies. "Hobart, take a whiff of this Jap."

"You kiddin'?"

"No. You gotta remember this smell," Smotts explained, "when these rascals sweat out their rice diet and try to cover it up with cologne, they smell real distinct."

Tipton smelled and nodded.

"You see, Hobart, nothin' foul, just distinctive. I've smelled this before. Now I know. When you smell 'em, be on your toes."

After gathering everything of value from the dugout, Dyer ordered, "Move out." He motioned for his men to follow him through the area of demolished buildings. Cautiously sifting their way through shattered lumber, sheets of rusted corrugated tin, and buckets of scrap metal, they saw that the Japanese had abruptly left what had once been a camp to flee the shelling. A dozen stiff jelly-eyed corpses were left behind.

The line of defense the Japanese had established between Lake Susupe and Afetna Point lay dead ahead. The men observed a well-fortified position on a dominant ridge. From several plateaus, mortars and heavy machine guns peppered Red Beach Three, keeping the Marines positioned there pinned down. There was no way they would survive a frontal assault on the Japanese position.

Dyer and his men worked their way toward the left side of the ridge until they found a spot where they could climb up. Using a human pyramid, the Thieves scaled the jagged coral one by one to reach the top of the ridge and discovered enemy fortifications below, facing both to the north and south. Moving along the apex Smotts led the way, inhaling then pointing out and marking the Japanese positions below, four to five on each side.

There were too many pockets for the Marines to jump down and take them out man-to-man, so Dyer asked for options.

Yunker offered, "Back at that Jap camp, there's pails of rusty nails and scrap metal. We could put blocks of TNT in the pails and adjust the fuse to go off just before it hits the ground." No other opinions were needed. Dyer sent Yunker and five others back to the camp to salvage up to ten buckets of rusty shrapnel. When they returned within an hour with the goods and a coil of rope, the Thieves went to work.

Estimating the distance from their location on top of the ridge to the base of the plateau, the Marines cut sections of rope and tied them off on trees or rocks above each of the enemy positions. On the other end was the pail of rusted metal and TNT, timed for fifteen seconds.

When everything was ready, Dyer gave the signal. The fuses were lit and the pails thrown over. With staggered and resounding booms, the ridge rolled and rocked beneath their feet.

Half the squad scaled the ropes down to the plateau on one side; the other half, on the opposite.

Yunker's ploy worked. The few Japanese left alive writhed in pain, bodies torn apart by the rusted shrapnel. They did not suffer long. After machine guns and mortars were destroyed, a search of the interconnected caverns uncovered cases of Hokkan sake, crabmeat, tangerines, and other canned provisions.

Borawski opened a tin with his Ka-Bar and tossed one to Yunker.

"We're issued Red Heart," Yunker marveled, "and the Japs're eatin' this."

Using their ropes, they hoisted case after case to the ridge above, climbed up themselves, and took all they could carry with them back to their camp.

Bypassing the abandoned Japanese site, Dyer's squad walked through a lush area more fertile than the surrounding ground cover. As they passed a row of shattered small buildings, bullets suddenly pinged off debris and made plopping sounds as the slugs burrowed into the soft earth. The Thieves dropped their plunder and themselves to the ground. Borawski was the first to spy a lone tree, unscathed in the devastation. It had to house the sniper. He unloaded his machine gun into the foliage, ending the threat. The squad brushed themselves off, gathered their loot, and waited for their corporal to give directions.

None came.

"Dyer!" Tipton called out. Retracing their steps, the Thieves fanned out and searched. Their squad leader was nowhere to be found.

Soon, a faint cry of "Help!" led the men toward the demolished buildings, but by the time they got there the voice had stopped.

"Dyer?" Smotts spoke cautiously.

"Get me outta here!" The voice called out.

Smotts followed the cries for help to an area of bright green fountain grass and a hole in the ground. Circling around it, the squad looked down. They had been walking through the latrines for the Japanese camp.

"Oh, Christ!" Tipton gagged, and turned away. The others suppressed their laughter.

The location of the outhouses was overgrown, and Dyer had fallen into one.

"Get me the hell out of here!" Fat flies swarmed around him.

Yunker took a deep breath, reached down, and pulled Dyer out. Now on solid ground, Dyer stood covered from head to toe in human waste and flies. The men all kept their distance, and no one dared to laugh or make a wisecrack.

"You're…" was all Yunker could manage before being silenced by Dyer's piercing glare. With all present and accounted for, the squad headed back to the command post. Instead of leading his squad back, Dyer brought up the rear—a quite distant rear.

As they approached the coconut grove, Ski observed nine men in the lead and one lagging far behind.

"What gives?" Ski asked Smotts as he entered camp.

Smotts told the lieutenant about the shit storm Dyer had encountered, Ski called out to Strombo to get a scrub brush and a bar of soap. The two met Dyer before he reached camp. Handing him the brush and soap, Ski ordered his corporal to the beach, "And don't come back until you're clean."

"I'll keep you company," Strombo said, being careful to keep up-wind.

"A regular Roman holiday," Dyer replied.

• • •

Organizing scattered units, preparing for the push inland, and bracing for the next counterattack absorbed most of the day after the invasion. The narrow beachheads had been made invulnerable, but progress was not what Howlin' Mad Smith had envisioned. Enemy resistance continued to be dogged, and the Marines' advance resolutely harassed. U.S. casualties reached almost four thousand.

That afternoon, Riseley received a copy of a Naval intelligence communique reporting that the Japanese Fleet had set sail for Saipan. Two U.S. submarines had discovered a large force of enemy carriers, battleships, cruisers, and destroyers moving from their base at Tawi Tawi in the Philippines toward the Marianas. The enemy's estimated time of arrival: two days.

The Japanese Fleet's rapid approach made it necessary to get all supplies and materials ashore immediately, in order to enable the U.S. Fleet to depart and engage the Imperial Navy before it could reach the Marianas. Howlin' Mad Smith ordered ships to unload all equipment and ammunition. The Army division held in reserve would also have to land sooner than anticipated.

Supplies were ferried in continuously throughout the day. Shore parties worked loading and unloading until dusk. Riseley received a message to send men to help with the process and passed that request onto Ski.

Smotts, Kenny, and Tipton went grudgingly back to the beach. Arriving at the point of debarkation, the trio busied themselves unloading boxes and crates of ammunition, rations, and weapons from the ships to the shore.

The soldier in charge had different ideas.

Smotts relayed the order to his buddies "They want us to unload their piano first."

"You're shittin' me!" Kenny's jaw dropped.

"For their goddamned Officer's Club." Smotts spit out the words in disgust.

"What are we, some type of moving company?" Tipton asked.

"Sonofabitch dogfaces haven't even begun to fight, and we gotta unload their piano?" Kenny fumed.

"Hey doggie!" Smotts yelled to the soldier in charge. "I know where we can move this piano. Right up your general's..."

"Shut up! Quit your belly achin' and get to work!" The soldier yelled back.

"What? Why I..." Kenny's Irish began to show.

"You heard me," the soldier snapped. "Shut up and get to work."

"Oh, that rascal's gone and done it," Smotts grumbled. "He's right. Let's get to work." The three positioned themselves around the piano.

"A one, and a two," Smotts counted, "and a three!" They lifted the piano over the railing and threw it overboard, into the sea.

"It slipped." Kenny apologized as he walked past the soldier in charge. Tipton added, "Oops."

Smotts explained in a deadpan voice, "You might want to fire us 'cause we're a crazy bunch. We're nuts. There's not many like us in the Army, I suppose. That's why we joined the Corps."

•   •   •

While the Marines prepared to protect the small toehold they had established on the beaches, the Japanese made their own plans. Initial Allied intelligence had indicated the presence of a tank regiment on Saipan. In his hope to "Drive the American Devils back into the sea," General Saitō had made plans for a massive counterattack, deploying an entire battalion of infantry, supported by almost four dozen tanks.

When the Marines encountered only a few enemy tanks during the first Banzai, scuttlebutt circulated: "It's gonna be everything tonight. More tanks."

The odd-duck mind of Philip Johnson concocted a plan to make it truly "later than you think" for the Japanese. While foraging in a blown-out pillbox, he stumbled upon some cases of sake and accidentally broke a bottle. Watching the liquid spread out and soak the ground gave him an idea. Johnson gathered all the sake he could find and hauled a case back to camp. All his buddies watched, puzzled, as Johnson poured out the contents of each bottle, fastidiously placing the empties back in the case. He disappeared and returned with a tin of gasoline pilfered from Army supplies.

Johnson sloppily filled the bottles with gasoline, tore his already tattered t-shirt into strips, and shoved a strip of the fabric into the top of every bottle. When he finished, he looked up to find Ski curiously staring at him.

"Molotov cocktails," Johnson explained. "For the party tonight."

"You get that idea from one of your radio shows?"

"*Light's Out.*"

Ski ordered the rest of the Thieves to scatter and scrounge for any bottle they could find, and to pilfer more petrol.

After crafting their crude anti-tank weapons, the platoon worked past sunset digging defensive trenches forward of their protective line.

At some point during the overcast moonless night, the Banzai would come. Listening posts, established far forward of the lines, readied to radio any sight or sound of activity back to command. The Marines dug in, braced themselves, and waited in silence. Time slowly ticked by— 2000…2100…2200…2300…

At 0330, the unnatural silence was broken, first by the faint sound of squeaking gears, and rattling caterpillar tracks churning.

"Here comes the kitchen sink!" Johnson yelled.

As the squeak and rattle grew steadily nearer, the sound of chants and blood-curdling screams accompanied the mechanical rumble. Once again, Navy guns were called upon to illuminate the night sky with flares, revealing humped black silhouettes—dozens of tanks with bodies swarming on top. More Japanese surged forward on foot. At 0345, the first wave hit the Marines.

The hellish sounds of screeching artillery shells, salvo after salvo of exploding mortars, and volleys of machine gun fire provided the soundtrack for the halting shadows pulsing forward through strobe-like flashes of light.

As the tanks rattled and clanked onward, the intermittent flickering of light illuminated figures protruding from the open hatches. The Japanese commanders perched on top of their tanks shouted directions to the drivers inside. The Thieves, lurking in the dark, waited for an instant of light to reveal their target. In that moment, a pull of a trigger left the tank without its commander, and the Marines followed up with a Molotov cocktail smashed into the tank's turret. The gasoline, quickly ablaze, ran down through cracks into the tank, causing its munitions to explode and roasting those inside.

Finding great success with their improvised gasoline bombs, the Thieves hunted tank after tank throughout the night.

The tempest ebbed and surged for hour upon hour. The blackened field of battle was speckled with fires burning everywhere, from smoldering tanks to the fuel-soaked ground itself. A sudden flash from an illumination shell revealed the air to be thick with oily smoke.

One enemy tank eluded destruction. It clattered toward the Sixth Regimental command post until it got stuck in one of the Marines' defensive trenches, at which point the crew inside attempted to bail out. The first to try didn't make it out of the hatch. One shot left his dead body blocking the exit, discouraging those still inside from even trying. The tank began lurching violently back and forth, its caterpillar tracks digging away at the trench until one tread snapped. The Thieves' supply of cocktails having run dry, Knuppel jumped on the tank and slipped a concussion grenade past the dead body, dropping it inside. Sudden, frantic cries ended with a muffled explosion.

The attack lasted until 0700. Once again, the Banzai had failed.

CHAPTER EIGHTEEN

Hell Is on Us

"There are only twelve tanks left in our regiment. Even if there are no tanks, we will fight hand-to-hand. I have resolved that, if I see the enemy, I will take out my sword and slash, slash, slash at him as long as I last, thus ending my life of twenty-four years."

—Tokuzo Matsuya, 9th Imperial Tank Regiment

June 17, 1944
Sixth Marine command post between Hill 500 and Mount Tipo Pale

The Thieves' cocktail party was a success. After dawn broke on the second day after the landing on Saipan, it revealed over two dozen smoking and smoldering enemy tanks. The Japanese attack had been poorly planned and executed. That was obvious to Riseley. But that morning he received disappointing reports of heavy personnel loss, more dead and dying to be added to the mounting casualty list.

It had now been fifty-two sleepless hours since general quarters had been sounded on the *Bolivar*. The Thieves were growing antsy, itching to get behind the enemy lines and make their mark.

"Boss, when do we get to do our jobs?" Evans asked quietly as the two stood outside Riseley's command post. "I ain't belly-achin' but my guys are tired of babysittin' Gentleman Jim. We should be doin' what we was trained to do. Besides," he grinned, "I gotta start baggin' my limit or else I'm gonna be disgraced by Arello and Duley. Can't lose my bet with 'em."

A destroyed Japanese tank. *From the collection of Joseph Tachovsky*

"I know we've been doing our share of babysitting, Don, but guarding the CP is more than just keeping the Old Gent safe," Ski replied. "Tell your boys our day will come. Soon. When Howlin' Mad lands, we get to work. How much disgrace are we talking about?"

"Fifty bucks."

As he awaited orders Evans explored the Japanese tank that had been disabled the night before. Climbing on top, he grabbed the corpse that lay halfway out of the hatch and tossed it to the ground like a rag doll. "Hey Boss!" Evans called out to Knuppel. "It looks in pretty good shape, and there's still some ammo."

"Check it out," Knuppel replied.

Evans reached down into the turret, pulled another lifeless form out by the scruff of the neck and threw it aside. The body had its stomach blown out, and the intestines trailed behind like a kite-tail. Reaching in again, Evans tossed a third enemy soldier to the ground.

Japanese tanks were smaller than U.S. models, and the outsized Evans had a difficult time getting through the hatch. When he stood up inside, his chest and head stuck way out. He crouched down to survey the shambles—bits of flesh, organs, and blood from the concussive effect of the grenade were spattered everywhere. Disappearing for a few minutes, he searched for maps and anything else of value. An ivory-handled samurai sword lying on the floor caught his eye.

Evans popped back up, "I think we can still use this thing." Hollering to Ski who approached, "Hey Boss! Catch. Merry Christmas!" Evans tossed the sword to his lieutenant then asked, "Where do you want me to shoot?"

Ski had noticed Japanese activity just to the north, on the side of Tipo Pale. If it wasn't an enemy command post, it was an assembly point. "See that plateau? Up the mountain side?"

Evans acknowledged with a thumb's up.

"Fire on that."

With the tank's sighting mechanism wrecked, Evans removed the block, opened the breach, and bore-sighted the tank gun by looking down the barrel. He raised it, judged the distance, and picked up a 57mm shell crusted with thickening blood and scraps of skin. Evans nonchalantly cleaned the shell with his bare hands and jammed it into the breach. His head and shoulders emerged from the turret.

"Fire in the hole!" he yelled and pulled the lanyard. The tank responded with a thunderclap.

"Raise the barrel and rotate the turret to the left a little bit," Ski directed.

Evans cleaned off another shell, loaded, and fired again. The second shot hit the mark, and Evans let out a triumphant cry of delight.

"Good work, Don!" Ski congratulated him. "Keep it up until the ammo's gone."

A dozen more shells battered the mountainside before the ammunition ran out.

"Ski!" It was Yunker coming up. "Back home on the farm, I used to repair caterpillar tread like that all the time. I think I can fix it."

"Do it. That tank'll come in handy." Yunker started surveying the broken track. Ski ordered the others, "Find more ammo for the tank!" and then told Evans, "Yunker's fixing the tread. You can keep your toy!"

Fellow farm boys went to help Yunker while other Marines excitedly scrounged through disabled tanks nearby.

"What's the racket, Ski?" McLeod asked as he approached, followed by Riseley.

"My boys acquired a new…"

Riseley cut the lieutenant short, bellowing to Evans, "Get out of that damned tank before the Japs start lobbing mortars at us." Riseley turned to walk away but pivoted to bark, "And destroy that tank immediately. We're moving out."

"Dammit," Evans groused quietly to himself.

"It woulda been nice to keep that tank. It might've come in handy," Ski told McLeod, who shrugged and walked away as well.

Knuppel shook his head.

A block of TNT was placed inside the tank and detonated.

At 0730 General Howlin' Mad Smith ordered a new offensive from his flagship, the USS *Rocky Mount*. The Sixth Regiment received orders to push inland and advance toward the foothills of Tipo Pale. And when Howlin' Mad said push, the Marines pushed.

Mid-morning the 40 Thieves were ordered to move out toward the front lines in support of a Marine unit bogged down in a vicious firefight.

Since Lewis's breakdown on the day of the landing, Ski had been able to keep him busy at the command post. He had been useful with administrative duties, and negative commentary from the men had ebbed. He still looked like a shell of his former self, but there had been no more episodes. Keeping him out of harm's way had been a convenient luxury for the past two days. But now the entire platoon was being deployed, and Lewis would have to join this mission. There were no two ways about it.

Ski shared his concern with Knuppel and Schieber before the Thieves moved out. "We've got to roll the dice on this one and see how he reacts."

"He hasn't gone off his nut since we landed, but if he jeopardizes the mission..."

"That won't happen. I'm not gonna let it happen. I'll have him carry the walkie-talkie so I can keep him in my hip pocket."

The bursting sun beat down through the orange haze as Ski led his men on point, double time, with Smotts by his side. He kept Lewis directly behind him, carrying the forty-pound SCR 300 radio on his back. The rest jogged in single file. Mullins trailed behind, ten yards ahead of Strombo, who brought up the rear. A few hundred yards ahead, a rugged hill separated the platoon from a valley on the other side. The sound of violent combat could be heard in the distance. The twang and whoosh of mortars, bullets snapping off in rapid succession, orders being screamed, the faint cries of "corpsman," and the sounds of death grew louder with each step the men took.

The platoon reached the foot of the hill and came to a halt. A narrow trail meandered between jagged rocks, dense foliage, and vines. The arduous climb would take precious time away from helping the Marines on the other side.

Running, and breathing in rhythm with his footfalls, Lewis had managed to control his fear. But as he stood at the base of the hill the throbbing noises from the valley preyed on his mind.

"Old dead dog!" Ski called out to the platoon, looking directly at Lewis who followed. But gradually Lewis's face grew taut, panicked. He fell farther and farther behind. Ski glanced back. No Lewis, but he couldn't stop.

Mullins, second to the last in line, walked by Lewis sitting on a rock halfway from the top of the hill. Perplexed, he looked down at the pale, frightened man and said "C'mon." Lewis avoided eye contact as Mullins passed. Strombo followed.

"Here." Lewis offered the radio-backpack, which he had taken off, to Strombo. "You take it, and I'll wait here."

"What's wrong with you?"

"Malaria. Please. Take it."

Strombo shook his head and accepted. Mullins and Strombo continued the climb together.

"What's up with Lewis?" Mullins asked, seeing the radio on Strombo's back.

"He said malaria."

"That's a crock. He's more skittish than a whore in church."

"He's scared shitless." Strombo said to Mullins, trudging forward. "What's he gonna do when this is all over, and he's back in the States? Christ, what if he runs into one of us?"

"He better not run into me."

"He's gonna have to live with that for the rest of his life," Strombo said, glancing back to see Lewis walking rapidly back to camp. "I'd laugh if it weren't so damn sad."

With every inch they climbed up the barbed rocks, the noises became more sporadic, and they soon waned into a dead silence as the platoon reached the summit.

The barren valley had been ravaged in a savage skirmish; a haze hovered above the smoking ground. Boulders, stumps, and leaves were pock-marked by bullets, every tree shattered, with palms seared and drooping.

Both sides had apparently pulled out in a hurry. No signs of life remained—only scattered helmets, weapons, and shell casings. Everywhere nothing but torn, blood-soaked clothing, bandages, and bodies. Ski looked around for Lewis, to radio Riseley. Spying the radio on Strombo's back, he motioned for him.

"Where's Lewis?"

"Heading back to camp. He said he's got malaria but if you ask me…"

"Enough," Ski snapped, uncharacteristically. "Turn around." Strombo complied. After radioing Riseley, Ski approached Knuppel.

"Take two squads down into the valley and reconnoiter. And when we get back to camp, remind me to talk to Doc Webber about Lewis."

"What about Lewis?"

"Malaria."

Knuppel rolled his eyes. He gathered two squads and cautiously maneuvered the men over the simmering earth. The caustic air made it a struggle to breathe.

Seeing any dead Marine was always a sickening blow. When passing a dead comrade, a Thief always paused, removed the poncho from the dead man's pack, and carefully covered his face to protect it from flies. The stiffening Japanese, however, were left to rot in the sun after their packs were picked clean.

From somewhere amid the charred debris, a faint cry of "corpsman" could be heard.

"Those bastards…" Leaving wounded buddies still alive in enemy territory angered Borawski. "Let's go," he said to Mullins and Strombo, unconcerned that it might be a Japanese trick. The pair searched through the rubble of broken bodies and found a badly injured Marine who had feigned death.

"Am I glad to see you guys." He attempted a smile despite the great pain of his injury. A 50mm shell had torn through his thigh, leaving a hole the size of a child's fist.

While Strombo, Mullins, and Borawski helped the injured Marine, applying sulfa powder and bandaging the wound with ripped strips of t-shirts, others continued searching the area.

Smotts, Kenny, and Tipton came upon a depression where the Japanese had bivouacked but had left in such haste that their combat packs lay strewn in heaps.

Japanese combat packs frequently contained maps, diaries, and other strategic information regarding enemy positions and troop strength. And each held something more valuable to a Marine—a "Good Luck Flag."

The Yosegaki Hinomaru, or Good Luck Flag, was a traditional and sacred gift given to Japanese soldiers leaving for war. Friends and relatives wrote messages of success and well wishes on a flag for the departing soldier to carry with him into battle. The flags were light, didn't take up much space, and became valuable souvenirs for front-line troops. Up to twenty could easily fit into a Marine's backpack and later be sold for a handsome profit. Rear echelon troops and Army Air Corps pilots paid as much as fifty dollars for one flag.

"Hobart, Red, these pickins are good," Smotts said as he opened his fourth pack and took his fourth flag.

Not even a three-day veteran, Tipton had already learned this drill. Each Marine took his share of the spoils, either for intelligence purposes or, if the items were light and easily carried, personal gain. Most packs had flags, and Smotts scavenged fourteen. Tipton claimed a decent share, and Kenny acquired five and a tantō, a small ornate officer's sword. He planned on sending it to his girl Eve back in the States as soon as possible.

The squads reassembled on the summit, but Borawski, Mullins, and Strombo—slowed by caring for the injured Marine—had not caught up. They had placed him on top of his poncho and were carrying him along.

Evans, Duley, and Arello with a Good Luck Flag. *Courtesy of Steve Evans*

Despite the pain from his leg being jostled, the Marine smiled. The "million-dollar wound" had bought him a ticket home. But the three had taken only a few steps when puffs of ash and debris began to erupt from the ground. An enemy sniper had come to life. The three quickened the pace, making the ride rougher for the injured man.

His smile disappeared. "You guys should make a run for it."

"Knock it off!" Borawski replied.

The bullets pecked away at their feet. Mullins knew that the low fire meant the sniper had to be on higher ground. He let go his hold on the poncho, bringing the group to a brief halt. Strombo and Borawski adjusted their grips and continued along purposefully, unconcerned. From the sound of the shot, Mullins spied the sniper on a cliff less than one hundred yards away. The barrel of a rifle protruded from a stump. A few seconds before he heard the shot, he saw the barrel jerk up.

"That sonofabitch," Mullins muttered to himself.

Besides the barrel, the only other thing visible to Mullins was one canvas-covered sandal sticking out from behind the stump. He took careful aim, gently squeezed the trigger as he exhaled, and hit the foot. The sniper immediately jumped and kept hopping up and down.

As the enemy sat on the stump and bent over to take off his sandal, Mullins slid the bolt, loaded another cartridge, and squeezed the trigger again. The second bullet went through the back of the sniper's head. The body somersaulted to the ground.

Once they had safely rejoined the platoon, four others relieved Strombo and Borawski and carried the thankful Marine the rest of the way. The Thieves returned to camp and sunk to the ground, drunk with fatigue. Smotts groaned as he began to unlace his boondockers to check his blistered feet.

"Ski, I'm supposed to remind you…" Knuppel was cut short by McLeod, who ordered the Scout-Snipers to rush to a small airstrip near Charan Kanoa in support of the Army.

Earlier that day, an Army outfit had advanced toward the airstrip, encountering minimal resistance. By mid-afternoon they had reached the runway and established a defensive perimeter. Almost immediately, thunk…whoosh…mortars rained from the sky. A Japanese unit encamped upon a ridge on the eastern side of the field unleashed a merciless barrage. Mortars and machine gun fire had driven the soldiers back.

"Old dead dog!" Ski yelled and took off running.

"Dammit." Smotts laced his boots back up, grabbed his pack, and tore down the hill after his lieutenant. The rest scrambled and ran like bats out of hell along the beach, then down a road toward the airfield. Ski and his platoon ran past the Army soldiers who had hastily retreated to the western high ground. On his right he observed the Japanese-held ridge. The Army's trucks, arms, and ammunition stood unprotected in the middle. The Japanese could easily recapture the airstrip and the Army's supplies. The Imperial Army held the upper hand, holding a dominant position and outnumbering his 40 Thieves, but Ski spotted an ace in the hole: there was only one road down to the runway.

The mortars and gunfire now targeted the Thieves, who were running, zig-zagging their way to the base of the ridge. Directly beneath the enemy, they were out of the line of fire. Ski ordered his men to take cover among the rocks and trees along either side of the road, and he put Mullins in charge of creating a roadblock.

Mullins hollered out for Moore, the BAR-man. Although still somewhat weak from his earlier bout with malaria, Moore considered his

Browning Automatic Rifle to be like a musical instrument; he would let no one else touch it.

They waited, ready to blast, delay, or destroy anyone or thing that might try to pass and retake the airstrip.

The noise of a truck rumbling down the road could be heard from above. The sound grew louder, and the vehicle burst into view, followed by soldiers on foot. Moore aimed for the tires while Mullins sprayed the cabin, turning the disabled truck into an effective roadblock. Japanese soldiers surged around both sides of the dead vehicle, but short bursts of bullets and red tracers drove them back.

The Japanese tried several times to retake the airstrip, but the Thieves repelled each attempt—until Marine reinforcements arrived, in the form of Hellcats and Corsairs. The snarling planes drove the Japanese from the ridge. More ground troops arrived, which secured the area.

Having cleared the airstrip of enemy resistance, the Marines gave the "all-clear" signal for the Army to move in.

Before leaving, Ski had his men take five.

As Strombo, Mullins, and McBride sat on the ground having a smoke, an Army captain walked over.

"How old are you guys?" the captain asked. "Maybe nineteen, eighteen?"

"Yeah," Strombo answered, "most of us."

"All volunteered I suppose," the captain continued to make conversation.

"We're Marines," McBride replied.

"My guys," the captain pointed over to his company, "were all draftees. They're in their late twenties, early thirties…most of them have families…kids," the captain paused. "You know, war seems like it's fun when you're nineteen or eighteen," the captain offered, somewhat embarrassed. "But when you get older, it doesn't seem like fun. A fella scares more easily. At least I know I do."

The Marines sat in silence.

"When you get older you just don't have the..." The captain cut himself short. "Well, wars are won by the young."

After a long pause Strombo finally replied, "Sad but true."

"I guess that's all I had to say. I'll let you boys get back to what you're doing." The Army captain returned to his unit.

If I were older, Mullins thought for a moment. If I were older, I don't know if I could be doin' what I'm doin'. I wonder how Ski does it?

Ski approached. "What was that all about?"

"That captain came over to give us a little pep talk," Strombo replied. "Well, let's move out. Old dead dog!"

•   •   •

While they had been away, Riseley had moved his headquarters further inland into a vacated Japanese command post between Charan Kanoa and Tipo Pale. The Thieves begrudgingly protected the perimeter that night, grabbed whatever rest possible, and wished that Howlin' Mad would come ashore.

There was no significant enemy activity that night.

As the Marines solidified their hold on Saipan, General Saitō's every effort to drive the American Devils back into the sea failed. The Japanese Army was in shambles, entire infantry battalions had been destroyed, only one tank company remained, with almost no artillery.

Saitō sent a dire message to Tokyo:

> Communications have been destroyed. I have three companies at my disposal; the whereabouts of other units are unknown. The enemy is gradually gaining ground under the support of fierce naval gunfire, bombing, and strafing. The southern half of the island is under enemy control. Our field headquarters has moved to the mountains 1,800 meters east of Garapan. The enemy is advancing from the south of Garapan and is rapidly closing in on us once again. Our Army is consolidating

for a showdown fight between Tapotchau and Tipo Pale. Secret documents were completely burned at 1830 yesterday.

Upon reading the communique, Foreign Minister Mamoru Shigemitsu observed, "Hell is on us."

CHAPTER NINETEEN

All the Devils Are Here

"...the Scout-Sniper boys spent more time behind the Jap lines than our own. They would sometimes get very angry because they were supposed to hold their fire until certain information had been sent to headquarters."

Commander Glenn English, U.S. Navy, Sixth Marines' Chief Surgeon, from an interview with Robert Sherrod

June 18, 1944
Saipan

The Thieves' wish came true. General Howlin' Mad Smith left the USS *Rocky Mount* late on the previous day and established his command post in Charan Kanoa. It was time for Ski to let his boys loose behind enemy lines. When he broke the news to his platoon, the energy level rose. The Marines were like a hungry football team released from the locker room.

First up, Evans. In the waning daylight, Ski referred to a well-creased map as he briefed Knuppel, Evans, Arello, Duley, Emerick, Orozco, Smotts, and Moore on that night's mission. The men listened intently as boot polish used to blacken faces and hands passed from one Marine to another, dog tags were taped, and sniper caps replaced steel helmets. Boondockers came off and sneakers went on, except on Moore's small feet.

"Riseley's orders are to remain silent and shoot only if necessary. This is what you boys trained for. Get to work." Ski stood back. "Old dead dog!" Armed with their array of knives, strangulation gear at the ready, and rifle safeties clicked on, the Thieves left camp.

They were given the password for the night, Lili Marlene, and passed the frontline sentries. Passwords always incorporated the letter L because of the difficulty the Japanese had pronouncing it.

Silently the Thieves moved through the dark of night, skirting the western edge of Tipo Pale. The pale moon was periodically obscured by passing clouds. Smotts, ahead of the rest on point, listened to the jungle sounds—trying to discern between animal and enemy movements—and inhaled deeply.

Following a Japanese trail marked by phosphorous notchings on trees, Smotts was brought to a dead stop by a rustling on the ground. He waited. It grew near. His heart raced as he slowly slid his Ka-Bar from its sheath. A figure gradually emerged from the rustling foliage, and Smotts smiled with relief. The twenty-pound rat crossed the trail and scampered off into silence.

Hours passed before Smotts came to another abrupt halt. Turning to the men behind him, he gave a nod that meant, "Those rascals are nearby." Now deep behind enemy lines, the Thieves moved with deliberation. Smotts tracked an ever-stronger scent that led him to a clearing with a number of buildings. Clouds began to thicken, eliminating the benefit of moonlight for observation. Creeping closer to get a better look, the Thieves crouched in a clump of brush as a light rain began to fall.

Two motorcycles and six or seven bicycles were parked near a building with a Rising Sun flag draped over the door. It had to be a command post. Knuppel motioned for his men to buddy up and signaled orders. Smotts and Moore tallied the personnel and equipment. Evans, Arello, Duley, and Emerick circled farther right to scout a plateau above a series of caves. Orozco, staying with Knuppel, gingerly unfolded his poncho, put it over himself, and lay flat on the ground. Turning on his flashlight, Orozco began to draw a map as Knuppel whispered coordinates and terrain features to him.

Orozco fumbled with his flashlight as he sketched. Knuppel swiftly adjusted the poncho to block the beam of light. The raindrops became fatter and more frequent as a Japanese officer left one of the buildings to patrol the area, walking along the periphery of the camp. He moved toward the shrubs that hid the Thieves.

Orozco and Knuppel lay still, not even breathing. The enemy soldier carried a long billy club on a string around his wrist. He twirled the night-stick like a baton as he walked.

The rain fell to the ground in a muted splash but made a slight plopping sound on Orozco's poncho.

Hearing the odd-sounding rain drops, the club-wielding soldier inched closer to the plopping and poked into the shrubs. Orozco lay motionless; Knuppel's hand slid over the hilt of his stiletto. The club prodded in and out near Knuppel's face, barely missing him. The next probe hit Orozco in the small of his back. Puzzled, the enemy soldier probed more roughly. Orozco yelped. Before the enemy soldier could yell out an alarm, Emerick bolted behind him and wrapped his Mafia necktie around the soldier's throat, brutally snapping him off his feet.

The Thieves had their fingers crossed that the pinging of the rain on the corrugated tin roofs of the buildings had muffled the flurry of activity. They waited for a response from the Japanese inside.

There was none.

Orozco finished the map under his poncho and slipped it in a plastic pouch along with other notes taken.

Emerick dragged the body into the shrubs and kept the billy club. The Thieves left, taking a different route back to camp.

Mud made it difficult to walk silently. The suck and squish of sixteen footfalls announced the plodding Thieves' passing. Yet they moved along unobserved until Smotts smelled the aroma of cooking rice. Through the darkness he spied a glimmer of fire and ten Japanese soldiers huddled over a pot.

Not thinking the American Devils could be so far behind the lines, one of the Japanese approached the Marines, assuming they were fellow members of the Imperial Army on patrol. He motioned for the Americans to join his group: "Konbanwa!"

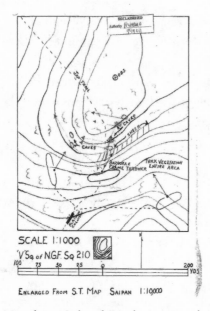

SCALE 1:1000

'V Sq of NGF. Sq 210

100 75 50 25 0   200
                                      YDS.

ENLARGED FROM S.T. MAP SAIPAN 1:10,000

Map from Colonel Riseley's journal.
National Archives

"What the hell should we do, Boss?" Evans asked.

"Wave." Knuppel said, and they did.

Other Japanese voices hollered greetings.

"Dah-mah-ray!" Knuppel yelled back.

"Whaddya say?" Evans whispered, as the group quickened their pace.

"I told them to keep quiet."

"Didn't work…"

The Japanese warily grabbed hold of machetes and fixed rifles with bayonets.

"Run!"

The Thieves fled down the muddy path and rounded a bend. Momentarily out of sight of the Japanese, Knuppel stopped abruptly and hid with Orozco and Smotts in the dense foliage on one side of the path; Evans and the rest took cover on the opposite. They waited.

The sound of the Japanese running through the mud grew closer until they passed and stopped.

A voice spoke in English. "Come on, guys. It's okay, we're Marines from Eighth."

The trick didn't work. Rooted in the mud, the Thieves were ready for the enemy. The Japanese gave up the chase but half-heartedly hacked at the undergrowth as they walked back to their dinner. The sound of the slashing machetes and jabbing rifles drew near.

One enemy soldier paused when his bayonet grazed something. It was Emerick's arm. His teeth clenched, Emerick swung his newly acquired billy club with all his might, crashing it into his enemy's skull. The dead man's peers acted quickly, but they were no match for the

Thieves and their Silent Killing skills. The fight lasted only seconds. The Imperial corpses were dragged into the ditch.

Miles away from their own lines, wet, tired, and hungry, Knuppel and his men backtracked to the enemy camp for a rice dinner. Their disappointment at finding the rice filled with maggots was soon replaced with joy at discovering a dry and well-provisioned cave.

After they gorged on tinned delicacies, each Marine took an hour's stint standing guard near the mouth of the cave. Smotts, still keyed up, took the first watch.

"The password," Knuppel told the Marines dozing off or still awake, "is Vernas Fingle."

"Vernas Fingle?" Smotts asked.

"She's a real high-stepper from back home." The answer came with a smile. "Orozco, you're up next."

After an hour, Smotts jostled his replacement, "Get up." Groggily, Orozco took his turn armed with a machete the Thieves had found in the cave. Crawling out into the night air to stretch his legs and rouse himself, Orozco walked a short distance away and didn't hear Moore come out to relieve himself. Hearing grunting and a heavy shoe kicking a stone behind a tree, Orozco whispered, "Password!" He approached the sound with the machete raised over his head.

Startled, with his pants around his ankles, Moore didn't respond.

The challenge came again. Hearing no "Vernas Fingle," Orozco brought the blade back behind his head to swing it down on the crouching figure. But as he swiftly lashed out, the machete became tangled in the tree's vines and fell out of his hands.

"Jesus! I forgot the damn password!" Moore whispered through clenched teeth. He picked up the machete.

"Who can forget Vernas Fingle?" Orozco said—as if in apology.

"Here." Moore handed the machete back. "Vernas Fingle...Vernas Fingle..." Moore kept repeating as he finished up.

The next morning, nearing the front lines, Moore told Knuppel, "That Vernas Fingle is a fickle little mistress." I better find some sneakers, he thought.

"Lili Marlene!" Knuppel called out to the American sentries. Making their way back to camp via a road near the shoreline, the Thieves saw several blown-out and abandoned coconut-log pillboxes facing the ocean. As they walked, planes appeared out of a cloud bank and zoomed overhead. Japanese Zeroes.

How in the hell did they get through, Knuppel wondered.

The Zeroes had not escaped detection. Hot on their tails were two Hellcats. The fighter planes came diving down on the enemy, and the Thieves had a front row seat at the dogfight.

Safe inside their own lines, the Thieves let out loud cheers, raucous applause, and gasps of amazement at every maneuver as the aerial show unfolded. USMC Hellcats trailed the Zeroes with wing machine guns blazing. One of the Zeros went down almost immediately to shouts of triumph from the audience. The two Hellcats then set their sights on the sole survivor. The Marines eagerly anticipated the next kill. The Zero made a steep dive with one Hellcat right on its tail. The Thieves cheered as the Hellcat let loose a hailstorm of bullets—until they noticed the slugs were heading toward them.

The Marines scattered for cover wherever they could. Knuppel quickly dove into one of the abandoned pillboxes. Down he plunged into the darkness, on his hands and knees. Immediately he realized his mistake. The pillbox was full of decomposed Japanese dead. Knuppel slid through the hellish mass of jelly-like sludge and bones, with the other Thieves right behind him.

"Back out!" Knuppel yelled. "Get the hell outta here. It's full of Jap slime!" They knew because they could smell it, but they were pinned down.

"We can't, Boss!" Evans said.

"Christ...I'm gonna lose it." Knuppel gagged, wallowing in the human sediment.

It seemed like an eternity, but the dogfight ended swiftly. The moment he could escape, Knuppel threw his gear in the sand and ran into the ocean. Furiously scrubbing himself and his clothes with sand, he tried to rid himself of the slime and stench.

After scouring his body and clothes, he believed himself clean and waded back to the shore. But the foul odor had permeated his clothes and pores. His comrades recoiled from him.

"This is sickening!" Knuppel tore the clothes from his body and raced back into the sea to scrub some more. The men exchanged glances, Orozco took off his T-shirt and attempted to clean Knuppel's slime- and sand-crusted gear. When Knuppel came back to the beach again, his beet-red body was raw with bloody scratches and scrapes from the vigorous scrubbing. Evans quietly offered him the rifle and bandolier that Orozco had cleaned.

"Here, Boss."

Without a word, the naked Knuppel slung his gear over his shoulder, and the march back to camp resumed. The sergeant led the way with his bandolier, rifle, and less modest "gun" on display.

CHAPTER TWENTY

Dark Eyes

"The hardest part of the whole damned thing was seeing all those poor natives.... We'd find 'em in caves. They'd been hiding for weeks, half-starved with no water. I saw children drinking their own urine from cups made out of leaves. It was a horrible thing."

—Roscoe Mullins

June 19, 1944
Sixth Marine Command Post, somewhere between Charan Kanoa and Mount Tipo Pale

During the walk back, Knuppel covered himself with clothing acquired from cleaner, fresher enemy corpses the Marines passed along their way. Entering camp, he broke away from Evans for a three-helmet Navy bath with real soap. Evans presented the gathered intelligence to Ski, and before Knuppel had finished lathering, Ski delivered the information directly to Riseley and McLeod.

The Thieves had done their reconnaissance well. Within hours of McLeod's relaying the coordinates to the Navy, a massive artillery barrage was laid upon the enemy encampment. It was eliminated, and more precious ground was gained along the western coast, unopposed. Saipan's capital city of Garapan was now within sight.

Both warring generals were disappointed. The three-day siege that Howlin' Mad Smith had anticipated was grinding into its fifth day, with less than half the island won; and Saitō's men had failed to drive the devils back into the sea. However, the Imperial Army still had control of the twin peaks of Tipo Pale and Tapotchau. What remained of the Japanese garrison stood determined to make the battle as costly as humanly possible.

In communication with the Navy, McLeod learned that most of the American Fleet had sailed from Saipan, leaving only a handful of old battleships and cruisers to protect the island's invasion force. The bulk of the U.S. armada was pursuing the Imperial Navy, which was steaming toward the Marianas en masse from the Philippines. More Japanese troops and firepower were on their way to save Saipan, Hirohito's Treasure.

Anticipating that General Saitō would seize the opportunity, Riseley gave condition code "Black" and braced to fend off the threatened invasion: besides the enemy fleet on its way, closer reinforcements from nearby garrisons on Tinian and Guam could evade the U.S. Navy and land on Saipan. It wasn't a question of "if" but "when." The Thieves received orders to head back to camp, dig in, and stand guard over the command post.

"The Old Gent just made his first mistake," Smotts said to Kenny as they dug a nice comfortable foxhole.

"Dirt never felt so good," Kenny answered in anticipation of a good night's sleep.

After ninety hours of little or no sleep, the foxholes dotted around the perimeter of the camp seemed as luxurious to the Thieves as Pullman roomettes. They paired up and climbed into their earthen suites. As one man rested on a bunk of dirt, curled up on his poncho and tucked into mosquito netting, his partner was supposed to remain awake on guard. But periodically all fell sound asleep.

Riseley awoke before daybreak the next morning and took his kit bag to his usual spot under a tree for his morning shave. As he looked down into the water in his helmet, he saw a reflection of someone above him in the tree.

"Ski!" Riseley squawked, face in a lather, rushing back into his tent.

Hurrying over, the lieutenant was greeted by the irate colonel wiping the shaving cream from his face and motioning to the tree.

Looking up, Ski saw an unarmed Korean slave wearing nothing but a pair of shorts and a paper-thin shirt.

Maurice Mehlin with the Korean slave. *Courtesy of Bill Knuppel*

"Shimpie shee-nigh-day....Eee-so-gay" Ski ordered the Korean.

The Korean replied in broken English that he wasn't afraid and hurried down.

Offering him a drink of water, Ski probed the unwelcome visitor for information.

The Korean pointed to the north and recounted how he had escaped from a Japanese work detail. He had been taken from his home in Korea years ago and had been on Saipan for only a few months. Hiding in caves and traveling by night, he had made his way to the Marines, walking by the entire platoon while they slept. Sitting beneath the tree, he had become frightened and climbed the tree before sunrise. Upon being shown a map of the island, he pointed out where he had spotted and eluded Imperial troops along the way.

Riseley was glad to have the information, but not pleased that the Thieves had let the Korean get so close to his command post. "Ski, you're damn lucky that wasn't a Jap. From now on you make damn sure your platoon has my camp secured."

The Thieves set up trip wires around their foxholes and the perimeter of the command post. They tied thin wire onto brush, stretched it across trails, and attached it to grenades whose caps had been unscrewed. That way they wouldn't explode. Instead, they'd make a popping sound like a firecracker. The whole camp was encircled with the early warning system. If anybody tripped the wire, no one would get hurt, but the popping noise would act as an alarm indicating that there had been an infiltration.

There would be no more infiltrations.

Day and night squads of Thieves roamed around Saipan wreaking havoc in, around, and mostly behind enemy lines. They kept themselves busy killing sentries, blowing up ammunition dumps, and mapping enemy emplacements. They didn't spend the day where they worked during the night, and they never came back the same way they went out.

During the day the sun bore down on their backs, and at night they wished for more clothes than the salt-stained rags they called uniforms. Ascending the heights of mountains or descending the valleys' depths, Ski's 40 Thieves silently hunted, searched, and destroyed, becoming a terror to the Imperial Army. Evans no longer worried about being disgraced by his Southeast High buddies, Arello and Duley, who were doing a good job to keep their bet competitive.

With no battle immediately before them, Riseley gave his Thieves the order of the day: scout the bypassed cliffs and caves in search of either the enemy or the native Chamorros. If the enemy, do what came naturally—destroy them. If Chamorros, the Marines would have the more difficult task of trying to persuade the natives to surrender.

Persuasion would be difficult. The Chamorros had been saturated with Japanese propaganda claiming that the Marines would be brutally cruel—that falling into American hands would mean torture and murdered babies. Many might choose suicide over surrender.

Scouting the caves proved to be a rugged proposition. Starved, sick, and frightened Chamorros could be hiding in the darkness, alone and unwilling to come out. Or enemy soldiers using civilians as human shields and waiting to pounce. Or there could be nothing at all. There was only one way to find out. Someone had to walk inside.

Dyer led a squad to scout the caves. Walking through a rock canyon with sheer walls seven feet high on both sides, the men were spaced in ten-yard intervals. Causey brought up the rear, scanning the tops of the walls, thinking that the Thieves might be sitting ducks. He spotted a grenade coming from above.

"Hit the deck!" Causey yelled, and the men dropped.

The grenade landed far in front of Dyer and blew up with a tiny "pop", sending sand and hundreds of fragments sailing through the air. Even if the explosion itself caused no damage, the shrapnel could be devastating. But thanks to Causey's warning, no one was injured.

The Marines assumed defensive positions along the base of the canyon walls.

"Let's go!" McBride urged.

"There was probably just one of 'em," Dyer stated, "or we'd have gotten it worse. He's long gone by now."

The Thieves continued their march, passing a village of crude huts virtually untouched by the war and eerily without any sign of life, save for a puppy that followed Causey. Soon the Marines discovered why the village was lifeless. Dozens of Chamorros swung back and forth in the breeze, hanged by the neck. Other natives lay strewn on the ground with their throats cut—men, women, and children still in their mothers' arms.

If the propaganda hadn't succeeded in convincing the natives to take their own lives, the Japanese took on the job.

Near the village a series of caves pocked a ridge, accessible by a narrow trail. The squad split up, with Dyer's group proceeding past the first series of caves while Mullins and four others remained at the nearest cavern.

"Shimpie shee-nigh-day!" Dyer yelled inside.

Faint rustling sounds put the men on edge, rifles readied.

"Day tay-koy!" He continued. "Me-zoo ya tay-bay-mo-no oh ah-gay-mah-show!"

They waited to see if the pigeon Japanese for "Don't be afraid!" "Come out!" and "We have food and water!" had been understood.

Slowly a figure emerged from the darkness. A shape neared the light at the mouth of the cave. A skeletal woman appeared, then quickly disappeared.

"She's scared of the rifles. Lower them." Dyer ordered. "Shimpie shee-nigh-day," he assured the woman as she re-emerged. A crucifix could be seen through her clothing, which was little more than rags. Both she and the child she carried appeared as flesh-covered bones, filthy, and full of sores. She stared numbly at the Marines. Dyer made a move to help the woman by taking her baby. She screamed, yelled many things not written on the Combat Phrases card that Dyer awkwardly held in his hand, and ran back into the cave.

"Shimpie shee-nigh-day!" Dyer tossed in a canteen and once again reassured the woman, "Don't be afraid." Sounds of much agitated movement inside the darkness culminated in the woman's reappearance—with five or six others trailing in the shadows behind her. Dyer's men wanted to raise their rifles, but he motioned for them to keep them down. The woman pointed to Dyer's Ka-Bar and then at her baby.

Dyer understood. "Boo-kee nah-shee nee koy," he patted his chest, indicating that he came unarmed, giving his Ka-Bar and weapons to McBride behind him. The tiny woman looked up at the smiling Dyer and gently offered her child to him.

The woman motioned to others in the cave, and more squinting Chamorros cautiously came out into the sunlight. They were so weak that they stumbled out barely able to carry crying children. Emerging from their hiding places in caves with no water or food, they were malnourished, threadbare, and in dire need of medical attention.

Mullins helped a naked mother and her two young children out of the cave. He gave her his blanket as clothing. While getting the blanket out of his gear, he remembered he had some hard candy. Mullins took two of the sweets and motioned that the children should eat them. They looked apprehensively at their mother, who nodded her approval. Their young eyes lit up at the juicy sweetness. Mullins gave away all his candy. "If this isn't the most pitiful detail," he said quietly to Causey, who picked up the tagalong puppy and handed it to a little girl.

Dyer looked into the dark eyes of the little baby smiling at him, not even noticing its foul smell. He took off his shirt to wrap the infant. For

A Marine helping Chamorros. *Courtesy of the United States Marine Corps*

a few minutes the hardened Marine's heart broke to see what the war had done to these innocent people.

Dyer cut a most impressive figure as he led his squad on the road to Charan Kanoa—bare from the waist up, a Browning Automatic Rifle over his shoulder, a pistol in a shoulder holster around his chest, and a child in each arm.

All told, the Thieves gathered over a dozen women, children, and elderly men. Each Marine carried a child as they made their way to the sugar mill at Charan Kanoa. Corpsmen had turned the sugar mill into a makeshift hospital for the wounded. Next to the hospital, a stockade had been built to house the Chamorros and other civilians.

•   •   •

That afternoon, Ski planned on finding Doc Webber to see what could be done about Lewis, but work once again got in the way. More

Chamorros at the Stockade at Charan Kanoa. *Courtesy of Roscoe Mullins*

caves needed to be scouted, more Chamorros moved to safety, more pockets of resistance eliminated.

The push along the coast was progressing well, but the enemy emplacements on Tipo Pale and Tapotchau ground the Marines to a halt.

"Ski!" McLeod called.

The Third Battalion had been getting hit hard by Japanese mortars, absorbing several direct hits.

"Take care of it," was McLeod's terse order.

Ski led Moore, Smotts, Kenny, Hebel, and Jackson through the jungle to report to Major John Rentsch, who had assumed command of the Third Battalion after the commanding colonel had been injured on the day of the landing.

Relieved to see the Scout-Snipers, Rentsch brought Ski up to speed. "It's quiet right now, but about an hour ago, mortars fell like they had eyes. There must be a spotter nearb…"

Rentsch's words were cut short by a whistling, the volume increasing at a feverish pitch. Instead of scattering like the others, Ski and his men looked up to locate the sound. The whistle abruptly terminated in a whoosh, then a clunk.

A 90mm mortar shell had broken through the canopy of dense foliage and landed ten feet from Smotts. He stared at the shell on the ground, amazed that it hadn't gone off. Falling through the dense foliage, the mortar hadn't hit the ground on its point, but landed flat on its side. It hadn't exploded right away, but the men were afraid it could be on a timer. After waiting a few minutes, Smotts disassembled the shell.

"From the way the branches are broken," Ski told Moore, "it looks like it came in low from that direction." He motioned to the north and east.

"Could be out a mile or two," Moore replied.

"I'm gonna find that spotter," he told Moore. "You take the boys and locate the mortar. Old dead dog."

Moore left, bringing up the rear, with Smotts on point.

Smotts hobbled slowly. Days of wet socks had brought on a bad case of trench foot. Maneuvering through the dense jungle, he knew what to expect. The unexpected. Twenty yards ahead of the rest, he inhaled deeply, limping with his bayonet fixed in front of his eyes to help cut through the foliage.

He moved silently, listening and sniffing for a distinct odor.

Nothing. But then Zing! Zing! Zing!

Three silent shots of searing pain in the back of his head sent Smotts crumbling to his knees. It's the end of the line, he thought.

Kenny was the first to reach Smotts, whom he found on the ground. Kenny whispered "What?" and shooed away a swarm of hornets.

Smotts was puzzled that he could still be alive after taking three bullets to the head. Feeling for blood, he found three welts instead. In the dark shadowy jungle he had accidentally sliced open a hornet's nest with his bayonet. Never having been shot before, he imagined that the stinging sensation was what it might feel like.

His nerves frayed, Smotts laughed crazily as the rest caught up.

"Quiet!" Moore whispered, and Smotts immediately obeyed.

"Christ," Kenny worried under his breath. "He's off his nut."

"What's wrong?" Moore whispered again.

"I'm good," Smotts assured. "I just got bit. A hornet's sting never felt so good."

Back on his feet, Smotts picked up on the odor he'd been tracking. It grew steadily, leading to the mortar position. The Japanese fled in a hurry, leaving the mortar and shells behind. Smotts disassembled the shells while Hebel, Kenny, and Jackson destroyed the mortars.

●   ●   ●

The next day brought an unexpected visit from Doc Webber. "Personal hygiene check," he called it. Watching Smotts limping, Doc called him over. "Sit down," he ordered.

Removing moist boots, Doc gingerly peeled away what was left of the disintegrating socks, revealing mottled red feet covered in green mold. Smotts winced as Doc cleaned his feet with an antiseptic, patted them dry, and doused them with foot powder. Rummaging in his own pack, Doc handed Smotts a pair of new socks.

"Put these on. And make sure your boots dry out."

Doc examined the rest of the men for jungle-rotted feet, issued halazone tablets for dysentery, and rationed Atabrine for the Guadalcanal veterans. When Ski's turn came, two of the Salty Sons managed to catch up.

"Seen Dulcich?"

"Haven't seen Joe." Doc replied, "but I know he's all right. Did you hear about Edwards?"

"What about the Skipper?"

"Killed by our own Navy. Yesterday. Reconnaissance planes mistook a fire at his headquarters as a marking signal and dropped a five-hundred-pound bomb on it." Doc, lancing a boil, avoided eye contact with his friend. "Dozens killed. All the command staff. More wounded. Lucky for Joe he was on patrol when it happened. He's the only officer left, so he's running L Company now. It's Joe's show with a handful of NCOs and a bunch of privates."

The news about Edwards made Ski forget about Lewis.

●   ●   ●

With an important pivoting movement to the north accomplished, General Holland Smith ordered that June 21, the sixth day after the landing, be spent reorganizing, resupplying, patrolling, and mopping up. The push would resume the following day.

At 1700 McLeod relayed good news to the men at the command post. "No more Code Black. We just received word our fleet's on their way back. It barely took two days. Our Navy routed them," he beamed. "The Japs turned tail for Okinawa. Our pilots are calling it a 'Turkey Shoot.'"

McLeod then directed Ski and Knuppel to the command tent. Inside, they stood amid the regimental officers. The gathering was quiet.

"Tomorrow," Risely began, "we're going to begin the push into the valley between Tipo Pale and Tapotchau." From the command post both Ski and Knuppel had noted enemy movement and activity in the rocks, trees, and dense brush below.

Riseley gave the directives to all the battalion COs while McLeod referenced maps. The Thieves' brain trust stood and listened. "What's your take on it, Ski?" Riseley asked.

"Well, Jim, that's pretty heavy brush country down there. No doubt the Japs have machine guns covering the whole area. One way or another, we'll get the job done, but it might be a good idea to lay down a half hour of phosphorus shelling before our troops move in. They'll have an easier job of cleaning it out if we got rid of some of the vegetation... and maybe we'd burn some of them out as part of the bargain."

The request was briefly discussed among the brass. "We'll look into that," Riseley said. "In the meantime, gentlemen, get your men ready. Dismissed."

Once outside, Knuppel wiped the sweat off his brow with his sleeve. "You know, Ski, I think you know a hell of a lot more than some of those colonels in there."

"I don't know about that," Ski shrugged and then stopped Knuppel. "You okay, Bill?"

"Sure. Top notch," Knuppel smiled. "It's just hot as hell…sweatin' like a fiend."

Ski nodded. "Tell the men to be ready at dawn." He and Knuppel walked off.

Vic Kalman, a Marine correspondent, had recently arrived at the Sixth command post and made it his base of operation. A reporter for *Leatherneck Magazine,* Kalman needed to be in the thick of the action, and he'd heard that the 40 Thieves were in the thick of it.

As the sun disappeared into the coconut trees, Evans, Arello, and Duley walked into camp. They had been out hunting. Not for the Imperial Army, but any food better than C-Rations. The three carried over a dozen chickens and some vegetation they had foraged.

"Dinner." Evans beamed.

"I thought you weren't supposed to touch any domesticated animals," Kalman remarked.

"Domesticated?" Duley feigned shock.

"These are wild," Evans quipped. "Hey, Boss," he asked Knuppel, "how do ya think we should cook these things?"

"We've still got time for a fire. Let's boil them in our helmets…maybe put in some papaya and coconut milk.

The chicken was ready to eat at dusk with plenty for every one of the Thieves—Kalman, McLeod, and Riseley too. Knuppel tried to eat, but his stomach didn't feel right. Evans took some of the chicken to Riseley, who was about to inquire about its acquisition but after tasting it simply asked, "Who's Betty Crocker?"

The tender and juicy chicken had a hint of pepperiness that nicely countered the sweet of the coconut and papaya.

"This is almost, remind you almost, as good as my mom's chicken paprikash," Ski gave Evans his highest compliment.

With every morsel of meat and drop of broth devoured, full-blooded belches signaled resounding approval. Fires were kicked out. Once the sun set on Saipan, darkness ruled the night; Japanese bombers might visit, and any fire became a target beacon. The 40 Thieves sat in a circle in the dark, resting against trees and enjoying an after-dinner smoke. Stomachs were full; they relaxed.

Kalman chatted with the men. Some, like Emerick, enjoyed the stage and blew smoke, laying it on thick.

"...there's only one way to find out," I says. "So I started up to this ridge, dontcha know, filled with Japs. Japs all over the place. 'Come back! Come back!' my squad leader was yellin' at me but I pretended not to hear."

The guys around Emerick poked at the ground with sticks, looking down to hide their smiles.

"Just as I get to the ridge, a machine gun opens up on me, and I hit the deck."

Kalman wrote feverishly, doing his best to keep up with Emerick.

"I'm pinned down, dontcha know. I stick my head up and peck-peck-peck the bullets whiz by. This goes on for, I dunno, it seemed like hours. Finally, I says to myself, 'What the hell, I didn't come here to live forever.' I stand straight up with those bullets flying past me and I throw a grenade and BAM, I blew them Japs to smithereens. Ya know, they named that ridge after me. I'll spell my name for ya. It's E..... ."

Kalman eventually got around to Evans, who was standing against a tree. In response to a question from the reporter, the big Jayhawk offered "We've got the best fighting outfit in the world. But Marines aren't supermen, excluding maybe Emerick over there. We've been lucky so far, all of us. Tomorrow, we may not be so lucky."

Elsewhere, the night was quiet.

CHAPTER TWENTY-ONE

Evans, Arello, and Johnson

*"In my mind's eye, I can see it as though
it happened yesterday."*

—Bob Smotts

June 22, 1944
Foothills of Mount Tipo Pale

The morning began with Colonel Riseley's denial of Ski's request for a phosphorus shelling. McLeod delivered the news, not in the typical brusque manner of an XO. He agreed with Ski, but they'd do without.

The red morning sky backlit the foreboding pitch-black peaks of Tipo Pale and the rocky hills that formed the island's jagged backbone.

Ski summoned Knuppel, who reported pale, with teeth chattering.

"Jesus, Bill," Ski remarked, "you look like hell."

"You're no Van Heflin yourself," Knuppel quipped weakly. He shook in his sweat soaked dungarees. "I just got bit again. I'll be fine."

"Go down to Charan Kanoa and let Doc check you out,"

"If we're gonna make the push today, I wanna do my share of the pushing." Knuppel argued.

"Bill, you're in no condition…" Ski paused.

"Condition?" Knuppel managed a laugh. "You make it sound like I'm pregnant."

"Well, you're not showing as much as that usherette, but report to the hospital anyway," Ski told him. "And if it's a boy, name it after me—now that's an order."

"What did the brass say about the phosphorus shelling?" Knuppel asked, before leaving.

"No dice."

Ski left to join his men and brief his corporals. Schieber asked if Lewis was to be included and received the terse response of "Yes."

At 0600, the push for the mountain began.

Throughout the morning Marine line troops methodically progressed toward Tipo Pale, bypassing pockets of stiff resistance. While the 40 Thieves tackled the dangerous job of cleaning out those problem areas, K Company led the push toward Tipo Pale. Moving slowly on a path that snaked its way along the base of the mountain, K Company aimed to reach the summit via the southeastern slopes.

Around 1000, K Company entered a small finger-like ravine infested with well-concealed enemy riflemen and machine gunners, on the hill's lower approaches. A firefight ensued. Within an instant the company captain and executive officer were wounded and two platoon leaders killed.

It was a bloodbath.

Marines fell in rapid, machine-gun-like succession. Quickly two-thirds of K Company lay contorted on the ground, dead or wounded. Burbeth Whipple, the last officer standing, assumed command. Faced with fierce opposition, Whipple fell back out of harm's way and radioed for the evacuation of the wounded.

Whipple received Riseley's response: trucks were on their way, and Whipple was to take what was left of K Company, veer to the left of the Japanese, and continue the push toward the summit of Tipo Pale, along the northwest side.

Riseley ordered the Scout-Snipers to wipe out the resistance that had ravaged K Company.

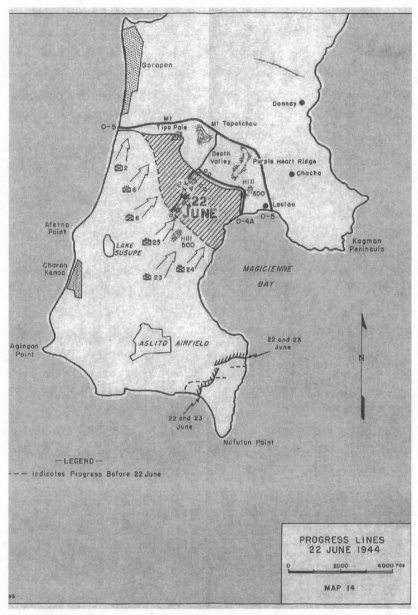

The state of the battle for Saipan on June 22, 1944, seven days after the American landing. *From* Saipan: The Beginning of the End, *written by Major Carl Hoffman for the Marine Corps*

"Old dead dog!" Ski gathered his men.

At 1232, Smotts led his platoon up a narrow, winding dirt road that led to the ravine where K Company had been decimated. Twenty yards ahead of the main body of the Thieves, Smotts hobbled along silently on feet still tender despite the dry socks and foot powder. He listened for the sound of a bolt being drawn back, looked for a glint of metal in the tangled roots of a banyan tree, and took deep breaths of the thick, stagnant air.

The platoon moved along in synchrony. Four squads spread out, with Smotts on point twenty yards ahead of Evans's group. Valenciano brought up the rear. Evans's squad was followed by the next squad in the same formation fifty yards behind, then the next, and the next, in varying intervals. Moving in this fashion, they would avoid massing in large groups, so that if hell broke loose, they would avoid decimation, unlike K Company.

Every man had heard what happened, and was aware what could happen to them, miles ahead of the front lines in a box canyon jungle. Doing the dirtiest and most dangerous work, they had been lucky so far, but the third time—or even the second—could be their charm.

Not very far in, Smotts paused. He had been catching a faint scent off and on for a few hundred feet. Then he smelled it more distinctly—and spotted someone darting inside a cave. He crouched until the rest of his squad caught up. Smotts briefed Evans, and Evans sent Valenciano back to alert Ski and the rest of the platoon, then motioned for Smotts, Arello and Duley to move to the opposite side of the cave.

Evans boldly walked over, called inside, "Day-tay koy!" and waited.

No one came out.

"Tay oh ah-gay-ro!"

Evans motioned for Johnson and Jackson to go inside. Johnson crawled on his stomach while Jackson pressed tight against the cave wall. Minutes passed without the sound of even one shot. Johnson and Jackson found two wounded Japanese soldiers, a captain and a sergeant. Johnson kept his sights on them while Jackson hastily searched the underground chamber for others, and for booby traps.

"All clear!" Jackson called. Evans went in while the rest of his squad stood guard.

By the time the other squads arrived, Evans had the enemy soldiers outside. Johnson and Jackson were conducting a more thorough search. Ski ordered Dyer to keep his squad a short distance behind. Arello and Duley remained forward to protect the point with Smotts.

"Oh-kah-kay!" Ski ordered the prisoners. They did not comply

"He said, sit down." Evans pushed the Japanese sergeant to the ground. The captain stood defiantly at first, but soon acquiesced. "They know damn well what we're saying, Boss."

A brief interrogation went nowhere. The two warriors sat with teeth clenched and heads bowed. The search of the cave also uncovered nothing of importance.

Thinking that the Army intelligence officers back at camp might get something out of them, Ski asked for volunteers to escort the Japanese there.

Most wanted to kill the prisoners immediately. No one wanted to waste their time escorting the prisoners back to camp.

One member of Corporal Schieber's squad volunteered. "I'll do it," Lewis said quickly.

Dumbfounded, the platoon exchanged glances. Ski saw his men's unspoken commentary: "Who in the hell leaves now?" "Chickenshit." "Good riddance." "We're better off without him."

His men had grown to know their lieutenant as even-tempered and calm regardless of the situation. If an occasion arose where he did get angry, he'd grow quiet and simmer.

The lieutenant waited a minute and asked, "Are there any *other* volunteers?"

Nobody spoke. The men drew in the ground with bayonets, struggling to keep quiet. No one wanted to leave just before the going got tough; they wanted to be there for each other. Every one of them was prepared to sacrifice himself to save a buddy, but nobody was sure about Lewis. Everybody knew it would be best if he just went away. Ski knew it, too.

"All right, Lewis. Take them back to the CP." Ski turned to the prisoners, "Tah-tay."

They did not stand up. He ordered Evans and Johnson, "Get 'em up and strip 'em down."

"Rise and shine! And give God the glory." Johnson mimicked his lieutenant, breaking the tension of the moment and drawing half-smiles from his buddies. He grabbed the Japanese sergeant by the scruff of the neck and dragged him to his feet.

"Strip down." Evans said, not bothering to speak their language anymore. The captain did not comply until Evans prodded his shoulder with the barrel of his rifle. The Japanese officer stood up, went nose-to-nose with Evans, and made a sudden move. Evans did not flinch. The Japanese officer grinned and slowly stripped down. With their hands tied behind their backs, the prisoners marched off with Lewis behind.

"Don, let's keep up the push," Ski said. "Old dead dog."

For the rest, it was "Take fifteen" while they waited for Evans's squad to move out. Men sat on rocks or the ground and lit up while they waited. Yunker and Borawski sat next to each other, savoring a smoke, using a log as a backrest. Cigarette in mouth, Yunker reached back with both arms to stretch. Behind the log he felt a box. Turning around, he discovered a field telephone. He nudged Borawski.

"Ski!" Yunker called, picking up the telephone box and moving it onto their side of the log. Ski came over, took hold of the wire that led from the box, and started pulling. The wire led in the direction where Evans was headed.

"Don's walking into an ambush," Ski muttered, then barked, "Yunker! Catch up to Evans and have him pull back."

Ahead, Smotts pushed on, the rest of the squad trailing behind. Arello followed him at an interval of about thirty-five feet, Evans and Duley came next, then Johnson, Jackson, Orozco, and Emerick, with Valenciano bringing up the rear about twenty yards behind.

Smotts reached a small box canyon and paused before entering. The path had leveled off into an open area. To his right, the road fell off abruptly into a gully full of fifteen-foot-tall trees choked with kudzu vines. On the left, a sheer wall mottled with thick foliage and needled coral hemmed the other side. Every few feet, fissures had been cut into the gnarled walls. Looking into the barren, tranquil canyon, Smotts observed no signs of a skirmish and thought, this can't be where K caught it.

Normally the constant noise of gunfire and explosions could be heard from somewhere on the island at all hours of the day or night. Now only the wind rustled the leaves.

Smotts found the stillness odd.

His tired eyes walked the path he would soon take. He let the sling on his Springfield out all the way and switched the safety off. With the rifle on his hip ready to fire, and ears wide open, Smotts slowly moved forward into the canyon, methodically scanning the mottled face of the sheer wall.

He reached the other side and waited for the rest of his platoon to come into view. Silently he raised his left hand as a signal to proceed.

While some of his buddies tentatively entered the canyon at ten-yard intervals, Smotts slid into the shade of a fissure to escape the close, heavy heat and lit a cigarette. The cool smoke felt refreshing as he drew it deep into his lungs. Slipping out of the fissure to check on his squad mates' progress, he noticed an entire company of Japanese two hundred yards ahead on a ridge. He motioned to Evans, bringing the squad to a halt. As Evans signaled for his men to fall back, the foliage of the trees suddenly stopped rustling. Smotts's eyes darted toward the new quiet.

Quickly, he drew a deep breath—and that distinctive odor entered his lungs.

Before he could yell out a warning, sheets of bluish-white flame erupted from the walls of the box canyon.

Four woodpeckers had opened fire in unison.

The squad fell to the ground, lying motionless in the road. Smotts looked at the bodies and thought that no one could still be alive. He was cut off. Between him and the rest of his platoon lay his buddies strewn all over the path, and dozens of Japanese. It was the first time he had ever felt fear. The St. Vitus's dance claimed his hands; his heart raced.

Valenciano heard the fire and hurried onto the scene. He and Smotts couldn't see each other, but they shared the same thought: their squad had been wiped out. Valenciano stepped back to return to the main body of Marines, slipped along the side of the path and tumbled into the ravine below.

During a lull in the firing, Smotts bolted from the cut-out and fired three shots in rapid succession. Jumping off the path, he landed on tree-tops in the ravine. His shots distracted the gunners and allowed his buddies who had been playing possum to spring into action.

"Now!" Evans jumped to his feet, a grenade in each hand. Everyone fired, save for Arello who remained on the ground.

Evans reared back to throw. Instantly a burst of fire brought him to his knees as he hurled the first grenade. Before he could throw the second, all four machine guns peck-peck-pecked in unison at Evans. The incessant fire peppered his torso, and the second grenade feebly fell out of his hand. Evans crumbled, the bullets continuing to chew his body into a pile of blood, flesh, and rags.

Arello clawed at the dirt, trying to move, but the machine guns taunted the injured. The Japanese were keeping Arello alive as bait: shooting around him enabled them to slaughter any other Marine who might try to help. Orozco was the first. One 7.7mm slug in his right arm and another grazing his chest drove him back. Johnson was next. When his legs were shot out from under him, he became bait as well.

Ski heard the bursts of machine gun fire in the distance and ran toward the sound. His men followed. With the arrival of new prey, two other machine guns opened fire from behind. The entire platoon was trapped.

Of the injured, Arello was closest, lying face down near the ravine. Johnson lay sprawled farther away. During lulls in the gunfire, Arello could be heard feebly calling out, "Corpsman."

Mullins and Strombo exchanged glances.

"Let's go, Marvin." Mullins raced out as Strombo, a step behind, strafed the foliage with covering fire. A slug pierced Mullins's left arm but he grabbed Arello by the scruff of the neck with his good one and dragged him to safety.

Strombo cut off Arello's pack and rolled him over. His dungarees were soaked in a brush stroke of blood and caked dirt that extended from his left shoulder through his chest and down to his right groin.

"My Christ," Strombo muttered. Arello, partly conscious and disoriented by the pain, babbled words Strombo found difficult to understand.

"Is it bad?' Arello managed with great effort. Strombo did not answer as his Ka-Bar cut away Arello's shirt so he could inspect the wounds. He moistened a piece of the cloth with water from his canteen and gently cleaned Arello's face.

"Am I going to die?"

Strombo looked at Mullins, unsure as to how he should answer. "You're gonna be fine," Strombo lied. He thought the lie might give Arello some hope, that it might provide some bit of solace for him, not knowing how bad it was.

"Don...Norman..." Arello clutched hands filled with earth, hanging on to the last few moments of life.

"They're fine...and you're gonna be fine, too," Strombo began to dress Arello's wounds while others around him returned fire and threw grenades. He cut apart Arello's pants and emptied his canteen on the bullet holes that riddled his body. Intent on Arello, Strombo heard none of the hellish din that popped and pecked about him, he only heard the hissing and bubbling sounds of the sulfa powder hitting his buddy's wounds. Arello tensed, spasmed, and held tighter to the dirt in his hands. Then, letting go of the earth, he grasped Strombo's wrist and tried to say something. His eyes glassed over, and he looked directly at Strombo yet through him, as if he weren't there. Then the air went out of his body.

As Arello died, he experienced "Angel Lust," a term used to describe the erection men sometimes experience when dying traumatically. Ejaculation may even occur during the final death throes.

"Maybe dyin' ain't so bad after all," said Borawski.

"I guess we'll find out for ourselves soon enough." Strombo closed Arello's eyes, took the poncho from his buddy's pack, and covered his body to protect him from flies—flies that had already begun to swarm around what was left of Evans.

Ski organized a defense as the fierce firefight continued.

Still using Johnson as bait, the Japanese lured another victim. Lonnie Jackson ran out, carrying his rifle at port arms. There was a short burst of fire as he neared Johnson. The bullets hit their target, but they didn't make the dull thudding sound of lead penetrating flesh. Instead, there was a sound like a rapid chopping of a tree. Jackson scurried back to safety. Breathless, he sat down next to Yunker.

Yunker stared in amazement at Jackson, whose face was bloodied with fragments of wood stuck in him like a porcupine.

All eight bullets intended for Jackson had traversed his wooden rifle stock, chewing it to splinters. A ninth bullet had lodged down the barrel. Jackson was bloody from the wooden shrapnel, but not seriously harmed.

"You're one lucky sonofabitch. Hold still," Yunker picked at the wood fragments. "If I ever have a boy," Yunker wet a rag and dabbed off some blood, "I'm gonna name him Lonnie. Then he'll be born lucky."

Ski didn't have many options. If he could get some of his men on top of the ridge, they could destroy the Japanese from above. Three-man teams attempted to scale the sheer rock wall to no avail. A human pyramid fell short, with Moore crashing to the ground several times.

The hopeless situation ground into its second hour. Ammunition was running low, and Johnson still writhed helplessly while the four machine guns relentlessly pecked away. "Get it over with!" he yelled at the Japanese.

If a runner could get past the machine guns behind them, a mortar strike could be called in. Causey, the fastest, volunteered to make the dash. Ski noted their coordinates, sketched the enemy emplacements on a map, and gave it to Causey.

"Go!"

The Marines trained every rifle and grenade they had on the two enemy machine guns hemming them in, allowing Causey to race down the path. He appeared to have made it.

Now wait. Another hour passed.

Not knowing how long it would take for the mortars to arrive, or if Causey had even made it back, they waited.

Soon a faint whistling could be heard in the distance. It grew louder and louder.

"Hit the deck!" Ski yelled.

Causey had made it. Mortars rained down. Shells hit with accuracy, destroying the machine gun emplacements behind, allowing the platoon to retreat.

The Thieves took off running. Yunker made a dash to get Johnson lying on the path, but the Japanese turned him back. He was about to try again, but Johnson discouraged his buddy. "You gotta make it home to tell my mom!" His eyes burned into Yunker with the silent plea. Yunker knew what Johnson wanted him to do. They had voted on it back on Hawaii, not to leave a buddy behind alive to be taken prisoner. Yunker shouldered his rifle.

"Do it!" Johnson yelled.

Before Yunker could pull the trigger, he heard a voice behind him say, almost as if putting a child to sleep, "Sweet dreams…" and a shot rang out.

Yunker didn't turn to look and see who it was. He didn't want to know.

The four machine gunners concentrated fire upon Johnson, now that he was no longer bait. Yunker watched angrily as bullets decapitated his friend.

Ski had waited for Yunker, and the two ran hard down the path and joined the rest. On the trek back, the angry swirling talk was about revenge. They all knew that the two Japanese prisoners had set them up.

•   •   •

Having climbed down the kudzu vines, Smotts found himself alone. He could hear the Japanese hunting him. He crouched over and sought cover in caves or dense underbrush. The enemy poked into the brush with their bayonets, passing just a few feet from him. They called out to him in English that they were sent to rescue him.

Smotts drew upon the survival skills he had learned, concealing himself in a hastily constructed spider trap for what seemed like hours. The soldiers passed by him several times before giving up the search. When he thought it was safe, he stole his way down to a lower road that led back to camp. A short distance ahead, Smotts saw a figure limping along. He approached the man cautiously. The figure abruptly turned, ready to open fire.

Valenciano.

No two people were ever happier to see each other.

"You're a sight for sore eyes, Val." Smotts took Valenciano's arm around his shoulder to help him walk. "Ankle busted?"

"I think just twisted."

They hobbled in silence until Valenciano asked, "You see it?"

"I'll see it for the rest of my life"

•   •   •

Not wanting to be away for long, Knuppel had returned to camp from Charan Kanoa by 1600. The prescribed Atabrine lowered his temperature to one hundred degrees, low enough for him to discharge himself. Arriving to find Lewis already back, he approached him angrily. "What's the excuse this time, Lewis?"

"I brought back prisoners," Lewis replied.

The answer didn't sit well with Knuppel, who began a tirade that did not end until McLeod intervened.

At 1810 the battered and bloody Thieves straggled back, including Valenciano, leaning heavily on Smotts. The men disarmed wordlessly, refilled canteens from the Lister bag, and sank to the ground. Corpsmen hurried over to help the wounded. One bullet had gone through Orozco's arm, the other nicked his rib cage. Cleaned and bandaged, he was declared fit for duty. Valenciano's ankle was broken. He joined two more severely injured who were loaded onto jeeps and taken to the hospital in Charan Kanoa.

After a quick head count, Knuppel approached Ski. "Don?"

Leaning his M1 against a tree, the lieutenant replied, "Johnson and Arello, too... You missed one helluva party, Bill."

Schieber threw his pack to the ground angrily and sought out Lewis.

"It should have been you." All eyes watched as a shoving match, with Schieber doing most of the shoving, escalated. The men egged Schieber on. Ski hurried over.

"Enough!" He dragged Schieber off, then said to Lewis, "Go into Jim's tent, now!"

He had put out one fire, but another ember burst into a flame. The rest of the Thieves, in groups of three or four, spied the two Japanese prisoners sprawled on stretchers. Army intelligence NCOs were feeding them pineapple and canned peaches while politely questioning them. At the sight of the ravaged platoon, the enemy captain and sergeant exchanged glances and smiled like a pair of smirking cats at the Marines who happened to make eye contact with them.

One of the Thieves broke away from the others, nodding at them to watch. He sauntered toward the prisoners—M1 on his shoulder—and saluted a greeting to the Army NCOs.

The enemy captain's white teeth sneered at the approaching Thief. The sergeant whispered something in Japanese and laughed, taking a bite of pineapple.

Returning the prisoner's sneer, the Thief said "Pardon me," and moved past the NCOs. Calmly, he placed the barrel of his M1 to the captain's head and pulled the trigger. Then he shot the sergeant. One bullet each.

The Army interrogators were stunned. "What the hell?" one of them, spattered with blood, blurted out.

"They moved," another one of the Thieves replied. "Pity."

Duley walked over and stared down at the two shattered skulls. He thought about smashing them beyond recognition but stopped.

Once the shock wore off, the blood-spattered Army interrogators lashed out. "Someone's going to be court-martialed for this!" one of them threatened. "I'll see you all court-martialed!"

"Who's your commanding officer?" the other demanded. "I want to see your commanding officer right now."

Ski walked over and stood, his sunken eyes staring into theirs.

The Army NCOs barked out, "You're all going to Mare Island for this!"

After minutes of absorbing their tirade, Ski turned coldly away.

"Hey, you. Come back here! I'm not finished with you."

Ski approached two of his men, took their rifles, and walked back to the Army sergeants. Colonel Riseley watched from his tent.

"Come on. Let's go." Ski threw the rifles at them, they fell to the ground, and the Army NCOs awkwardly picked them up.

"I said, Let's go! Old dead dog! Right now!" he erupted. "You want to court-martial my boys? Come on, let's go!"

The two intelligence men fumbled with the rifles. "You can take a little walk in their shoes and then you can court-martial my boys when we get back. If you get back." The two didn't move as Ski walked away, "One of you can take the point, and be the last to die, and the other can bring up the rear, and be the first to die." He stopped, turned around and walked back to the immobile men.

"What's that?" Snatching the rifles away Ski asked. "Don't wanna die today?" He stood inches away, nose to nose. "All right, this is how it's gonna go. If you want to see the sun come up tomorrow and have a nice morning's sunrise, then you better use what little intelligence you have and forget all about this court-martial crap." He pointed to the dead prisoners. "My boys are worth more than that. So, go back in your tents and shut the hell up."

Ski saw Riseley watching, turn around, and go back into his tent.

The lieutenant regained his composure. "Get rid of your handiwork," he said to his men, then left.

Jesus, Knuppel thought, I've never seen Ski that mad.

Smotts kneeling over Evans (identified by Marvin Strombo). *Courtesy of Roscoe Mullins*

CHAPTER TWENTY-TWO

The Road to Garapan

"Harry: I give you my solemn word. THIS time it's
not dangerous.
Chester: Not dangerous?
Harry: No.
Chester: That's what you said when you had me wrestle
a gorilla. It's not dangerous?
Harry: All right, those guys mean business.
They're killers, murderers.
Chester: Besides that, they're unfriendly."

—Bing Crosby and Bob Hope, The Road to Hong Kong

June 23, 1944
Southern Slope of Mount Tipo Pale

The next day, an entire company from the Second Marine Regiment suffered dozens of casualties trying to flank the pocket of resistance. They withdrew as well. Riseley ordered the area to be bypassed.

Before leaving the hospital in Charan Kanoa, Knuppel had been given bits and pieces of mail for the Sixth. One letter with a return address from Kansas City caught his eye. The flap had opened, showing one page of paper covered in tidy, gentle handwriting. He pushed his own letters in a pocket and found a secluded spot to read the letter.

My Dear Donny,

The news from your way is encouraging, but we know casualties have been many. You may know we are anxiously awaiting word from you directly that you are safe. We really feel that you are, but we need assurances. It seems so terrible that we have to give up so many of our fine boys. All the news reels are running the first pictures of the invasion of Saipan, and last night we saw the landing barges loaded with Marines going in, and we know you were among them.

I am so glad Norman and Tom got to visit you. What did you mean saying "We might be together for some time?"

Dottie called and read me a letter which they had just received from a lady just outside of Honolulu, a sugar planta-tion owner's wife. She had entertained Hank and some other boys at her home for a Sunday nite supper. She wrote a grand letter. Mr. Harrington is better now and has gone back to work but must take extreme care of his health from now on.

How many of the boys we know are with you?

Remember we are pulling hard for you boys because we love you dearly.

Much love, Mother

As he read the letter, Knuppel heard his own mother's voice in the words of Evans's. It hit him. His buddy would never read this news from home. The reality stung. He folded the letter and tucked it back into the envelope to give to Ski.

With Arello killed in action, the secret of the two Army volunteers could not be kept from Colonel Riseley. Ski sought out his colonel and told him the entire story of how Evans's boyhood friends had become Scout-Snipers.

"They wanted to show Don they were just as good as Marines," he finished.

"Good men?" Riseley asked.

"Two damn good Marines," he replied.

"Well, we'll have to send Duley back to the Army."

"Understood. Changing to another topic—Lewis."

"Already transferred out." Riseley replied.

Duley prepared to leave the Marines and rejoin the Army's Division on Saipan. Assuming his temporary Thief might be punished, Ski wrote a letter for him to take back:

> Privates Norman Duley and Thomas Arello, U.S. Army and most recently U.S.M.C., have been on Saipan in combat with the Sixth Marine Regiment Scout-Sniper Platoon. It was a privilege working with them, they are two fine men. Privates Duley and Arello served with distinction and bravery with Thomas Arello giving his life in the line of duty. If disciplinary measures are being considered against Private Norman Duley for his being AWOL from his unit, I would highly recommend against it. He is a credit to the Army and the Marine Corps. Duley and Arello served their country with honor."

"This might help, if they try to jam you up." He handed the envelope to Duley and walked him to a waiting jeep.

Scuttlebutt spread from foxhole to foxhole. One by one the Thieves gathered to bid Duley farewell. Most shook hands, a few saluted.

"You know," Smotts said to Orozco, who was standing next to him. "I had no idea that rascal was a dogface? Did you know?"

"Nope," Orozco flashed his Ipana smile. "If they had more like him, we'd be outta this hell-hole by now."

The story of how two soldiers had deserted the Army to join the Marines had swept over the island before Duley reached the Army camp.

After Evans, Johnson, and Arello died, emotions ran hot among the Thieves. No repercussions arose out of shooting the prisoners or Ski's lecture to the Army intelligence NCOs. But Ski felt the need to call his diminished platoon together.

"There's going to be more killing and being killed ahead of us," he began. "So, we have to control our emotions. I have to. If I get pissed off and start to let my anger make decisions for me, like yesterday, I'm not an effective Marine. In the field, I'd be a dead one. I know it's hard, watching buddies get shot up, but you…we've got to keep our composure. More of us are going to die before this is over, so we've got to deal with it better.

"If you can keep your head," he paraphrased Rudyard Kipling in conclusion, "when all else are losing theirs, then you're more likely to keep your head. On your shoulders. Where it belongs…my sons."

It was back to work for the Thieves. Being reduced to only three squads meant even less rest. By the evening of day eight after the landing, the Sixth Marines had pushed to the top of Mount Tipo Pale and begun to reorganize and consolidate lines. Riseley moved his headquarters into a vacated Japanese command post on the northern face of the mountain.

For two days, June 24 to 25, Rentsch's Third Battalion once again had been butting heads with a pocket of Japanese resistance, this time on Tipo Pale's northern slopes. Communications with Rentsch had been severed, a nuisance that retarded the advance of the entire regiment and that of the entire division.

General Howlin' Mad Smith kept pressure on Riseley to step up the push. The colonel and McLeod, his XO, had a new strategy to deal with the problem area. A fresh battalion would pass through Rentsch's men, leaving one company to contain and mop up the area. The remainder, along with the Third, would then continue the push forward. McLeod volunteered to direct the process.

On June 24, nine days after the landing, Ski escorted McLeod down the slopes of Tipo Pale. From time to time they chatted about the old days—Iceland, New Zealand, Guadalcanal, Tarawa. They had been through it all together; McLeod was the officer who had recommended Ski for his Silver Star. Ski would never say it aloud, but in his opinion McLeod should have been commanding the Sixth. With no disrespect intended toward Riseley, he merely held McLeod in great esteem.

As the two approached Rentsch's position, the reason for the Third's struggles became apparent. The American force was trapped in a small gorge, with mortar rounds going up one side and down the other. Ski and McLeod could hear the whining shells—and also Japanese voices in the distance, taunting, "Die, Marine, die!" Artillery support for Rentsch's battalion was impossible because of the close proximity of Imperial troops. Forward progress had ground to a halt.

As the death toll mounted on Saipan, reinforcements had arrived to replace the casualties. Gung-ho and fresh-faced green boots sporting clean uniforms had poured in by the thousands—unseasoned lieutenants and privates alike, who didn't know any better and needed direction. With no time for tutorials or hand-holding, McLeod began to bark orders and directions as Ski walked back to camp. Rentsch's men responded instantly.

The next afternoon Dyer and his squad returned from an overnight mission behind enemy lines on Mount Tapotchau. Mullins proudly carried a large Japanese Naval telescope on a tripod.

"Came across an observation post on Tapotchau." Mullins smiled. "Looks like the Japs skedaddled 'n' left it behind. We thought the Old Gent and McLeod might like it."

"I'm sure they'll appreciate it," Ski accepted the gift and headed toward headquarters. Upon entering, he waited as Riseley consulted with another Marine, an officer by all appearances from the cleanliness of his uniform.

When their conversation hit a lull, Ski opened the legs of the tripod to present the gift. "My boys found this on Tapotchau and wanted to give it to you and McLeod."

Riseley accepted unsmilingly, then tipped his head toward the stranger. "Ski, this is Russel Lloyd, my new XO." Ski and Lloyd exchanged nods.

"Is McLeod staying with the Third?"

"Ken McLeod was killed yesterday." Riseley told Ski. "A sniper got him, one bullet. Out of all the men there, the Japs picked him off."

The Road to Garapan. *Courtesy of Bill Knuppel*

Ski took a moment to digest the news. "We've been getting in so many green replacements, some kid must've saluted or called him sir. He was a damn good man."

Nothing more needed to be said. One man died, and another took his place. Every Marine was expendable.

That night the Sixth Regiment's command post had moved farther down Tipo Pale, setting up camp near the road to Garapan. The good news of the day was that Mount Tapotchau had fallen after several days of bitter and costly battles. Marines now commanded the deadly twin peaks and could fight downhill.

The 40 Thieves had grown restless over days of uneventful mopping-up patrols and inactivity while they waited for the Third Battalion to make headway. Roscoe Mullins and Marvin Strombo, just a few miles south of Saipan's capital, could see the town's southern edge.

They settled down for evening C-Rations, shooing away big, fat flies. Periodically they'd experience a juicy crunch.

"Flying croutons," Mullins wisecracked.

Both buddies had become lean. Salt-hardened uniforms hung from hips and square shoulders on bronzed bodies. Strombo's curls had grown into a mop; Mullins's strawberry-blond hair was sun-bleached almost white.

"I don't know about you, Marvin, but I'm getting as jumpy as a fart on a griddle with all this sittin' around." Mullins blew a fly off and then gobbled down a forkful of food.

"Maybe we can talk Ski into a day trip tomorrow," Strombo suggested.

"Where?"

"Garapan." Strombo nodded to the city in the distance. "Listen Roscoe, we know we're not going to be the first into Paris or Berlin...probably not even Tokyo. So, let's be the first U.S. troops into Garapan."

The pair quickly polished off their tins of stew and sought out their lieutenant.

"Garapan? What for?" Ski puzzled.

"We've been sitting around for days." Strombo paused, then almost begged, "Don't we need to send out a patrol? Somebody's gotta reconnoiter Garapan."

"We're antsy," Mullins added.

"The Second Regiment's about a mile south of the city," Ski said. "That's in their sector. If their CO gives the green light, you can go."

The next morning, the trio walked along the beach. The sun climbed slowly in the clear blue sky, rising above the jagged hills to the east.

At their meeting with the Second Regiment's CO, Ski spoke convincingly about the value of sending a patrol in to scout Garapan.

The officer tried to talk them out of it. "Once you're there, we can't help you if you get into trouble. You're gonna be in no-man's land. If the Navy starts shelling or if the Japs begin an offensive, you're on your own. I won't risk my troops to get you out."

"We understand," Ski replied.

The CO reluctantly gave his okay, and Strombo's day trip was on. He and Mullins returned to camp and asked others to join them. Moore, who had recently received a field promotion to corporal, would lead. The three of them, plus Causey, Jackson, and Emerick, grabbed their gear, and the six left down the road to Garapan—Strombo bringing up the rear, with Causey ten yards in front of him.

Not long after they passed through the Second Regiment's lines, the Marines walked by a clump of dense growth on the beach side of the road. Something odd about it attracted Causey's eye. As he walked he turned his head, keeping an eye on the foliage. When Strombo reached it, sunshine fell upon gleaming metal. Causey saw a rifle barrel aimed at Strombo's back.

"Down!" Causey yelled and opened fire with his M1. In response a barrage of bullets spewed out from other hidden rifles. Jackson wheeled around. His Browning Automatic Rifle sprayed red tracers back and forth. One Japanese stood to throw a grenade, but Causey brought him down with a single shot.

Jackson's tracers hit another Japanese in the buttocks; he ran to the ocean and sat down in the salty water. Strombo took aim and exhaled as he squeezed the trigger. A bullet smashed into the man's skull.

The firefight lasted less than one minute but netted nine Japanese dead. One escaped, running as hard as he could, toward Garapan.

"I thought that was gonna be the last thing I ever did," Causey said rubbing his bullet-grazed ear while the other Marines searched the bodies for flags, diaries, and information.

"Swamp Rat, I owe you one," a grateful Strombo told Causey.

Encountering no other resistance, they reached Garapan's city limits. Ahead lay Saipan's capital; to their right, a field of over one hundred fresh corpses, victims of the unrelenting bombardment.

Amongst the Japanese dead, Strombo saw what appeared to be a small WWI cannon, similar to one he had seen somewhere back home in Montana. The object seemed to shimmer as the tropical heat rose from the ground. Strombo broke off from the group and carefully maneuvered through the corpses, keeping his eyes on the ground, in case any of the dead came to life.

When he approached the cannon, it vanished. His eyes had played a trick on him, but it had seemed so clear that it puzzled him when it wasn't there. In its place lay a dead Japanese captain, as peaceful as if he were sleeping. Something about the sleeping captain drew Strombo closer. Initially careful not to touch anything for fear of booby traps, he gazed at the placid face. No visible wounds, very little blood, Strombo guessed that he had been killed by a mortar strike.

Rummaging through the warrior's pack, he found many family photos: mother, father, and their children in a mountainous village strikingly similar to his home in Montana. Looking back at the face, he momentarily saw himself. He's no different from me, Strombo thought. Standing up to leave, he noticed the captain's Good Luck Flag peeking out of his uniform. Knowing the flag to be sacred to the Japanese, he decided against taking it, then reconsidered.

Kneeling at the dead captain's side he said, "If I don't take it, somebody else will." He removed the flag and tucked it into his dungarees. "I promise I'll give it back to your family someday." After unclipping the samurai sword from the officer's belt, he raced off to rejoin the rest.

Ahead of them, the capital city appeared devastated. Most buildings had been leveled. Amid the rubble and debris, the crushed bodies of soldiers, civilians, and animals lay strewn about, bloating in the heat of the sun.

"I thought somethin' might be left," Strombo said. "There's nothing here but a bunch of straw-covered huts."

"And a smell so bad it'd stink a dog off a gut wagon," Mullins added.

The group dispersed to scout the few buildings that still stood.

Moore came across a general store unscathed, although its bulk food and other mercantile goods lay scattered across the floor. An old-fashioned scale hung from the ceiling. Bolts of silk spilled from shelves. An officer dead by his own hand lay curled next to sacks of sugar. Moore searched the body, admiring the dead man's nice canvas sneakers.

A few nights before, on patrol with Dyer, Moore had almost gotten the group into trouble when his heavy field shoes clacked against a rock, alerting their prey. After a brief firefight, Dyer told him, "You'd better find yourself some sneakers, some place, before you get us all killed."

Garapan. *Courtesy of Roscoe Mullins*

Sneakers had been the diminutive Moore's chronic problem since the beginning. But the corpse's canvas shoes fit perfectly. Problem finally solved.

Mullins found his way into a bank. Half the building stood untouched, but the door to the safe had been blown open by the shelling. He stood, mouth agape, staring at stacks and stacks of paper yen.

I struck it rich filled his head. He set to work gathering his fortune. Emptying candy and other non-essential items out of his pack, he stuffed it with yen. When the pack was full, he stuffed bills into his shirt until buttons almost burst.

The Thieves lurked about Garapan for hours, not encountering any living enemy. They knew the Japanese were there, hiding beneath the rubble of corrugated metal, concealed in blown-out buildings but withholding their fire. Based on their experience, the Thieves assumed that the enemy believed them to be the vanguard of a much larger Marine force. Japanese rifles most likely had the Thieves in their sights with trigger fingers readied.

Mullins and Strombo rendezvoused about 1450. "Marvin…ever see the hair on the back of a dog's neck stand up?" Mullins asked.

"Yup," Strombo said. "I feel that way right now. We should get the hell out of here."

The six regrouped, laden with spoils, to begin their trek out of Garapan. They noticed two Japanese walking outside a building and crept out of sight.

Causey and Emerick unburdened themselves of their plunder and silently stole behind the two sentries. In unison, each cupped one hand over a sentry's mouth and sliced his throat open with a Ka-Bar held in the other. Gently, they lowered the bodies to the ground.

Emerick looked inside the building and waved for the rest to come over, "Looks like we won't have to walk home after all." He smiled. "It's a bicycle shop."

Everyone shopped for a bike except for the over-burdened Mullins, who lamented, "I'm carrying too damn much shit." He waddled behind the riders, feeling like Fatty Arbuckle in a silent movie.

From time to time the five rode in a figure eight, circling back to Mullins, his shirt bloated with yen, a Japanese helmet on top of his sniper cap, a sword on a belt slung over one shoulder, his own rifle and an Arisaka over the other, and tins of crabmeat and other edibles stuffed in his pockets. Strombo rode his bike alongside Causey who adroitly balanced several bottles of plum brandy. Moore carried several brightly colored kimonos he planned on sending home to his mom and sisters.

They had been gone just a few hours, but their return caused an uproar. Only Japanese rode bicycles, so as the Thieves pedaled toward Marine lines, rifles were leveled against them with triggers poised to be pulled.

"Don't shoot!" Causey yelled. "We're Marines!"

"What the hell?" the sentries laughed. "There's a bunch of Marines riding in on bikes!"

"Lamour, Lake, Lombard, Lamarr!" Strombo shouted any starlet's name that began with "L" to prove they weren't Japanese.

Knuppel ran to get Ski. "You gotta see this."

In peddled five of his Thieves on Japanese bicycles, laden like they'd been Christmas shopping at Macy's.

"Don't shoot!" Jackson joined in yelling. "We're Marines! Marines coming through!"

As they cycled in circles to allow Mullins, on foot, to catch up, it looked like a circus show.

"We're Hope and Crosby on the Road from Garapan!" Strombo chimed in.

Everybody started laughing, and one sentry asked loudly, "Hey! Which one of you daisies is Dorothy Lamour?"

"What a lash-up," Ski laughed with Knuppel.

"Ski! Catch!" Causey threw a bottle of plum brandy to his lieutenant as he rode past.

"Thanks for the day trip!" Mullins beamed. "Our report's in the bottle."

Their reconnaissance escapade became the talk of the camp. Correspondent Vic Kalman, present with notepad in hand, had his next article for *Leatherneck Magazine*. "Some of the craziest, fiercest, most lovable Marines on Saipan," Kalman wrote, "are in the Scout-Sniper platoon under the command of First Lieutenant Frank Tachovsky, twenty-nine, of New Brighton, Pennsylvania.

"Tachovsky's Terrors have wreaked havoc in, around, and mostly behind the enemy lines. They've killed numerous Japs and blown up ammunition dumps.

"But all their exploits are not recorded in the annals of the high command. And it is their 'unofficial' escapades which are becoming Marine Corps legends.

"Take the 'Garapan bike patrol,' for instance...."

CHAPTER TWENTY-THREE

Emerick

*"There's one man I remember in particular, and that's
Wild Bill Emerick. He looked a lot like William Bendix.
He was a character and one hell of a Marine."*

—*Bill Knuppel*

June 27, 1944
Northern Slopes of Tipo Pale

"Counting your nest egg, Mullins?"

Two corpsmen stopped next to the foxhole where Mullins was
giddily stacking and straightening his yen.

"Don't let your mouth run off before your brain's in gear. This is
gonna buy a whole lot more than a few Hershey bars and cigarettes."
Mullins kept his head down.

"Can I see one of those?" one of the corpsmen asked. An apprehensive Mullins offered him one bill. After examining it he said, "You
shouldn't be counting your chickens before they're hatched."

"Whaddaya mean?"

"Ever see Jap paper money before?"

"Nope."

"Hate to be the one to break it you," the other corpsman said, "but that stuff's only good in the latrine. That's military yen. Occupation money. It's worthless, unless you're a Jap."

Mullins's bubble burst.

"Sayonara, Rockefeller." The corpsmen walked away laughing. "You may get somethin' for it after all. Toilet paper's like gold around here. Guys might buy it for wipin' their asses!"

It had now been almost two weeks since the Marines had landed on Saipan. Two weeks of wearing the same clothes, night and day. Two weeks without a bath or any attention to hygiene and barely enough water to drink. Two weeks with little or no sleep while suffering through bouts of malaria and dysentery. Two weeks of C-Rations that left the men's tanned skin stretched tight across rib cages.

Two weeks of working behind enemy lines, constantly under fire, fighting an unrelenting enemy who would not surrender. More than one man wondered when and how it would ever end. The days were scorching hot; the evenings provided little relief. Hell continued.

"Ski!" Riseley called out. "Yesterday corpsmen out scouting for wounded came across some Japanese forward of our lines. It's pretty rugged country, and they're pretty well dug in on that ridge." He pointed to an elevation three hundred yards to the east toward Tapotchau. "Take care of it."

Due to attrition, Ski had to cobble together squads and teams as best he could for sending out on missions. Emerick was tagged to lead two teams onto the ridge.

"You're Marvin, right?" Emerick approached Strombo, who was sitting with Mullins. "Brother of that loudmouth from the Eighth?" Being from different squads, Strombo and Emerick didn't know each other very well.

"I'm Strombo," he corrected Emerick.

"Well, it's about time we worked together," Emerick said nicely— something that was unusual for the brusque club-fighter. "You guys wanna give it a go?"

Strombo and Mullins stood up and joined Emerick's other volunteers: Causey, Jackson, and Tipton. They set out for the ridge with Mullins leading the way. Strombo walked next to Emerick, followed by the others, with Causey bringing up the rear.

"Dontcha know I was in the Canadian Army before Pearl Harbor," Emerick broke the ice with Strombo. "After we got involved, I went AWOL—lock, stock, and rifle barrel. Hell, I thought if I'm gonna be fightin' I'll fight with the Marines. The first letter I got on the Canal wasn't from my wife, it was from the Canadian government. Asking me to return my rifle." He laughed and showed a letter he carried in his breast pocket to Strombo, "It's my favorite keepsake."

"You send the rifle back?"

"Nah, took it home before I shipped out. I'll give it to my kid when he's old enough."

"You got a kid?" Strombo asked.

"Yeah, a boy. 'Master Emery.' The wife got pregnant right before I left to join the Canadians. Club fightin' was chump change. I couldn't find any good payin' work in Chicago...I had a wife, a baby comin' along, and the Canadians paid thirty-eight dollars a month," Emerick said with a wink.

"That's ten bucks more than we get!" Strombo said in amazement.

"Yeah, but it wasn't a tough choice to take the pay cut. I'm fightin' for my boy. Dontcha know, I've never even held him," Emerick showed a ragged picture. "Here, just turned three."

Strombo looked at the chubby little boy and handed the photo back just as they reached the foot of the ridge. The rocky facade, pocked with caves and heavy underbrush, could conceal one or one hundred Japanese. There was no way of telling.

Slowly they made their way up along a narrow path. When they came across the dark opening of a cave, Mullins shouted, "Day-tay koy!" If there was no response, Mullins threw a grenade inside.

Methodically, the squad climbed to the top. Once there, they fanned out in pairs, investigating every nook, cranny, and crevice they came across, no matter how small. "Day-tay koy!" was followed by rifle bursts and grenades.

Strombo and Emerick looked down on a shale ledge five feet beneath them. It looked like the surface of the moon with craters large and small. Silently, Emerick climbed down, then motioned for Strombo to join him. Jackson and Causey noticed the pair climb down and walked to the edge. Emerick pointed to a larger crater that went straight down into the shale and motioned for Strombo and the others to be quiet.

Emerick walked toward the opening, signaling for Strombo to follow. As he readied to throw a grenade down, a head appeared out of another opening off to the left behind Emerick, who didn't notice.

"Look out!" Strombo yelled as he rushed forward to take Emerick out of the line of fire with a running tackle. Before he could, a blue streak flew out of the cave. The dum-dum hit Emerick in the back. Japanese dum-dums, bullets with their tips cut off, deliver a greater destructive power, entering in a small spot but exiting like a shotgun blast.

Emerick flew forward and landed flat on his face. He lay motionless as Jackson fired at the opening. Strombo thought Emerick was dead until he suddenly stood, staggering, bleeding, and struggling to breathe. Bullet fragments had hit his lungs, and his chest was bleeding from a dozen different places. He gurgled and wheezed.

A wounded buddy's body never seemed heavy to Strombo, regardless of size. Heaving the husky Emerick across his shoulders, Strombo walked him over to Jackson and Causey above on the ridge. It took the strength of both to pull Emerick's dead weight off the ledge and carry him a short distance away.

Strombo went back to roll a hand grenade down the opening, but before he could the head lobbed one up at him. It smoldered a thick dense smoke. Everything began to move in slow motion. Strombo moved toward the grenade to kick it back, but he stumbled on the pebble-covered shale and fell. His face hit the ground next to the smoking grenade. More worried about his eyes than his life, he took off his cloth Scout-Sniper cap and put it over the grenade.

"Dammit." Strombo, lying on the rock with his hands on the cap covering the grenade, kicked himself for not wearing his helmet. Billows of smoke oozed out. The grenade would blow his hands off, but that's what his instincts told him to do.

There was no explosion.

Leaping to his feet, Strombo kicked the grenade down into the cave, and followed it with two of his own. Back-to-back explosions brought a terrific reply of gunfire erupting straight up from several of the crevices. Strombo ran for the ledge and struggled to climb up. Several Japanese heads began to appear out of the shale.

Mullins and Tipton heard the commotion and arrived in time for Mullins to help his buddy while Tipton threw grenades to cover their escape.

The gurgling Emerick rallied, to the amazement of all. Periodically he jabbed at Mullins and Causey, who were trying to carry him. Because he was fighting those who were trying to help him, his comrades had to handle him roughly, which infuriated Emerick even more. He brawled with such fury that it took the strength of all five to subdue him. Then, when they got him to camp, Emerick fought against being taken to the hospital in Charan Kanoa and continued to rage until he expended all his adrenaline and collapsed. At last, corpsmen could load him onto a jeep.

CHAPTER TWENTY-FOUR

Kenny

"You know, so many of the things I did are forgotten or changed in my mind, but there are some things that are just crystal clear."

—Bob Smotts

June 27, 1944
Sixth Marine Encampment, Northern Slopes of Mount Tipo Pale

Later that afternoon, Riseley sent an entire company of Marines to clean out the hornet's nest now known as "Emerick's Ridge." It would take two days to achieve success.

The Marines pushed onward, driving General Saitō further north to yet another command post, a cave about one mile north of Mount Tapotchau. Riseley knew that the general's pleas to Tokyo for reinforcements would go unanswered. The nearest Japanese troops, on the adjacent island of Tinian could offer no help, huddled deep within their own earthen shelters for protection from continual Allied bombing. The next-nearest troops, stationed on Guam, could try to sail for Saipan, but they would never penetrate the U.S. Naval barricade that ringed the island.

General Saitō had delayed Howlin' Mad Smith's plans, but little more. The Marines pressed on regardless of the bravery of the Japanese garrison. Every counterattack that Saitō had launched had been repelled with great loss of life and equipment. Weaponry and tanks had been destroyed, lines of communications disrupted. All hope had slowly bled from Saitō, who had suffered setback after setback and now was unable even to issue orders to his troops that remained scattered about the island. He radioed Tokyo:

> Having lost the influence of the Emperor due to the weakness of our representatives, we have not been able to work at our best. Please apologize deeply to the Emperor that we cannot do better than we are.
>
> However, the right-hand men of the Emperor are rejoicing because they are not in places of death during the fight. But we will defend our positions to the very end, though that be death, to guard the Treasure. Although, my forces have few weapons and little fighting strength, we do have large numbers.
>
> Still, there is no hope for victory.
>
> Praying for the good health of the Emperor, we all cry, Banzai!

Twelve days after the landing, Howlin' Mad Smith instructed his Marines to hold their present positions until the Army had moved abreast. They would continue the push the following day. During the lull, the areas around Tipo Pale and Tapotchau were secured, and more reconnaissance patrols went into Garapan.

One of the patrols failed to return by 0500 the next day, delaying a scheduled artillery barrage, the prelude to the day's push. Before dawn, Riseley called out "Ski!" and his lieutenant reported.

"The First sent out a squad yesterday, and they haven't returned," Riseley explained. "They're holding us up. Find them and bring them back."

"Knuppel!" Ski passed the orders down the chain of command to his sergeant.

"Moore!" Knuppel called further down the chain. "Get a squad together."

Smotts and Kenny were the first to respond to his call.

The Thieves stole through the early glow of dawn in single file, staggered five to ten yards apart. Smotts, inhaling, as always, had the point, with Kenny directly behind. The rest followed, slogging their way through the dense jungle on a narrow dirt trail.

As they entered a clearing the path became wider and spiraled up a small hill that could be one of those spots the Japanese would defend to the death. The squad paused.

"Take five," Knuppel said. Some men sat on the ground, others stood, lighting up and sipping tepid water from canteens. Smotts sat beside Kenny and bummed a cigarette from his preoccupied buddy. Kenny used the opportunity to add a few more lines to a letter for his girl, Eve. Their whirlwind Stateside romance had the couple faithfully corresponding, planning on marriage after the war. Kenny dreamed of the home they'd build together and how different it would be from the one he'd left behind in Detroit.

Knuppel approached Smotts, who searched for a match. Knuppel offered his Zippo.

"Thanks," Smotts handed the lighter back.

"That hill should give us a pretty good view," Knuppel said. "If a squad's nearby we should be able to see them from up there." He handed Smotts a pair of binoculars. "When you're done with your smoke, head out."

Smotts ground his butt into the dirt, gathered his gear and started off.

"Wait a minute." Knuppel gave it a second thought. "You've been on the point all day. Kenny you go."

"Here, Red." Smotts handed Kenny the binoculars.

Kenny folded up his letter to Eve, slipped it into his pack, and took his turn on point.

Following the path that snaked its way up the hill, Kenny passed several patches of jungle that dotted the hillside of large rocks, ledges, banyan trees, and thick foliage.

When he had walked about half a mile he reached the top. Upon a ridge with a commanding view of the countryside, Kenny scanned the terrain with the binoculars, carefully surveying the entire area below. After a thorough search, he signaled to those below that the other squad was nowhere in sight.

Smotts sat, watching his buddy's progress back down the hill, straightened, and then lit a bent cigarette he had found in his pack. To Smotts, a silent movie began.

A Japanese soldier emerged from a screen of trees behind Kenny. Smotts and others of the squad frantically jumped up and waved their arms trying to get Kenny's attention, with no success. The soldier slithered up behind Kenny and rolled a concussion grenade in front of him. First Smotts saw the soundless pop of an explosion; then Kenny sunk quietly to his knees, clutching his ears.

Silently struggling, Kenny crawled to escape. Before he could manage to stand, another enemy soldier appeared from behind a banyan tree, put a rifle to the back of Kenny's head, and pulled the trigger. Smotts saw the bullet hit before he heard the shot. A splattering of blood spewed from his forehead as Kenny's body lurched forward, falling face first into the dirt.

"Let's go!" Knuppel hollered, and the squad raced up the hill, hoping against hope that Kenny might still be alive. Moore and Smotts took one side. Knuppel and the others the opposite.

While Smotts and Moore ran, shots rang out from the other side, where Knuppel's group had come face to face with the enemy.

Moore stopped and shot into the tangled roots of a banyan tree. Somehow a Japanese soldier had contorted himself and hid in the twisted knots. As Moore fired, the Japanese tried to escape. Thirteen bullets hit their mark, but the enemy kept crawling. One final shot directly to the head finished the job.

Japanese swarmed everywhere—from behind banyan trees, out of crevices, jumping down from above. All ran toward a trail that went into thick elephant grass that was almost ten feet high. Expended cartridges spat out of Moore's BAR as the enemy escaped into the grass.

Smotts spotted two Japanese about seventy-five feet away, their crouched figures silhouetted against the grass. He quickly shot twice from the hip, and both shots missed. The enemy ran toward the grass bent over, keeping low to make a smaller target.

The second time he fired, Smotts aimed. Two clean shots peeled off in rapid succession. He saw the armor-piercing shell hit them in their buttocks. They didn't go down, but instead ran further, fueled by adrenaline.

Smotts fired at others, who fled for the safety of the tall grass, but it was unclear if he had hit any of them. They disappeared, darting onto the trail.

"Let's go!" Moore urged. The two split up and gave chase, running hard, hearts thumping. Twenty feet in, Smotts tripped over one slumping body and a few feet further over another. The shells that had hit their buttocks had traveled through their torsos and exited out their necks. In case either was still alive, Smotts made a hasty assurance with his bayonet.

Out of breath, Smotts stopped and stood alone in the middle of the grass-like maze.

He listened but heard nothing except the pounding of his heart. A slight breeze nullified his sensory gift. Not wanting to call out for Moore, Smotts kept his rifle at his hip, ready, and slowly made his way out of the grass and back to the top of the hill.

Walking onto a small ridge, Smotts looked down the trail that he and Moore had ascended earlier; he saw his squad halfway down the hill. He had been so intent on chasing the Japanese that he had lost track of time. The squad had given him up as MIA.

He was about to yell to them but noticed a slight movement on the rock ledge three feet beneath him. The plateau had a small cavern dug into the hill; a Japanese soldier lay below him in that cavern, partially exposed. Armed with a light machine gun, the enemy was waiting for a clear shot at his buddies below.

He hadn't noticed Smotts, who now had to decide quickly and quietly, "How?" Firing his rifle would make too much noise, and if he used his bayonet, the enemy might cry out. There might be more lurking about.

Because the Japanese soldier was wearing a cloth cap instead of a helmet, Smotts decided to smash in his skull with the butt of his rifle.

Daniel Kenny. *Courtesy of Bob Smotts*

The rifle butt made a dull thud driving the cap into the bone. Immediately, the soldier bolted up as if he were a spring and went for Smotts, but fell back down. He flopped about wildly, jumping up to run away, then crumbling in a heap. Smotts picked up a large rock and brought it down hard, crushing the skull and finishing the job.

Then Smotts saw Kenny on the ground and paused. In the heat of the melee, he had forgotten.

Flies had begun to swarm around and into the head wound. Smotts crouched beside the limp body and shooed them away. He thought about rolling his buddy over to take one last look. The matted blood from the gaping wound in the back of his head dissuaded him. Kenny's bright russet hair had become a congealed ruddy brown; there could be nothing left of his face.

Smotts sat with his buddy for a moment. He didn't want to leave him, not like this, as if Kenny were just debris. He opened his buddy's pack and Eve's letter fell out, landing in a pool of Kenny's blood. Smotts wiped the envelope clean on his dungarees and put it back. He would've liked to stay longer, maybe bunk next to his friend one last time, but knew he could not.

"I'll let Eve know." Smotts covered the body with a poncho. "Goodbye, Red." He took Kenny's pack and left to rejoin his squad.

CHAPTER TWENTY-FIVE

Dyer

*"The toughest thing Ski faced, would be sending
people out on missions knowing that they were going
to get shot up. That was something he had to live with.
He had to make that decision of which ones go out
and either live or die."*

—Marvin Strombo

June 29, 1944
Sixth Marine Command Post, Northern Slopes of Mount Tipo Pale

Semper Fi: Always Faithful.

Back at camp, Smotts rummaged through Kenny's pack. Numb, he carefully examined each item, pulling out a crumbled pack of cigarettes, C-Rations, chewing gum, and the tantō sword wrapped in a handkerchief. He finally found a small "Memorandum" notebook containing a list of the ships his buddy had sailed on, names of camps and islands, notes from map-reading classes on Hawaii and Stateside addresses for everyone in the platoon. The only other person listed was Eve from Oceanside.

Since the couple had not yet married, there would be no official "WE REGRET TO INFORM YOU" cablegram for her, only one letterless day after another. Smotts felt she should be told. He wrote a letter to Eve, telling her about Kenny's death, and how much he had cared for her. Smotts packed the sword, his own note, and Kenny's last, unfinished letter into a box that he would mail when he could.

Howlin' Mad Smith's push had been delayed another day. While the Marines waited for the Army to advance abreast of their lines, one more day of inactivity brought a bittersweet remembrance of home.

Since leaving Eniwetok in early June, there had been little or no contact with family and friends back in the States. The Corps wanted it that way. "We're treated worse than dogs," Mullins groused to Strombo.

"To make us meaner," was the reply. And it was working. The Corps had succeeded; the Devil Dogs were winning the battle.

There was little benefit in a Marine's being distracted by a letter from parents or sweethearts. "Therein madness lies," Doc had counseled Ski long ago. A homesick Marine was of no use, and a Dear John letter made matters worse; the Marines doled out mail sporadically.

But on the fourteenth day after the invasion there was an impromptu mail call. There were bags of letters and packages—missives from Smotts's girl Alma Jean, Moore's little sister, Yunker's mom, and a crayon drawing of Dyer in uniform from his baby sister. Knuppel received a 78rpm Voice-o-Graph recording of his dad's band, The Kraut Makers, performing "Cocktails for Two." He laughed. "Where in the hell am I gonna find a phonograph on this damn island?"

Ski held in his hand over a dozen letters and a postcard from Roxie. Not having the time to read the letters, he shoved them into his combat pack and glanced at the card.

The colorful note contrasted with his unclean hands. The more he looked at it, the farther away he felt from that other, long-ago life.

Riseley called out, "Ski! The line troops are starting the push tomorrow. We need to know what's out there."

After consulting with Knuppel about who was up, Ski called out "Dyer."

Folding up his sister's artwork, the corporal reported for duty. "The old man wants us out tonight," Ski told him, and went on to discuss the mission with Dyer in detail. There was nothing new about any of it; this had been the daily routine for over two weeks. Men were chosen, and they did their jobs; most came back, a few wounded. Everything seemed as normal as normal could be. The sun had just

Postcard from Roxie to Ski. *From the collection of Joseph Tachovsky*

set. Guys sat, napped, ate C-Rations for supper, cleaned gear, and smoked. Strombo looked up from grinding his cigarette into the dirt to glance in Dyer's direction.

As he lit another Lucky, Strombo stared at Dyer. Through the tobacco haze, he saw his buddy standing silhouetted against a changing sky. Dyer's drawn white face appeared pale as moonlight. Strombo blinked and continued to stare as the smoke dissipated. He thought his eyes played tricks on him. The world went mute. Mouths moved, yet he heard nothing.

Unable to take his eyes off Dyer, Strombo wondered if Ski saw the same sight, or if he himself was hallucinating. He wanted to ask Mullins, who was sitting next to him, if he noticed anything odd, but he found he couldn't break the spell to speak.

Everyone else was moving around in the world of sound, routinely cleaning rifles and sharpening knives, but in Strombo's noiseless world he could only gaze toward the dream-like scene. Dyer stood up slowly.

He knows he's not coming back. Strombo's thoughts churned with the realization. Christ, he's as white as a sheet. How does he have the guts to get up? If I were him my knees would turn to jelly. I'd fall down. How in the hell can he stand?

"And take enough men with you." Ski was still briefing Dyer. "And listen for the names we've memorized: Saitō, Nagumo, Obata, Suzuki, Oka, Goto. You know what to do." Ski finished.

When Dyer called for his squad—"Old dead dog!"—Strombo snapped out of his trance.

He worried about cracking up, losing it. He couldn't ask his buddy Mullins if this was how it starts. And how would he know? Jesus, is this how it began for Lewis?

Strombo lit another Lucky and looked down to see if his hands had begun the St. Vitus's dance. He was relieved to find them steady.

Mullins, part of Dyer's squad, rose to head out. "See ya, Marvin J." He gave Strombo a tap on the head. Strombo calmed at the sound of his buddy's voice. He exhaled and watched the squad assemble.

Dyer directed his men, "One canteen, no rations. Mullins, take the point with a shotgun. Tipton…"

Before leaving, Dyer looked at Strombo one last time. As their eyes met, it happened again: no sound. The ashen Dyer pointed in Strombo's direction. Thinking he was pointing at someone behind him, Strombo turned to look, but no one was there. As he turned back around to meet Dyer's stare, time froze. The exchange lasted only a second, but for Strombo it seemed a lifetime. He understood. The cold fingers of death that Dyer had spoken of aboard the *Bolivar* had come for him.

Dyer nodded and held up his right hand to Strombo in a sort of salute. He was saying goodbye.

Mullins slapped Dyer on the back. "C'mon, you said old dead dog, so let's go." They left.

I could never do what he's doin'. He's the bravest man I know, Strombo thought as he watched Dyer disappear.

Dyer's Thieves moved into the still night. The sounds of sporadic gunfire or popping grenades had a strange, strangled quality in the heavy air. Even the resounding boom of an ammunition dump blowing up lacked intensity.

The night sky awed Mullins. A large, low-hanging moon made night almost as bright as day. The depth of the stars made him feel like reaching up to grab a handful.

They walked softly. The sound of their breathing created a worrisome rhythm. Mullins held up his hand to pause their movement. Having come upon a dense overgrown area that looked typical of a Japanese strongpoint, he waited for minutes, looked, and listened. Nothing. Mullins gave the all-clear. Dyer motioned for the Marines to proceed one man at a time. Waiting until the last man had cleared the overgrowth, Dyer brought up the rear.

Nothing.

They continued through the dense foliage, going miles from their lines. Their progress halted when the jungle ended abruptly at a ridge. The facade dropped down to a large horseshoe-shaped valley. A horde of Japanese—an entire regiment, possibly more, with heavy armaments—stood illuminated some thirty yards below.

"Jeez…" Dyer's raised hand cut off Tipton's whisper. The kid had never seen so many Japanese before. If Tipton spit over the edge he could hit one of them. The jagged face of the ridge was the only obstacle separating the Thieves from hundreds of enemy soldiers only a short distance away. Hearts raced with adrenaline.

They crouched. Dyer glanced at the luminous dial of his wristwatch. It was 0115. He motioned commands. Three stood guard. Tipton tallied the weaponry—tanks, heavy artillery, and field pieces. Mullins, compass in hand, worked on a map, quietly walking about and logging down compass headings. The more headings, the more accurate the map. Orozco and the rest moved cat-like, getting closer to listen for those memorized names and observe the terrain.

Through his binoculars, Dyer surveyed the scene and wrote in a small notebook in great clarity and detail. The brightness of the moon made it unnecessary to huddle under ponchos with flashlights.

They had hit the jackpot. It was indeed a regiment, designation unknown, possibly the remnants of many, including elements of the Forty-Seventh Imperial Brigade. Japanese soldiers were working on repairs of three or four tanks in uncertain condition. Over two dozen field pieces and artillery stood unattended. Orozco noted activity in and out of a small cave carved into the western side of the sheer facade, twenty yards away. The enemy soldiers' voices carried. He had always pronounced the opposing general's name as Sa-EE-too. He wrote down phonetically what he heard: SIGH-toe.

After gathering information, taking copious notes, and mapmaking, Dyer assembled the intelligence, recorded the time as 0230, June 30, 1944, and placed it in the waterproof portion of his pack. He and his men crept back toward camp.

Mullins continued on point as clouds began to drift across the sky, periodically bringing blackness to the otherwise bright night. Nearing the same overgrown area that had given them pause going in, Mullins stopped and motioned for the men to bypass the area. A dark figure he thought was Dyer signaled for them to keep going. Mullins obeyed. The moonlight momentarily waned as Mullins noiselessly passed through, followed by Orozco, who assumed the lead and walked onward. Mullins stayed to cover the rest. Two more made it successfully. As Tipton, Dyer, and others ventured in, the skies cleared. Bright moonbeams streamed down, allowing Mullins to catch a glimpse of gleaming metal in a clump of brush. At the same time as he pulled the trigger on his twelve-gauge shotgun, a woodpecker opened fire.

As the peck-peck-pecking broke the silence, Mullins hit the deck and pumped two more rounds into the overgrowth. Another Thief scampered through to join Mullins as Orozco raced back. Dyer lay face down on the ground, not moving. Tipton and the others bolted for cover.

It became quiet again. No one moved, not even to breathe. They were pinned down, the squad split in two. Mullins's initial blast had distracted the enemy soldier and interfered with the accuracy of his aim. Dyer was not hit. He tried to breathe as slowly as possible, to look dead.

Mullins and Orozco heard the Japanese jabbering—and a metallic clattering sound. "Jammed," Mullins whispered to Orozco, who inched closer to the sound. Removing the pin from a grenade, he gently lobbed it into the clump of brush. One small "pop" interrupted the stillness of the night.

Warily, Dyer arose. The squad followed his lead, breathing a sigh of relief.

"Whatever happens, it's imperative this gets back to Ski and the Old Gent." Dyer removed his pack and tossed it to Orozco. "Get going. You," he ordered two others, "go with him. Don't stop under any circumstances. That's an order." The three left.

Tipton walked forward. "You've been hit," he said, pointing to Dyer's arm, which dripped blood. "Let me look at it."

"Not now. You guys…" Dyer, cut short by sudden burst of fire from the opposite side of the trail, went down.

Mullins and the rest dove for the ground once again. Through the barrage, Tipton cautiously worked his way to where Dyer lay and dragged him to safety near Mullins. Circling the source of the fire, the other Thieves met two Japanese in retreat carrying their woodpecker. They finished off their encumbered enemy with Ka-Bars.

Thinking that Dyer had been playing possum again, his men waited for him to get up. He did not. Tipton rolled his squad leader onto his back.

Dyer's stomach oozed blood from multiple gunshot wounds. Tipton tended to him, feverishly cutting off Dyer's uniform, sliding the morphine needle into his arm, applying sulfa powder to the bullet-riddled flesh. Everyone handed Tipton their sulfa packets because Dyer had been hit so badly. There was so much blood.

The night's silence crept in once again.

Martin Dyer, Jr. was posthumously awarded the Navy Cross for his actions on June 30, 1944. *Courtesy of Bill Knuppel*

It was so quiet that Mullins could distinctly hear the sounds of Tipton tearing the packets, the hissing of the sulfa powder as it hit the wounds, and the gurgling of the bubbling blood. The only other thing Mullins could hear that night was Dyer calling out for his mother—until he couldn't hear that anymore.

CHAPTER TWENTY-SIX

Oliver

"Roscoe was there. He should know what happened."

—*Marvin Strombo*

June 30, 1944, 0400 Hours
Sixth Marine Command Post, Northern Slopes of Mount Tipo Pale

Orozco arrived at camp ahead of the rest of Dyer's squad and delivered the intelligence report to Ski. The information carried enough urgency that Ski took it directly to Riseley. A flurry of activity rushed through the headquarters—command staff roused from sleep, maps consulted, messages sent, coordinates relayed. A terse record in the colonel's journal summarized the hours: "My Scout-Snipers reported intense enemy activity to the front of our lines. Navy and the Twenty-fourth Marine Artillery contacted."

Shortly after dawn on the fifteenth day after the invasion, Saitō's most recent headquarters, tucked into a small cave about one mile north of Mount Tapotchau, came under heavy Naval and Marine bombardment. American Devils nipped at the Japanese general's heels. The enemy commander's tenure at his fifth location since the American invasion lasted only four days before necessity demanded another hasty

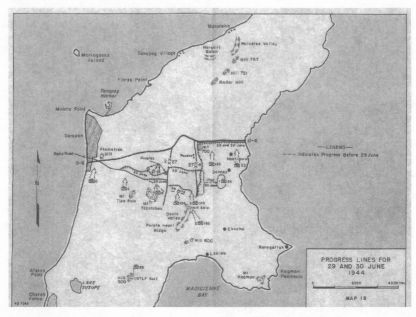

The state of the battle for Saipan on June 29–30, 1944. *From* Saipan: The Beginning of the End, *written by Major Carl Hoffman for the Marine Corps*

relocation. Saitō ordered his forces to fall back, reorganize, regroup, and coordinate a stronger line of defense. Across positions closest to the fighting, from Flametree Hill due east to the Pacific, Marines observed large numbers of Japanese migrating northward.

Fleeing further north toward the village of Makunsha, Saitō established a cave command post in an area east of Harakiri Gulch. What the Marines called "Paradise Valley" the Japanese knew as "The Valley of Hell." But even in retreat, the Imperial Army would make the Marines pay dearly for every inch of ground taken from their Emperor's Treasure.

Regrouping didn't take long. At dusk on July 1, a Banzai erupted along the front lines of the Eighth Marines, the regiment of Marvin Strombo's brother Oliver. Oliver's unit, encamped on the northern slopes of Mount Tapotchau, bore the brunt of the attack. Droves of Japanese crashed wildly into their defenses. Mad cries of "Die Marine, die!"

pierced Marine lines before the death lunge ruptured them. Fierce animalistic hand-to-hand fighting eventually drove the outnumbered enemy back, leaving the Eighth Marines bloodied with some wounded and many dead.

By nightfall of the seventeenth day after the invasion, Marine forces reached the outskirts of Garapan. Beyond, Tanapag Harbor was in view. The Japanese had lost another mile of Saipan.

With the enemy heavily concentrated on the northern end of the island, squads of Thieves continually patrolled forward of the front line. Moore led one group toward Flores Point with Jackson, Strombo, and Mullins among those getting the call.

Moving effortlessly though thick, murky air, the group made no contact with the enemy for the first fifteen hundred yards. Then they came across a series of four huts in various stages of decay and destruction. Two had been levelled.

"Check the debris," Moore directed. He had encountered enough Japanese lying in wait under sheets of corrugated tin or piles of wood to know to take every precaution.

Nothing uncovered in the rubble, Moore kicked in the door of the nearest standing hut. A thorough surveillance revealed more nothing. Reaching the last structure, Moore, Strombo, and Mullins paused by the front door while Jackson and others circled the building. Kicking in the door caused a commotion. There were four Japanese inside. Three were wounded and could barely move, but the fourth, a sergeant, reached for his weapon.

"Boo-kee Oh Oh-toe-say!" Moore warned. The Arisaka rifle dropped to the floor.

One of the injured Japanese immediately plunged a sword into his abdomen, crying out as he drew the blade sideways, disemboweling himself. Another held a grenade and began to bring it to his chest, but Strombo stepped on his arm—"Shee-nigh-day!"—and leveled his M1 at the man's eyes. The grenade fell from his hand, and Strombo kicked it away.

"Search them," Moore told Strombo and Mullins.

The pair removed weapons, searching pockets and packs as Moore stood ready, rifle at his hip. Strombo shouldered his M1 and crouched down, rummaging through the pack he'd taken from the sergeant, looking for documents, diaries, or maps. Pulling out a Good Luck Flag, he unfolded it in his hand. Several metal objects fell to the floor.

"Dog tags." Strombo held one up to show Moore. "Where did you get these?" he questioned the enemy sergeant. Not receiving an answer, Strombo studied them one by one—until one stamped name stopped him cold.

"Where did you get this?" he thrust a set of tags on a ball chain in the sergeant's face. "I said, where did you get these?" he demanded angrily. The defiant sergeant turned away.

In a cold rage, Strombo stood up. Simmering, with jaw clenched, he paced back and forth, staring at the chain in his hand.

"Marvin…" Mullins tried to get his buddy's attention. Strombo, rapt at the sight of the tags, heard nothing. "Marvin J.," Mullins repeated, touching his buddy's shoulder. Angrily shrugging off the hand, Strombo shot a glance at Roscoe, who had never before seen that look on his friend's face—pent-up wrath waiting to explode.

Strombo let the chain slip out of his hand. Mullins picked it up and read the name: Strombo, Oliver.

CHAPTER TWENTY-SEVEN

Seven Lives

"Hell is empty, and all the devils are here."

—*William Shakespeare,* The Tempest

July 3, 1944
Six Marine's Bivouac, a thousand yards inland from Garapan

General Saitō resigned himself to the fact that he had been unable to drive the American Devils back into the sea. The shattered artillery and thousands of bodies littering the island were a testimony to his failure.

On July 3, eighteen days after the American landing, the Japanese defense received several severe blows. The gravest was the fall of Garapan at last. Nothing remained except the skeletons of buildings, people, and animals. The smell of rotting human flesh was mixed with the more suffocating odor of putrefied oxen. The cloud of vile stench hovering over the capital city caused Marine pilots flying overhead to vomit in their cockpits.

After almost three weeks of constant combat, good news greeted the Sixth Regiment, when the Army relieved the battle-weary Marines on the front lines. With little enemy territory left to conquer, Riseley recalled the 40 Thieves from the field. Death and severe wounds had reduced their number to less than thirty.

The platoon set up a little bivouac behind the front lines about one thousand yards inland from Garapan, far enough away to avoid the gut-wrenching stench. Seizure of the capital provided enough water to afford the opportunity of bathing for the first time since the Marines had been aboard the *Bolivar*.

By the next morning the Thieves felt they could relax. Savoring their spoils of Ponkan wine, crabmeat, and canned tangerines, the men stripped for leisurely Navy baths and Ka-Bar shaves, cleaning themselves up as best they could.

"Ski!" Riseley's call to duty put a damper on their simple pleasures.

Knuppel, poised to lather up his stubble, sat off to the side with his half-naked corporals. "Christ...not off the line for an hour...What in hell could the Old Gent want?" he griped.

After consulting with the colonel for a few minutes, Ski approached his men.

"What's the word?" Knuppel called out.

"No word." Ski smiled, stood next to Knuppel, and took a big swallow from the offered bottle of Ponkan. Showing a folded piece of paper, he loudly got the attention of his platoon.

"Gentleman Jim wants me to relay this message to you boys...Listen up," Ski unfolded the note while his men set aside their Ka-Bars and soap, lit cigarettes, and listened.

"It's from Howlin' Mad: 'The Commanding General takes pride on this Independence Day in sending his best wishes to the fighting men on Saipan. Your unflagging gallantry and devotion to duty have been worthy of the highest praise of our country. It is fitting that on this Fourth of July you should be extremely proud of your achievements. Your fight is no less important than that waged by our forefathers who gave us the liberty and freedom we have long enjoyed. Your deeds to maintain these principles will not be forgotten. To all hands a sincere well done. My confidence in your ability is unbounded.'"

"Jesus." Knuppel paused. "It's the Fourth of July."

•   •   •

The military situation of the Japanese—cornered and pushed toward inevitable defeat—was becoming more precarious by the minute.

Official reports supported the common belief that Saitō's once mighty army had been reduced to odds and ends. Scuttlebutt painted his forces as poorly equipped and running out of supplies, wounded, and sick. With no means of communication, no hospitals to treat the wounded, and precious little food and water, the enemy could be nothing but demoralized and essentially finished. Marines hoped the finale might be another Kiska.

American forces swept north, and the front line narrowed. Holland Smith divided the island in two, with the Army assigned the western half and the Marines the east. With Strombo in their foxhole, Mullins—still concerned about his buddy's state of mind—distracted him with the same thought many were thinking: "It's gonna be over real soon, Marvin J. We've almost got the whole damn island."

The twentieth day after the invasion came and went with no hostile activity. Many civilians surrendered and were transported to Charan Kanoa. That evening, the brief respite over, the Thieves went back to work. Knuppel and Moore took squads out overnight to reconnoiter enemy territory.

As a burnt orange sun sank into the sea, the Sixth held the high ground. Riseley's command post, located on an escarpment behind the front lines, held a commanding view of the Tanapag Plain. Below Riseley, the Army had set up their camp in a wooded ravine a few hundred yards inland from the Tanapag Plain near Radar Hill. Sporadic machine gun fire from below broke the quiet. The harsh staccato sound echoed throughout the ravine, but Ski was determined to respond to mail received a week before, even if only with a brief note.

My Dearest Roxie,

Now it can be written that you were right, we are on Saipan. At present we are enjoying a little rest.

I received two letters several days ago and the postcard of June 5. I hope there will be some mail in soon.

There is very little that I can write. It has been pretty rough, and we are glad that part is over. We have lost some pretty damn good men.

I wish I could be optimistic of the future, but that is hardly possible. Fate holds the cards. In view of the fact that many will never return to their loved ones, the desire to be optimistic is almost lacking. One feels lucky and fortunate to still be alive.

I've washed your socks a couple times. They've shrunk quite a bit. It takes much stretching to make the heel fit but I still wear them.

Well, my dear, that is all for the present. I will write again very soon.

All my love forever. Your husband, Frank

At 1900 the continued sound of gun fire from the Army raised eyebrows and Riseley's anger. By 2200 he erupted.

"Ski!"

When he reported to his colonel, Riseley didn't give Ski a chance to say, "Yes, Jim," before barking orders. "Go down there and tell the goddamn Army that if they don't stop firing those machine guns, I'm going to come down there myself, take those weapons, and shove 'em up their ass!"

"Can I paraphrase?"

"No!"

Ski left Riseley's tent and walked through the command post's defensive perimeter, passing one of his men.

"Where you goin' Ski?" Yunker asked.

"Gotta pay a visit to those dogface boys and tell them to knock off the racket. The Old Gent's pissed."

"Sounds like Hellzapoppin'."

Ski walked through the moonlit highlands and then down into the ravine. Approaching Army defenses, he made enough noise to let them know he wasn't the enemy. Following the sound of intermittent firing, he happened upon a solitary travel-trailer, like the kind used on camping trips back home. Through a curtained window, a light glowed inside. Peering through the sheer curtains, he watched a soldier standing over a hotplate, flipping pancake after pancake.

What a lash-up, he laughed to himself. We're livin' on Red Heart, and this dogface in a supporting unit is makin' himself pancakes. Ski knocked on the trailer's door.

"Who goes there?" a voice from within challenged.

"I'm from the Sixth Marines..."

The door opened; Ski entered and asked, "Is there an officer around here?"

"I'm a lieutenant."

"Tell your captain that he better have your boys stop shooting those machine guns or my colonel is gonna come down and..." he paused, "take them away."

"What for?"

"Just tell your captain that's an order."

As Ski made his way back to camp, the shooting stopped. He kicked himself, I should've asked for some pancakes.

The next morning, Ski walked back down to speak with the Army captain in person. After repeating what Riseley had said, he added, "I wanted to make sure you understood my CO's request."

"My boys need to protect themselves," the captain replied. "They heard Japs and returned fire."

"With all due respect, sir, they weren't protecting themselves. If you go out there you won't find any dead Japanese. They're too clever.

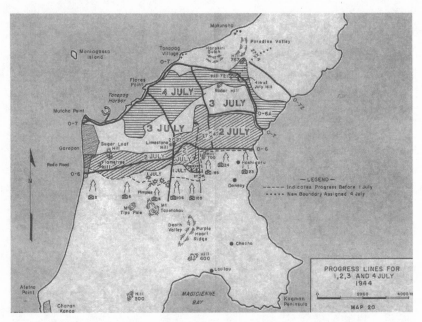

The state of the battle for Saipan on July 1–4, 1944. *From* Saipan: The Beginning of the End, *written by Major Carl Hoffman for the Marine Corps*

If they heard anything, it was probably a trick. Japs'll throw fire-crackers to make you shoot. All your guys did was let the Japs know exactly where your machine guns are. If there were any Japanese around, you'd know." He added, "You may want to move those machine guns."

The Army captain bristled at the reprimand.

General Saitō knew there would be no rescue or reinforcement for his troops. No hope was left. The Emperor's Treasure had been lost. That same morning, he issued a final order from his headquarters in The Valley of Hell:

I am addressing the officers and men of the Japanese Imperial Army on Saipan.

It has been more than twenty days since the American Devils attacked. The officers, men, and civilian employees of the Imperial Army and Navy on this island have fought well and bravely. Everywhere they have demonstrated the honor and glory of the Imperial Forces. I expected just that.

Heaven has not given us an opportunity for success. Our comrades have fallen one after another. Despite the bitterness of defeat, we pledge, "Seven lives to repay our country."

The barbarous attack of the enemy continues. Whether we attack or whether we stay where we are, there is only death. However, in death there is life. We must utilize this opportunity to exalt true Japanese manhood. I will advance with those who remain to deliver still another blow to the American Devils and leave my bones on Saipan as a bulwark of the Pacific.

As it says in the *Senjinkun*, [Imperial Japan's battle code,] "I will never suffer the disgrace of being taken alive," and "I will offer up the courage of my soul and calmly rejoice in living by the eternal principle."

Here I pray with you for the eternal life of the Emperor and the welfare of our country, and I advance to seek out the enemy. Follow me. Banzai.

The shame of defeat weighed heavily upon the aged Japanese officer. The devastated General Yoshitsugu Saitō committed harakiri after a last supper of sake and canned crabmeat in his sixth and final command post.

●　　●　　●

During initial tactical planning, Howlin' Mad Smith had anticipated that retreating Japanese would become compressed on the northern tip of the island. If they were to launch one final attack, the banzai might be launched from the town of Makunsha. He alerted the Army to that possibility on the twenty-first night after the landing.

Thieves out on the job were once again called back. With evening swiftly approaching, Knuppel decided against going all the way back to

Private First Class Francis Moynihan shaving Smotts, Private First Class Barney Wheeless, and Moore. *Courtesy of Bob Smotts*

Standing: Smotts, Wheeless, Mehlin, Moore, Mullins, Borawski, Private First Class Bernie Cumbie, and Moynihan. Kneeling: Marvin Strombo and Yunker. *Courtesy of Bill Knuppel*

Hebel, Mehlin, Jackson, Mullins, and Moore. *Courtesy of Bill Knuppel*

the Regimental CP. Instead his and Moore's squads bivouacked one hundred yards behind the Army's front line.

The Marines exhaled. Feeling safe behind the lines, everyone took it easy, enjoying the welcome time off. Besides the cursory rifle-cleaning, knife-sharpening, and getting their gear in shape, they clowned around.

The Thieves drifted off to sleep that night with a shared thought in their heads: the Japs are done.

But at 0300 on July 7, a dozen Japanese were slowly moving forward through the deceptive moonlight, carrying a red flag. Smaller probing groups of Imperial troops followed the flag bearers—darting in and out of the Army lines yelling "Kill! Kill! Kill!" trying to provoke a response and find a weakness. The American soldiers waited nervously in foxholes with bayonets fixed and withheld fire, bracing for impact and listening to the taunts of "Blood! Blood!"

Behind the probing groups of Japanese, three thousand well-equipped and able-bodied Imperial soldiers were massed, lying in wait. And behind them were thousands more enemy—walking wounded and civilians armed with "idiot sticks," crude spears of bamboo poles with knives tied to the ends or anything else that could be used as a weapon.

The harassing incursions continued for over an hour, until the enemy discovered a weakness, a several hundred-yard gap between two Army battalions. The screams and taunts dwindled into an eerie silence.

At 0445 the silence was broken by thousands of voices united in the deafening cry of "Banzai!" Flooding the gap with crazed fury, the horde stampeded forward, hitting the Army positions hard from the front, the flank, and the rear. Bayonets could not stop this assault, more violent and more savage than any previous attack. Twenty days of pent-up rage fell upon Army lines. Never-ending swarms of shrieking Japanese came on. Lines buckled and communications were severed. The two Army battalions—hundreds of soldiers isolated and fighting for their lives—were overrun by thousands of Japanese, each determined to take seven American lives, or die trying.

The noise of the attack jarred the sleeping Thieves awake. In a heartbeat Japanese were everywhere. Fighting with rifle butts, entrenching tools, Ka-Bars, whatever they could lay their hands on, the Thieves used every lesson they had learned. They didn't dare shoot and chance hitting one of their own in the madding chaos. No sooner did one enemy fall than two more took his place.

The Army's machine guns became so hot from continual firing that they froze. A Marine artillery unit to the rear became embroiled in the fray. Artillerymen had to shoot their 105mm howitzers level, timing fuses for two or three seconds after leaving the barrel, firing over forty rounds a minute.

At the Sixth's command post, Ski watched flashes of fire on the beach and heard the sounds drifting up. Machine gun fire, swords hacking flesh, popping grenades, and howling mortars were accompanied by screams of "Banzai" and "Blood!" Most sickening was the indistinguishable howling of the killers and those being killed.

Marine artillery kept the Japanese at bay until Riseley recalled the Sixth Marines to the front lines. What had begun at 0445 raged until 0700. It was over.

Under the glaring blue morning sky Knuppel, Moore, and their squads stood dull-eyed and spent amidst the mass of Japanese dead at their feet. The tempest of sounds had turned into the queer quiet of faint groans and the buzzing of flies. Dried blood had glued dungarees to bodies. Sweat streaked filthy faces. Hands could not release grips on knives, shovels, or rifles battered beyond use.

The Thieves looked out onto the Tanapag Plain. Bulldozers had already begun to carve huge trenches in the sand, preparing mass graves for the enemy dead. Thousands of mutilated bodies were starting to bake under the morning sun, creating that familiar nauseating stench.

"As far as you can see," Moore muttered, "there's nothing but spilled guts and brains. Everywhere."

"Saitō's grand finale," Knuppel added.

Skirmishes continued throughout the next day.

The two Army battalions that took the brunt of the attack had fought bravely but were nearly annihilated. Over three-quarters of their ranks were either killed or wounded.

There were no survivors among the attacking Japanese. The bravery and willingness of Saitō's warriors to die honorably and take "seven American lives to repay our country" made up for their lack of weapons.

CHAPTER TWENTY-EIGHT

Good-Byes

"It is easy to go down into Hell; night and day, the gates
of dark Death stand wide;
But to climb back again, to retrace one's steps to the
upper air—there's the rub, the task."

—*Virgil*, The Aeneid

July 9, 1944
Tanapag Plain

The hell of war did not end with the final banzai.

Many Imperial soldiers were willing to die and even embraced death, often by their own hand. Harakiri ensured an honorable death for some. But the most cunning and tenacious continued their personal battle vowing never to accept surrender or defeat. Disorganized remnants of Saitō's Army fled into caves, ravines, and the dense jungle. Pockets of sporadic resistance erupted.

Two days after the last banzai, the Thieves were patrolling north toward Marpi Point. Along the eastern wooded ridge, they found hundreds more Japanese who had committed suicide. They also watched as groups of the enemy vacated pillboxes in Makunsha to walk out into the ocean hand in hand to drown. Staring beyond the corpse-covered ground toward Marpi Point, the Marines saw nothing but water. The Emperor's Treasure had been taken by the American

Devils. Admirals and generals in ships off-shore declared Saipan "Secure."

That meant little to those in the field. On July 10, twenty-four hours after Saipan was declared secure, two thousand Japanese troops were killed on the island in fierce fighting. Ski and his Thieves knew that searching out the remaining enemy and delivering the final death blow would not be easy. "Rabbit hunts" on the mountainous island could take a life as easily as full-scale battle, as long as Hirohito was still refusing to surrender.

The Thieves found Chamorros in hiding, most of whom were now easily persuaded to surrender. Japanese civilians, having been indoctrinated with warnings of fate worse than death if captured by Marines, proved more difficult to deal with.

Imperial soldiers and hundreds of civilians had been condensed onto Marpi Point in the northward exodus. Hellcats and Corsairs that usually dealt death were now used to drop pamphlets written in traditional tategaki script promising safe conduct. G-2 interpreters used loudspeakers to encourage the elderly, women, and children to surrender, "Shimpie Shee-nigh-day!" The phrase "Don't be afraid" was repeated over and over, along with offers of food and water. A squad of Thieves joined the interpreters to escort traumatized and wary non-combatants who accepted safe transport and first aid.

But the mass of people crowding the edge of Marpi Point's sheer cliffs listened to the pleas yet appeared as resolute as their military brethren. Imperial soldiers stirred emotions in the horde, shouting defiantly and waving Rising Sun flags. Random *pops* were heard when Japanese soldiers threw grenades at civilians who attempted surrender.

As callous as Mullins had grown, something about the scene made him uneasy. Mothers flinched at every sound and looked for avenues to move out of the crowd. Children clinging to skirts were separated and swept away by the throng. Mullins advanced cautiously toward one young mother and baby, but Japanese soldiers kept him at bay, aggravating the tense situation by waving their weapons and yelling crazily.

Movement along the cliff became panicked. A strange throbbing chant began and grew louder, louder, louder. Their emotions driven out of control, mothers hurled their babies and small children from the cliff and then quickly followed, crashing body after body onto the jagged rocks below.

"My God." Mullins could not close his eyes. If he had, he would have missed the cliff's emptying in the blink of an eye. No one escaped the press of the mass suicide. Hundreds of broken bodies undulated on the surface of the sea, splashing back and forth at the base of the cliff.

Hours later Mullins confided to Strombo, "The worst thing about this whole god-damned war was watchin' those mommas killing their babies then themselves. There's nothin' anybody could do but watch. I'll never be able to forget. Never." No man who witnessed the mass suicide would ever be able to forget.

There was no way of counting exactly how many died on Marpi Point that day. Thirteen thousand Japanese civilians eventually surrendered, but not before approximately four thousand died from suicide or were killed by their own army. Of the garrison force of thirty thousand, fewer than three hundred Japanese soldiers survived, having been found wounded amid the dead. American forces tallied three thousand dead and more than thirteen thousand wounded or missing.

Bloody Tarawa was now demoted to the second deadliest battle of the Pacific war.

Rear echelon troops landed, Seabees went to work, and Saipan slowly transformed into an Allied base. Quartermaster camps became a common starting point for rabbit hunts with starving enemy soldiers stealing supplies and food. Working night and day, the Thieves had little time to rest.

Whatever free time was spent corresponding with loved ones back home. After several failed attempts to dash off a note to his worried wife, Ski found a few moments for his ritual of "My Dearest Roxie:"

A little work came up, so I could not write until today. More mail arrived yesterday and today that fills in the gaps up to

July 9. Many thanks, Roxie for your faithful writing. It is a grand feeling to get so much mail when it is passed out. We are getting a little more rest now. Today I bathed—about three helmets full of water—put on some previously washed clothes, and then washed your socks. I didn't wash the remainder of the dirty clothes because there wasn't enough water. In the letter of the ninth you wrote that today, Saipan is ours. Of course, you had that through the news. While true, small groups of them give us some trouble, from time to time. So, we didn't get overly excited knowing the island was announced as secure, and we can't lie down and rest peacefully. There is still much to do out here in the Pacific.

While war changes people, I don't suppose one notices it in oneself. One sees it in others. I don't see how anybody engaged in the actual fighting can get through this without undergoing some change.

You will have to excuse the writing; it appears to be a lot of scratch. My bunk amounts to a stretcher with little else appropriated. Since the fighting is over, we make use of the stretchers for bunks.

How I'd love to be home for Christmas. To hope so would be overly optimistic, I suppose. Most of us old timers out here feel that we'll get home when the war is over.

Now I'll run along. It is almost time for the evening meal, so I leave you for some C-Rations.

All my love forever. Your husband, Frank

With Saipan won, hopes ran high that the Marines would be sent back to Hawaii or New Zealand but the "much to do out here in the Pacific" included the immediate need to take the adjacent island of Tinian. From Nafutan Point on Saipan, the Thieves could see their next target, fourteen miles to the south. The topography of Tinian, which was slightly smaller than Saipan, favored the Marines. With fewer enemy troops and no Mounts Tapotchau or Tipo Pale, Tinian's flat farming land appeared less foreboding. Even if the terrain had been rugged, Tinian would have been worth the taking. It held an asset much coveted by the Allies at any cost, the finest airfield in the Pacific.

The Ushi Airdrome's runway was a thousand feet longer than Saipan's Aslito Airfield, long enough to accommodate the new B-29 Superfortresses—finally putting Tokyo within striking distance.

When Ski informed his platoon that the assault on Tinian would take place in a few days, Knuppel took him aside.

"We aren't in our right minds yet," Knuppel protested. "Saipan was a grinder all the way. Our Division was hit the hardest of them all, and the Sixth had the most killed and wounded out of all the regiments. And we're going into Tinian?"

"Bill, I'm just as disgusted as you that we got picked to do it."

There would be little time to rebuild the Thieves to forty. Ski and Knuppel would not have the luxury of reviewing applicants' Record Books. The battered platoon took what they could get. The old salts would have to provide on-the-job training for the new boots.

Except for Tipton and Causey, Tinian would be the third or fourth charm for every one of the original Thieves. They were neither angered nor awed at the mounting casualties and the deaths of their friends. There was no time or energy for those sentiments as they faced the next assignment.

Three days before the invasion, Tinian Town was the target of massive air strikes and Naval artillery bombardment. The Japanese, lured into thinking that the Marines intended to take the island by storm like Tarawa and Saipan, massed the Imperial Army around Tinian Town, and braced for the impending invasion.

On July 24, the Marines employed a bit of uncharacteristic guile, landing north of Tinian Town on the opposite side of the island and walking ashore unopposed. It was so picture perfect that Ski jokingly called it a "MacArthur Landing." U.S. Army General Douglas MacArthur—"Dugout Doug," as he was known to Marines—had become infamous for his "Hit 'em where they ain't" strategy in the Western Pacific. Targeting small, poorly defended enemy installations hadn't garnered him much of a fan club in the Corps.

By the time the Japanese realized what had happened, the Marines were firmly ensconced, and the push began.

Tinian was a Kiska. The battle was over within a week.

On August 6, the 40 Thieves returned to Saipan and bivouacked in a sugar cane field on the east side of the island, not far from the Aslito Airfield. When they were told the location would be their permanent camp, that there would be no return to New Zealand or Hawaii, it was Ski's turn to grouse to Knuppel. "We always get the shitty end of the stick."

On the other side of the island, the Navy's camp had tents with floor-decking and new Quonset huts for the Mess and Officer's Club, but the Marines had to build their own camp from scratch once again, using wood salvaged from destroyed buildings. In the meantime, the 40 Thieves slept curled up on stretchers on the ground, with tents promised to arrive—someday. They didn't wait. Instead they stole cases of liquor from Navy depots and traded the booze to Seabees for lumber and tents. Within a week they were living in the lap of combat luxury.

Ski understood that his boys had grown inured to nearly subhuman conditions in their two-month Roman Holiday sleeping in foxholes. So had he. If anyone back home could see the crude camp they constructed, mothers and fathers would object to living conditions unsuitable for human beings. The Thieves might have agreed, except that their new camp meant water for bathing, sleeping above ground, beer, hot meals, and more important, mail call.

Receiving mail was always a prized treat, but even more so after combat. Letters helped take the Thieves' minds off their descent into the hell of war. Reading and re-reading helped to bring them back, even if just a little.

A letter addressed simply, "Sarge, Sixth Marine Regiment, Forty Thieves" found its way to Knuppel. After opening and reading the first few lines, he stopped, smiled, and knew he had to share it with the rest of the boys. He found the platoon huddled around Mullins, who was busy jury-rigging some sort of contraption.

"What's he up to?" Knuppel asked.

"He's been braggin' about it long enough. He's making a still," Strombo replied.

Mullins had been holding an empty kerosene tin between his legs and driving a screwdriver into it with blows from a rock. He attached tubing to the tin and announced, "The mash's in the ground fermentin' away. Before you can say Jack Robinson, we're all gonna be drunker than skunks."

"Good luck with that," Knuppel smirked. "Hey everybody, listen up! There's a letter I wanna read to you. It's from Wild Bill."

Mullins paused from his work, and the rest happily turned their attention to their sergeant, glad to hear that Emerick had pulled through.

"It's addressed to all of us." Knuppel began to read: "To Sarge and the guys. Sorry about the Irish good-bye."

He paused, waiting for the roaring boys to calm down.

But now I'm livin' the Life of Riley back here in the States at a hospital in Texas. The swabbie nurses here are takin' swell care of me. One of them's a real tomato. The chow is decent, and there's plenty of it. A guy here, Freestone, had a hand blown off on Saipan. He knew Evans from the Canal. I told him Ol' Don didn't make it.

Smiles left faces, but only for a moment.

After gettin' perforated on that ridge, I didn't remember nothin'. The next time I come to, I didn't know where I was, or what was goin' on, and I kinda lost my marbles. I thought I was still up there on that ridge fightin', dontcha know, and I thought the docs and nurses on the hospital ship were the Japs! So, I picked up this grenade to throw at 'em, but it wasn't a grenade. What happened was, I crapped all over myself, and I was slingin' shit at 'em!

A waterfall of laughter slowed Knuppel's reading.

Dontcha know, the docs and nurses tried to get near me, but I fought 'em off with some left jabs and kept slingin' and peltin' 'em with grenades. Dontcha know, I didn't win that fight either, 'cause the next time I woke up, they had me tied down on the table like Frankenstein's monster.

When I found my marbles again, they told me what I done, and I damn near bust a gut laughin'. Since part of my lungs are still up on that ridge, you better name it after me! And you bunch of thieves better write me, ya hear? At this place we treat the postman like he's Santy Claus.

Semper Fi, Wild Bill

Mail call for Ski had produced an embarrassment of riches from Roxie, as always, dozens of letters and a few packages. But one scrawled note from Doc brought a smile. "Dear Ski: Your scholarly presence is requested to discuss the magnetic monopole problem. Meet me in Charan Kanoa at 1600. Ab ōvo, Jeromus Webborius, Doctorum Rectum."

Doc had learned that a hometown friend of his, Jimmy Goodman, was stationed on a ship anchored off Saipan. Doc invited Ski along for the visit—and to enjoy the luxuries offered courtesy of the Navy. There was a lot of activity on the beaches of Charan Kanoa, with landing craft going back and forth to larger ships anchored offshore. They found the friend's location and bummed a ride out.

Goodman met Doc on deck. The two friends excitedly shook hands and exchanged tidbits of news from back home. Quickly remembering his manners, Doc introduced Ski. "Jimmy, this is my good buddy, Ski, from Mount Blass, whose balls are made out of glass. When he hears 'Stormy Weather,' he bangs them together, and lightning shoots out of his ass."

After the laughter subsided, Ski reached his hand out in greeting. He really hadn't thought about his appearance much because he'd been living with his boys in the same condition for two months. He had taken a three-helmet bath a few weeks earlier. But when Goodman eyed Doc's buddy, he recoiled at the outstretched hand.

"Boy, you're a mess! I don't even know if I want to shake that hand. We gotta get you presentable."

Goodman led Ski to a shower, lent him a razor, gave him a towel and scrub brush, and said, "Get cleaned up. That's an order, Mount Blass." He then laid out a pair of his own clean khakis for Ski to wear and took the dirty ones to be laundered.

Looking into a mirror for the first time since the *Bolivar*, Ski understood Goodman's revulsion. He was filthy beyond recognition.

After a long lingering shower, he felt like a new man and joined Doc and Goodman in his state room to sip a before-dinner drink of bourbon on ice.

After a good hot meal in the mess, they sat down to share more bourbon and relive the Battle of Saipan for Goodman's benefit. Doc asked for three more glasses to be poured.

"What for," asked Goodman.

"For two buddies who didn't make it." Doc raised his glass. "And for one who might not make it."

Ski looked stunned. "What happened to Dulcich?"

When they left, much later, Goodman handed them each a quart of Four Roses. "Anything that will help you get through the night," he said.

That evening, Ski lay on his stretcher-cot under mosquito netting, sipping the warm bourbon out of the bottle. Having found a ragged piece of V-Mail and a pen, he began,

> My Dearest Roxie,
>   Doc Webber and I had occasion to go aboard one of our ships offshore. I hadn't seen Doc in quite a while. He sends his regards. We got there just in time for a nice supper of spaghetti and meatballs. The whole meal was enjoyable. We

had bread and butter instead of the hard biscuits we've been eating for over a month and ice-cold, clean water instead of hot, salty tasting water. I also enjoyed a decent shower.

The three of us had a good bull session, and it was good to catch up with Doc.

Every day I seem to hear about men of my acquaintance having been wounded or killed. I should have mentioned this earlier but had to wait until Tilly was officially informed. Captain Edwards is dead.

Doc said that Joe Dulcich was wounded, and rather badly. Doc worked on him as soon as Joe got to the hospital. A sniper shot him in the back and severed his spine. He's paralyzed in the lower half of his body. Doc didn't expect Joe to make it at all, but he's been evacuated. He'll be hospitalized a very long time. Then there is the paralysis. That is tough for Joe and Ruth. Sometimes the very worst cases eventually turn out better than our highest hopes. I do hope he will be alright. You should write Ruth. I've written Joe. It's tough on them both.

I'm sorry this isn't much of a letter, Roxie, but it will be something.

Good night for now, my dear. I miss you so very much.

All my love forever, your husband, Frank

Weeks after Tinian, a surprise visitor knocked on Ski's tent post. "May I come in, lieutenant?" a voice inquired before a head poked through the flap.

"Duley!" Ski welcomed him. "Good to see. Sit down. Drink?"

Duley sat on a crate and Ski pulled out a bottle of scotch and filled two tin cups.

"Thanks, lieutenant."

"Ski," he corrected. "What brings you by?"

"Well, I finally got permission to write home to Don and Tommy's parents to let 'em know what happened," Duley took a drink. "Our side of the story, I guess. I wanted you to read it and see what you think." He offered the lieutenant two sheets of paper. Duley explained, "The first page is about how we became Marines and what happened. It's the last bit I'd like your opinion about."

Dearest Family,

  The purpose of this letter is to enlighten you folks and the Evans and Arello families. I think that I have finally obtained permission to write everything that happened to us in the last several months. I am going to start from the beginning and hope that the censor doesn't cut anything out. Before I start, I want to ask someone from the family to take this letter over to the Evans and Arello families. Don't just call them up, as this will clear up the mystery of our movements. Also, I am enclosing two pictures of Don shown receiving the Silver Star just before we left for Saipan.

  On May 26, '44, Don very unexpectedly dropped in on me. I was lying on my bunk when he came into the barracks about 10:30 a.m. and surprised me. I was so tickled to see him. He had another marine with him whose name was Bill Knuppel. Immediately we set out to go find Tommy. We found him on KP, we talked awhile, and then Don and Bill and I left to go swimming over at the Schofield pool where I was the swimming instructor. Tommy said he would join us soon as he finished his KP duty.

  He met us about 1:30 p.m., and we went back over to my barracks to talk. We visited for a couple of hours when Don said that he would have to go as he had to be back on ship. Then the idea hit us, I forgot who suggested it, to go aboard ship with Don. We hated to lose sight of each other so quickly, as it had been two years since Tommy and I had seen Don. We changed quickly into our sun-tan khakis, tore the infantry braid off our caps, took out our ties, and presto!

We were transformed into Marines. We knew at the time Don's outfit was going into combat, but we were so reluctant to let Don go we decided to try and get aboard ship for just a few more hours together. We accomplished this with ease as the officer of the deck thought we were just Marines returning from pass. After several hours aboard we decided that maybe it was best to stay aboard and go into combat with the Marines, thus keeping us together. Combat held few terrors for us as all of us were veterans of several campaigns. The reason Tommy and I made this foolish decision was because we were both already AWOL and would face almost certain court martial if we returned. We figured that if we went into combat, they would be more lenient and perhaps we'd escape scot free. We had an idea where the task force was going, but we had made the fateful step and had to abide by our decisions. It was en route to Saipan that Don wrote the letter home mentioning our names. We had a wonderful time going down talking over old times. It never occurred to us that tragedy could strike our little plans such a fatal blow.

Finally D-Day came, and we prepared to hit the beach. We were as yet undiscovered, and Don and his friends had equipped us fully. We went in on the second wave and fortunately none of us was hurt.... We fought with Don's outfit until the 22nd of June. We were on a patrol about 200 yards ahead of the front line when we walked into a Jap machine gun nest. The three of us were fairly well spread out, Tommy was in front about thirty-five feet with another Marine, Bob Smotts. Don and I were next. Suddenly the machine gun fire opened up, and we hurriedly hit the deck. The fire was so intense that we were forced to withdraw as we were only a platoon strong. When we withdrew, we left behind several dead, the wounded were able to walk back. Among the dead

were Corp. Donald L. Evans of the 6th Marines, and Private
Thomas O. Arello of the U.S. Army 7th Division.

The fire was so heavy we (myself and the Marines) could
not get down to the bodies. After an hour and a half of fighting in which we were helpless....

Even if Duley's time in the platoon had been short, Ski could read
between the lines. He knew that Duley understood: "Once a Marine,
always a Marine."

"You did a nice job." Ski handed the letter back to Duley, and they
clinked their cups together—"Semper Fi!"—and drank a toast to Evans
and Arello. "Knuppel and the boys are talking about paying Don and
the others a visit. They're having a ceremony at the cemetery this afternoon. I know they'd be happy if you'd join us."

"My pleasure."

The mournful grey sky started to drizzle steadily as the platoon
left camp, trudging over muddy trails, heading northwest toward
the Second Marine Division Cemetery on the outskirts of Charan
Kanoa.

The men, with carbines and M1s slung over their shoulders, hiked
quietly for miles across hills and down into valleys through the tropical
rain, making their way slowly, silently, and purposefully.

By the time they reached the cemetery, the sky had cleared but their
dungarees were soaked and caked with mud.

They stood and gazed upon row after silent row of thousands of
white crosses.

Near the entrance, a crowd had gathered around a recently constructed stage. Making their way to the front, the Thieves stood in mud.
A chaplain stepped onto the platform.

"Today we dedicate the Second Marine Division cemetery here on
Saipan," the chaplain began. "You men have fought many battles on
many other islands in the Pacific with those who now rest here. We gather
to honor your fallen comrades, your friends who..."

The Second Marine Division cemetery, Saipan. *Courtesy of Roscoe Mullins*

The words faded to the background as Moore reflected on the day the notice for the Scout-Sniper platoon had been posted at M Company. Of the nine volunteers from his company, only he and Orozco were alive and still with the platoon.

Knuppel and Duley walked over first to Evans, then to Arello. They talked quietly about that day in the slop chute.

Yunker hadn't had a moment to think about Johnson until now. He did not look forward to his promised visit to his Sheepshead buddy's folks, but go he would. He must. He wondered how in the hell do you tell a mother that her son had his head shot off? You don't.

Strombo stood in front of Dyer's grave and remembered how his buddy had foreseen his own death. He knew he would never forget Martin Russell Dyer, Jr.

Smotts, who had wandered off, found Kenny's grave. The first thing he noticed was that his buddy's name had been misspelled. Killed in this hell hole, and the Corps didn't even get his name right, Smotts thought in disgust. He sat down to read his friend the letter that he was now allowed to send Eve.

"Buddies who fought on Guadalcanal and Tarawa are gone in one way, shape or formless being…" The chaplain's words wound down, and a Marine began to sing *Amazing Grace*. Eyes drifted from cross to cross, looking for names of friends and finding memories.

The voice of the chaplain drifted back, "The words that are said here today aren't important. More important is what was done here yesterday. And what will be done tomorrow."

Top: The graves of Daniel Kenny and Martin Dyer.
Bottom: The graves of Don Evans, Thomas Arello (center back), and Philip Johnson, whose name, like Kenny's, was misspelled. *From the collection of Joseph Tachovsky*

Every Day for the Rest of Your Life

"No one can imagine what it's like to be in direct contact with the enemy, killing. The loss of an arm or a leg you can learn to live with, but the loss of your soul is something that you may never recover. You won't know until your day of reckoning comes."

—*Frank Tachovsky*

Back in the States, families went about their day-to-day lives with thoughts and prayers for those overseas constantly in their minds. Families diligently scoured news reels and photographs in magazines and newspapers looking for glimpses of their loved ones. They would see their son or husband in almost any face that bore a vague resemblance.

Having received no letters for a month, the Thieves' wives and parents had no knowledge of the war in the Pacific except from newspapers or radio broadcasts, which reported heavy casualties.

In August of 1944, Merle Evans was finishing a letter to her son at the Evans home at 1807 East Seventy-Sixth Street in Kansas City.

Dear Donny,

Jean told me she had sent you a big picture of herself, tinted and all, and you didn't even acknowledge it. Why? Elaine says she writes you regularly. How are you and Dottie getting along?

Your Daddy is the superintendent at the downtown Wolferman's, but he isn't very enthusiastic about the job because he wrangles all day with his supervisor.

Otherwise, we all are well. Mrs. Flynn took her boy and your brother on a fishing trip in the Ozarks. They left Sunday night and will probably be back tomorrow. We don't know what the year will bring for your baby brother, of course. He'll be eighteen in September and will have to register. Southeast is trying to negotiate a deferment, so he can graduate.

Please write soon and tell us all about you, Tommy, Norman, and all your buddies. We miss you so much.

Much love, Mother

As she was sealing the envelope, a sedan pulled up in front of the house. On the same day, four other sedans visited families, another in Kansas City and one each in St. Louis, Milwaukee, and Detroit. Each car bore the same complement of messengers, two Marine officers and one chaplain, to deliver a telegram.

When the five porch doors opened, Merle and Herbert Evans, Marie and Louis Arello, Mary and Martin Dyer, Sr., Evelyn and Donald Johnson, and Margaret and Fergus Kenny all read the same terse notice.

DEEPLY REGRET TO INFORM YOU THAT YOUR SON WAS KILLED IN ACTION IN THE PERFORMANCE OF HIS DUTY AND SERVICE OF HIS COUNTRY NO INFORMATION AVAILABLE AT PRESENT REGARDING DISPOSITION OF REMAINS TEMPORARY BURIAL IN LOCALITY WHERE DEATH OCCURRED PROBABLE YOU WILL BE PROMPTLY FURNISHED ANY ADDITIONAL INFORMATION RECEIVED TO PREVENT POSSIBLE AID TO OUR ENEMIES DO NOT DIVULGE THE NAME OF HIS SHIP OR STATION PLEASE ACCEPT MY HEARTFELT SYMPATHY LETTER FOLLOWS
AA VANDEGRIFT LIEUT GEN, USMC COMMANDANT

The promised letter from the Commandant of the Marine Corps arrived three days later, personalized for each family. By the end of World War II, General Vandegrift would send over twenty-four thousand similar letters.

> My Dear Mr. and Mrs. Evans:
> It is a source of profound regret to me and to his comrades in the United States Marine Corps that your son, Corporal Donald Lee Evans, lost his life in action against enemies of his country, and I wish to express my deepest sympathy to you and members of your family in your great loss.
> There is little I can say to lessen your grief, but it is my earnest hope that the knowledge of your son's splendid record in the service and the thought that he nobly gave his life in the performance of his duty may in some measure comfort you in this sad hour.
> Sincerely yours,
> A. A. Vandegrift
> Lieutenant General, USMC, Commandant

For those of the 40 Thieves fortunate to return home, the war continued to take a great toll upon bodies and souls. The story of "Paul Lewis" is based on the experiences of a member of the platoon, but the other Thieves were hesitant to share the name of a buddy who lost the emotional battle. They knew it could have been any of them on any day.

In early August of 1944, Marvin Strombo received permission to write his parents and tell them of Oliver's death. But before he could, an attack of Dengue fever sent him to the hospital in Charan Kanoa. Waking after a week of delirium, he glanced at the bed next to him to see his brother Oliver. Still in a fog, Marvin at first thought that he himself had died. "That's the only explanation that I could think of for seeing Oliver again," he explained.

During the Banzai that had been launched against Oliver's outfit on July 1, a grenade exploded near him. The force knocked Oliver unconscious, sent his dog tags flying, and embedded shards of shrapnel in his upper back and head. Corpsmen found him alive among the dead. Surviving the Banzai would lead to a lifetime of pain for Marvin's older brother; the shrapnel in his head could not be removed, and it caused severe headaches that would never go away. Oliver attempted to lead a normal life and got married, but the relationship lasted for only a year, and he self-medicated with alcohol until his death.

If Bill Emerick had died on that ridge, he would have been remembered as a hero by his wife and child. Instead he returned home and battled with alcohol as well, driving away his wife and child. Physically and mentally scarred by the war, he was unable to fit back into the world he had fought to preserve. Two more failed marriages and estranged children left him with little of the swagger that he had exhibited as one of the 40. He drove away those who tried to love him, and most considered alcohol to be the cause of his death at forty-five.

Life also proved cruel to the smiling artist from New Orleans, Lieutenant Joe Dulcich. After multiple unsuccessful surgeries to repair his severed spinal cord, Joe had wasted from a one-hundred-sixty-pound Marine to a seventy-seven-pound skeleton. The sniper's bullet that struck Joe on Saipan in July of 1944 finally did its job, and he died on December 22, 1950.

Fitting into civilian life back home proved difficult for many of those even without physical scars. Gone was the regimentation that had governed their lives for the past four years; there were no more corporals or sergeants growling out orders, no more lieutenants to revere, no more living side by side with buddies who had grown to know each other better than anyone else in the world. The skills that kept a Thief alive in the war didn't translate into peacetime success.

When Smotts and two other Thieves received a month's leave for Christmas 1944, they were first sent to Treasure Island in San Francisco Bay for thirty days of psychological reorientation. "They felt the Scout-Sniper Platoon needed to be reoriented," Smotts said, "to face civilian life again. They told us that if we shoot anybody now, if we kill some poor ol' defense worker, at best we'll spend the rest of our lives in prison, and at worst we'd be in front of a firing squad." None of them made it home for Christmas.

Before their train ride from Treasure Island to the Marine base in San Diego, the three Thieves acquired some bottles of booze. Smotts and his buddies settled into the baggage car and proceeded to get soused. By the time the train reached San Diego, railroad workers found the three Thieves dead drunk and summoned MPs to roust them. Upon seeing Scout-Sniper stenciled on their dungarees, the MPs refused to wake them, and they warned the railroad workers to leave them alone. They recommended that the car be uncoupled and the baggage left alone until Smotts and his pals woke up on their own.

The pride and self-worth that came with being one of the 40, the elite of the elite, now meant nothing. The former Thieves competed for jobs with other returning troops who swamped the country with their search for work and security.

"You start out cleaning toilets," Smotts recalled, "and if you're lucky, digging ditches for ninety cents an hour. There were no good jobs. You had to do what no one else would do."

The GI bill provided some help for the returning Thieves. Hal Moore enrolled at Oklahoma A&M and joined the wrestling team. He excelled at the collegiate sport, vastly different from the life-and-death wrestling he had done during the final banzai. In 1948 Moore wore a different uniform while representing the United States, as a member of the Olympic wrestling team in London.

The lack of jobs and the Korean Conflict were good reasons to re-enlist and return to the lifestyle in which the Thieves had felt comfortable. Frank Tachovsky, having risen to the rank of major, would be stationed on Formosa, training troops for Chiang Kai-shek's Nationalist Army. Hal Moore, Marvin Strombo, and Walter Borawski rejoined the Corps, and all three accepted promotions to sergeant.

On January 13, 1953, Sergeant Borawski's platoon, assigned to the Jamestown Line, participated in an assault on a strongly defended enemy position. When his platoon commander was wounded by enemy fire, Borawski assumed command and was immediately injured as well. Although critically wounded, he refused evacuation and led his platoon to victory. Borawski died on the trip back to camp.

Walter Borawski joined Martin Dyer, Jr., as the second of the 40 Thieves to be awarded the Navy Cross.

For those of the 40 Thieves who lived, terrible nightmares plagued them all to their deaths. Frank's young bride met him in Chicago at the Great Lakes Naval Station in August of 1945. It had been three years since they had seen each other. Roxie had planned a romantic reunion at the Palmer House. She cried when her husband was reticent about going to bed and preferred to sleep in a chair. "What's wrong with us?" she asked. He could not explain.

"It's a funny thing," Frank would say. "When you're first overseas you dream about going home. But after you've been in combat, in direct contact with the enemy, killing, you're afraid to sleep, afraid to dream."

For the rest of his life, Frank never slept at night; to get any rest, he managed short naps throughout the day. On his death bed, he dreamed of a dark figure standing at the foot of his hospital bed. "It's the end of the world for me," he muttered.

Every night while they were growing up, Alfred Yunker's children awoke to the wild screams of their father tearing his bedroom apart in his never-ending battle with the trauma of the war.

Heavy drinking was one, perhaps the only, means of coping. In his nineties, Roscoe Mullins's nightmare of the officer's tomb ebbed in frequency, but certain sights, sounds, and smells triggered it once again. At first, "I thought I'd have to spend the rest of my life a drunk, like my Old Man," Mullins told a buddy. The nightmares became so bad he didn't want to sleep.

Also in his nineties, Bob Smotts recalled, "When I first came home, I shared a bed with my kid brother. The first night, I had one of my nightmares, where I'm fighting with the enemy. I had my brother by the

Martin Strombo in Japan delivering Captain Sadao Yasue's Good Luck Flag to his younger brother Tatsuya. *Courtesy of Marvin Strombo*

throat, and I almost killed him. My dad had to pull me off.

"The dream is the same every night: I see Kenny get killed, and then I start chasing the Japanese through the elephant grass as hard as I can run. I catch up to one Japanese soldier, and we fight, hand-to-hand. When I wake up, my heart is racing."

Newlywed Alma Jean Smotts would be startled awake at night by Bob's choking her. She soon became familiar with the early warning signs of Bob's nightmare and could wake him before the hand-to-hand combat began.

Marvin Strombo also had nightmares after the war. Sometimes it was something as innocent as the tone of a voice that made him dream of his first banzai. When Marvin's wife left him shortly after their fourth child was born, he found that being the single parent of four was the best medicine in the world to help him ease his demons.

Time marched on, decades passed, but year after year one thing weighed heavily on Marvin. The promise he had made to the dead Japanese captain in the field of corpses on the outskirts of Garapan remained unfulfilled. But finally, thanks to a series of articles written for the *Missoulian* by Kim Briggeman under the title *Honor among Thieves*, the family of the Japanese captain was located.

In August of 2017 the ninety-three-year-old Strombo made the arduous trip to Japan, kept his promise, and delivered Captain Sadao Yasue's Good Luck Flag to his younger brother Tatsuya.

Upon receiving the sacred heirloom, Tatsuya held it to his face, inhaled deeply, and said, "You have taken good care of my brother."

Honor among Thieves

"I wouldn't want to live it over again, but I wouldn't trade my life for all the gold in the world. And I pray every day for the people I've killed."
—Roscoe Mullins

"None of us ever talked much about the war because killing is nothing to brag about. I'll tell you one thing that's guaranteed, those that brag the most did the least. The reason I had trouble talking about what happened was that I feared I was beyond forgiveness for the things I had done."
—Bob Smotts

"If one has never been in combat against the enemy, one should shut the hell up concerning war."
—Jerome "Doc" Webber

"I have a hard time putting into words my experiences and feelings. The young men that I served with for years, that had their lives snuffed out in such quick order on those islands, they were just kids. Evans, Dyer, Kenny, Johnson, and Arello never had a chance at life. And so many Japanese boys who were just like us."
—Bill Knuppel

"For every Mother Theresa, there are many more Stalins and Hitlers. We are an odd species in that we can create Sistine Chapels and centers of great learning, yet consistently find ways for extreme cruelty to one another. You hope that someday the world will grow tired of war."
—Frank Tachovsky

"War is an awful thing. But if there were another, I'd go. I'd go so my sons wouldn't have to."
—Jesus Orozco

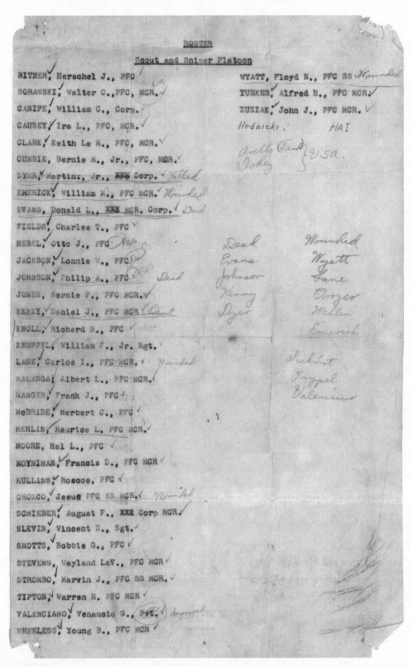

Roster of the Scout-and-Sniper Platoon, showing the dead and wounded. *From the collection of Frank Tachovsky*

The Making of
40 Thieves on Saipan

On September 10, 2011, Frank Tachovsky died.

Like most men of his era my father rarely discussed World War II. The exception to that rule was when he was looking at old photographs. There was a magazine clipping of him with another USS *Maryland* football player captioned "Fleet Stars" with "Goofy Guthrie" handwritten underneath. Dad would point at the other player and say, "He died on Wake." Otherwise, if the topic of Guadalcanal, Tarawa, Saipan, or Tinian ever came up, it would end any conversation.

Family and friends were well aware that Frank had been a Marine in the Pacific. The many reunions he was invited to attend meant that there was no hiding the fact he was a retired colonel: he went to the one for the USS *Maryland* and for New Zealand, but not for Tarawa. When he was asked why not Tarawa, he replied, "Why would I want to go now, when I never wanted to go the first time?"

Occasionally Marine buddies would surface. Frank golfed twice a year with Doc Webber and Goodman and exchanged letters with

Shit-sack Rhode and Snerd McIntyre. But there was one buddy, Knuppel, that Frank saw often when he wintered in Arizona. Although his other friends had first names, his Marine buddies were referred to only by nicknames or last names. And to them he was "Ski."

During his memorial service, several people spoke of his tenure as mayor. His youngest brother by eleven years, Otto, told how Frank would rock him to sleep as a child, singing *If I Had the Wings of an Angel*. But one man delivered a very different kind of eulogy.

> The first time I met Frank was in 1955 at the University of Wisconsin in Madison. We took an accounting class together, and he stood out because he was old. He must have been forty, and he was there on the GI bill. Knowing that I was from Sturgeon Bay, Frank introduced himself to me after class one day. From then on, I saw him in class and around campus from time to time.
>
> I was in Naval ROTC at the time. There was this one surly Marine, Sergeant Yunker, who was always on duty at the armory. I never saw him smile, and whenever he had occasion to talk to me, he'd bark out my name. He was there every day when I went to meetings. He was every inch a Marine.
>
> After an ROTC meeting one day I saw Frank talking to this usually stoic sergeant. But with Frank, he was uncharacteristically animated and obviously glad to see him, shaking hands and smiling. I thought it a little strange but didn't think much about it until it happened a few more times. I became curious. I went up to Sergeant Yunker after a meeting one day and asked, "How do you know Frank Tachovsky?" He immediately snapped back, "That man is Lieutenant Tachovsky to you, and when you speak of him, you speak of him with respect. I have been in the Marine Corps my whole life, and the lieutenant is the bravest man I know. He was our platoon leader on Saipan when a Japanese tank broke through our

lines. It had our outfit pinned down. The machine gun fire from it was intense. The tank kept advancing and was within a hundred yards of our Regimental command post. Our situation was hopeless. There was nothing we could do against it; we all thought we were goners.

Suddenly, a solitary figure ran out from my right. He stood in the middle of that withering fire without any regard for himself and fired a bazooka, disabling the tank and killing the crew inside. That was the lieutenant.

I wouldn't be here today, I wouldn't have my wife, I wouldn't have my family if it weren't for that man. Lieutenant Tachovsky saved my life that day, and he saved the life of every man in our unit, so when you speak of him, do it with respect."

If a pin had dropped on the carpet, you would have heard it. Everyone in attendance had grown accustomed to the face of the little old man in a wheelchair as Frank. There were many photographs on display of Frank and Roxie in their younger days, but they were images of people virtually unknown.

In the days following the funeral, I could not get that eulogy out of my mind. I did an online search of "Tachovsky, Saipan," which led to a Leatherneck website. Posted there was an article from the December 1944 issue of *Leatherneck Magazine.*

The post, by Chris Tipton, was prefaced with, "This was my father's platoon in World War II. He said the article was all true except for a few small errors. One of which was that, among Marines they were known as Tachovsky's Forty Thieves, not Terrors."

This discovery prompted me to open the footlocker Frank kept in the garage. Inside was a historical trove of letters, documents, articles, awards, and countless photographs of anonymous men—saved memories from long ago that had not been looked at for decades. Among the memorabilia were a Silver Star Citation; a Bronze Medal Citation; and

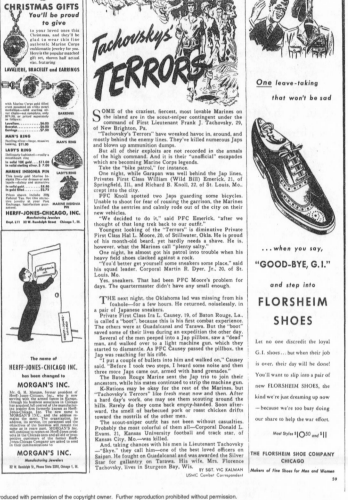

"Tachovsky's Terrors," a profile of the 40 Thieves. Leatherneck Magazine, *December 1944*

platoon rosters for Guadalcanal, Tarawa, and the "Scout and Sniper Platoon" on Saipan.

Curious, I contacted Chris Tipton, whose father Warren had been in the platoon. Chris, who is also a Marine, recommended a website named Hyperwar—USMC Monograph, and mentioned that the

Scout-Snipers were singled out several times in the Saipan section there—an unusual amount of attention for a small forty-man unit.

I retrieved the 40 Thieves' roster from the footlocker and scanned down the list of names—Borawski, Walter C.... Causey, Ira L.... Evans, Donald Lee.... Knuppel, William F.

I had met Bill Knuppel several times in Arizona when Frank had wintered there. We also visited him at his summer home near Flathead Lake in Montana. It was early November 2011 when I called Bill in Montana and arranged an impromptu trip. Armed with the platoon roster and photographs, I sat down with him and asked if that was his name on the roster. Bill didn't say a word. He simply smiled, stood up, left the table, and returned with a box full of memorabilia—his diary, a memoir he had written titled *Semper Fi*, a DVD of himself being interviewed, and photographs. Unlike Frank, Bill was a walking-talking Marine Corps historian. He began at the beginning, like he had told the story many times before. Frank and Bill's tour of duty together began in 1941 when the Sixth Marine Regiment, "the Old Pogey Bait Sixth," were sent to Iceland as the first U.S. forces deployed in World War II. Bill was with Frank on Guadalcanal and Tarawa, and, yes, on Saipan, he was Frank's platoon sergeant.

Unlike so many who tried to leave the Corps behind, Bill was a Marine for life, and he had no hesitation about sharing his remembrances. He looked over the platoon roster: "Emerick, he was a tough SOB, club fighter out of Chicago, looked like William Bendix," "Evans, he's a big brute," "Moore was a rough little bugger." Bill Knuppel told me about the day Ski asked him to be his platoon sergeant, about why the Scout-Snipers were nicknamed the Forty Thieves, about the time he and Evans went on liberty in Kona, and about the pig roast, Arello and Duley, the landing on Saipan, the first banzai, the Garapan bike patrol, and the last banzai. Over two hours after he got started, he pushed the box toward me and said, "This would make a good story."

The muse struck me. The title was obvious, *40 Thieves on Saipan.*

My mission began. Once I got home, I searched every man's name. Most had passed, but there were some men who might still be alive. I sent out a dozen awkward letters: "A name similar to yours was found on a Marine platoon roster for Saipan, and I am curious if you are that man...."

Bea Causey wrote a lovely letter to inform me that Ira had passed away. Carol Valenciano wrote that Val was living in Arizona but struggling with his memory. The families of Hal Moore, Richard Knoll, and Jesus Orozco all responded that their fathers had died. Like Frank, none of the men from the platoon had talked much about the war to his sons and daughters, but what little they knew they shared. The families of Evans, Knoll, Yunker, Tipton, and Orozco were helpful in providing access to letters, articles, and photographs.

Most of my letters went unanswered, but I was fortunate to have three members of the 40 Thieves reply. Bob Smotts, Roscoe Mullins, and Marvin Strombo earned my eternal gratitude for their willingness to discuss their service.

All were at first hesitant, but when I came armed with intimate knowledge of the platoon acquired from Knuppel—namely, the pig roast—they were soon at ease. The fact that I was the son of their commanding officer didn't hurt the cause. When I arrived for my visit with Mullins, he greeted me with, "You look just like Ski."

What they had been trying to forget for most of their lives, they now talked about without hesitation—commenting on pictures, articles, and documents. Marvin Strombo had a great memory for faces, and soon the anonymous men in the photographs began to have names—like Borawski, McBride, and Dyer.

At first the memories seemed a jumble of disjointed events but after the first series of interviews, one or two memories would have a common thread. I reported back to Knuppel to get his input on the new perspectives. Questions arose, and he began to remember more.

To clarify his new memories, I went back to Smotts, to Mullins, to Strombo, asking about "the push into the valley," "Martin Dyer," or

"Daniel Kenny." Information uncovered by a question to one of the Thieves would spark a new story from another, which would need corroboration, which meant taking to the road again...to Smotts...to Mullins...to Strombo...and always reporting back to Knuppel. The new recollections brought more stories. The circle tours of the country continued. One more visit to these old Leathernecks meant one more memory, one more word, one more phrase.

They had spent their lives trying to forget. Forget what they saw, forget what they did. They told of nightmares they had continued to have—watching friends die, banzais, people burning to death—nightmares they woke up from in cold sweats, hearts racing. At night it was June 15, 1944, all over again. Yet the men continued to tear the scabs off their old wounds and answer my questions.

After multiple visits with Knuppel, Strombo, Mullins, and Smotts, I had accumulated hours of video interviews, handwritten notes, letters, and emails.

As though there wasn't enough raw material already, I went back into the garage to retrieve the footlocker. There were more discoveries—including many cigar boxes full of letters that Frank had written to Roxie. Letters that she had saved, from 1941 when they first met at Mike Lyman's in Los Angeles, to their marriage in August of 1942, to Frank's homecoming in 1945.

It seemed almost voyeuristic, an invasion of privacy, reading the thoughts of this couple who would become my parents. As I sorted and read through the material, it was difficult to imagine that the Frank and Roxie of the 1940s were my parents. At this point in time, they weren't Mom and Dad. They were Frank and Roxie, two characters living through their own version of *From Here to Eternity*.

More information, more memories. At this point it was like a huge jigsaw puzzle with many pieces missing—and with some pieces that might or might not be part of this story. But by now I was determined to put the puzzle together.

I had gleaned a lot of general information about Marine activity from Chris Tipton's Hyperwar site, but I needed more specific information regarding the movements of the Sixth Marine Regiment. Fortunately, William Jones, commander the regiment's First Battalion on Guadalcanal, Tarawa, and Saipan, had written *A Brief History of the 6ᵗʰ Marines*.

Battle Cry! by Leon Uris gave me a wonderful sense of the tenor of the times, from one who lived it. Knuppel knew Uris, having served in the same H Company on Tarawa. In his book, Uris writes of a notorious group of thieves within the Sixth, recounting many of their antics. I asked Knuppel if that was his platoon. He smiled and said, "Somewhat." One episode involved the theft of an Army colonel's jeep. At first I assumed it was merely fiction, but later I asked Smotts if the 40 Thieves ever stole an Army Colonel's jeep. "No," he replied and paused. "It wasn't a colonel's jeep, it was a captain's…and we beat the hell out of that thing." Trying to find out whodunnit proved difficult. Even at ninety, nobody wanted to rat out a buddy—but I finally wrangled out of Strombo, "Borawski done it."

A valuable resource I found while researching at the National Archives in Bethesda, Maryland, was Colonel Riseley's "Daily Report" from Saipan. Colonel James Riseley commanded the Sixth Marine Regiment, and the Scout-Sniper Platoon fell under his personal control.

Other useful source materials: *Highpockets: The Man. The Marine. The Legend.* by Zona Gayle Murray, *U.S. Marine Corps Scout-Sniper: WWII and Korea* by Peter Senich, "On the Art of Hand to Hand: An Interview with Colonel A. J. Biddle" by James N. Wright, *Tarawa: The Incredible Story of One of World War II's Bloodiest Battles* by Robert Sherrod, and *Leatherneck Magazine*.

This book was first put together as an oral history, and when a publisher informed me, "Oral histories don't sell. Write it as a narrative," I was flummoxed.

In stepped Cynthia Kraack, an accomplished, award-winning author. A novelist with a background in journalism, she asked the questions that transformed letters and notes into an encounter with living, breathing young men going through hell. Her father, Roman Frisque, served in the Pacific during World War II and Korea—something that made the

Scout-Sniper experience her own personal journey of discovery. The slogan "Join the Navy, See the World," had piqued the wanderlust of a seventeen-year-old boy from a tiny Wisconsin dairy town. Cynthia's father left home, choosing the Navy over the Army because he dreamt of traveling the world and hoped a ship would take him to see the exotic places that he had only read about in books. In an odd coincidence, the first exotic place he saw was Saipan, following the invasion, aboard the USS *Guadalupe*. Like many children of vets, she has a box of his souvenirs and another of his medals, but no stories.

Cynthia pushed through a nearly impossible task, restoring flesh and muscle to the bones of the Marines' stories and breathing life back into the experiences of the men who lived *40 Thieves on Saipan*. For her, this book has always been about the men and their resiliency.

This book has benefited from the kindness and expertise of many: Adrian Schramm, Brian Bradshaw, Niko Courtelis, Neil Duffy, Andrew Stolinski, Charles Locks, Dr. Deborah Berrill, Richard Zuziak, Andrew Orozco, David Kyle, the nephews of Don Evans, Al Yunker, Jr., and the sons of Lonnie Jackson.

Writers depend on the skills of many to bring a book to market. Leticia Gomez, our Savvy Literary agent, shared depths of enthusiasm, knowledge, and a special human touch in marketing *40 Thieves on Saipan*. We are grateful for her guidance and care. The continued support of Alex Novak, publisher of Regnery History, and Margaret Vander Woude, managing editor, allowed us to believe the platoon would find an audience. With both brilliance and incredible patience, Elizabeth Kantor, senior editor, and Laura Swain, editorial assistant, made the journey from manuscript to completed work uncomplicated and rewarding. For others involved in the marketing and publicity of this book we also are thankful.

I sincerely hope this book is worthy of the legacy of selflessness, honor, and sacrifice of young men who were simply "a crazy bunch of kids" who did give a damn.

"We don't do enough for our veterans," my father frequently said. In honor of that sentiment, a significant portion of the royalties from *40 Thieves on Saipan* will be donated to organizations that help our veterans.

Semper Fi.

Index